CLASSICAL PRESENCES

General Editors

LORNA HARDWICK   JAMES I. PORTER

CLASSICAL PRESENCES

Attempts to receive the texts, images, and material culture of ancient Greece and Rome inevitably run the risk of appropriating the past in order to authenticate the present. Exploring the ways in which the classical past has been mapped over the centuries allows us to trace the avowal and disavowal of values and identities, old and new. Classical Presences brings the latest scholarship to bear on the contexts, theory, and practice of such use, and abuse, of the classical past.

Diversifying Greek Tragedy on the Contemporary US Stage

Melinda Powers

OXFORD
UNIVERSITY PRESS

OXFORD
UNIVERSITY PRESS

Great Clarendon Street, Oxford, OX2 6DP,
United Kingdom

Oxford University Press is a department of the University of Oxford.
It furthers the University's objective of excellence in research, scholarship,
and education by publishing worldwide. Oxford is a registered trade mark of
Oxford University Press in the UK and in certain other countries

First Edition published in 2018

Impression: 1

Published in the United States of America by Oxford University Press
198 Madison Avenue, New York, NY 10016, United States of America

British Library Cataloguing in Publication Data

Data available

Library of Congress Control Number: 2018938831

ISBN 978-0-19-877735-9

Printed and bound by
CPI Group (UK) Ltd, Croydon, CR0 4YY

For Meli

Acknowledgements

I wrote this book in 2016 over the course of a year while on sabbatical leave, but my interest in this project has been a long time in the making. It began in 2005, when my then soon to be PhD supervisor Sue-Ellen Case sent me an email stating that I should see Luis Alfaro's *Electricidad* and contact *Theatre Journal* to offer to write a review. That suggestion became a critical turning point for me, when I began to synthesize my study of Classics with a study of Performance.

This book would not have been possible without Sue-Ellen. A generous teacher and mentor, she gave me the gift of inspiration. Helene Foley has been another loyal guide. From the time I first met her, when I was a first-semester, first-year Columbia undergrad in her course on Greek drama, to her reading a draft of my first manuscript, until her most recent reading of this manuscript, she has been a kind, patient, generous, and dedicated professor. I am honored to have studied with these two great women.

Special thanks also to Nancy Rabinowitz, Manuel Simons, Shane Breaux, Jessica Kubzansky, Aaron Mark, Tim O'Leary, Peter Meineck, and Desiree Sanchez, who have also read an earlier version of the manuscript, either in part or in full. The final version has been much improved by their comments. Nancy, especially, has been a supportive reader and colleague, as well as Mary Louise Hart, who has been a source of encouragement over the years, and whose conversations with me about Luis Alfaro's *Mojada* and the cover art for this book have been most helpful. This work has been much improved thanks to everything I have learned from Thomas Postlewait, the editor of my first book, from whom I had the privilege of benefiting from his over twenty years of experience as editor of the award-winning Studies in Theatre History and Culture series for the University of Iowa Press. I also thank Oliver Taplin and Edith Hall. In addition to what I have learned from their pioneering work and kind support, their founding of the Archive of Performances of Greek and Roman Drama created a welcome home for me to explore my keen interest in reception during the glorious time I spent as a Master's student at Oxford. Many friends and professors from those days, too numerous to name, and from my years as a graduate student in

Los Angeles also deserve thanks, especially Del Chrol, Philip Purchase, Elena Kallinikidou, Carla Melo, and Hana Salussolia, who have all continued to be a source of ideas, support, and some much-needed comic relief.

Working as a professor at the City University of New York's John Jay College of Criminal Justice, which hosts a multicultural, multigenerational student body comprised of over 100 nationalities, has also influenced the development of this project, for the diversity of the student body is not just one of identity but also of perspectives and opinions. What I teach the students about history, theatre, and literature, they reciprocate in teaching me about life. Much of their enthusiasm, ideas, and perspectives has influenced my writing in this book, as have those of the students at CUNY's PhD Program in Theatre and Performance, where I have taught courses on Classical reception.

In fact, with the exception of two productions, all of the material here discussed has been collected over the course of time that I have been teaching at CUNY. Throughout this process, my wonderful colleagues at John Jay and at the CUNY Graduate Center, particularly Pat Licklider, Robert Davis, Adam Berlin, Peggy Escher, Richard Haw, Paul Narkunas, Nivedita Majumdar, Marnie Tabb, Allison Pease, Valerie Allen, Jay Gates, and Jean Graham-Jones, have created a warm and supportive environment for me to develop these ideas and eventually put them down on paper.

Grateful thanks also go to the theatre artists whose work I here represent. I am fortunate to have met and corresponded with many of them. Debra Ann Byrd, Petronia Paley, Jessica Kubzansky, Allain Rochel, Tim O'Leary, Aaron Mark, Manuel Simons, Mark Greenfield, Lois Weaver, Peggy Shaw, Peter Meineck, Desiree Sanchez, and Bryan Doerries have all generously granted me interviews either by phone or by email. Their powerful work continues to inspire and challenge me to think critically about the ideas, values, and emotions expressed in their plays and the ancient tragedies before them.

Accordingly, this book combines my interest in Classics and Theatre and Performance Studies, the two main fields in which I work. I am thankful for the comments of professional colleagues from both of these fields at a variety of annual conferences for the American Society for Theatre Research, the Association for Theatre in Higher Education, the Comparative Drama Conference, the Classical Association of the Atlantic States, and the Society for Classical Studies.

I am also grateful to the late Kathryn Bosher, who helped to organize the John E. Sawyer Seminar Series 'Theatre after Athens', sponsored by the Andrew Mellon Foundation, at Northwestern University. Kate's vision for the conference and work in developing the presentations into a volume for Oxford University Press gave me the opportunity to write and later revise some of the material that appears in Chapter 1 of this book. Her warmth, kindness, and intellect are sorely missed. Patrice Rankine, who edited my section of that volume, also helped me to develop this project. Through his invaluable comments on my essay, he pushed me to think further and 'be bold'.

Grateful thanks are also due to the Committee on Ancient and Modern Performance at the Society for Classical Studies, who provided the opportunity for me to present a paper on Luis Alfaro's *Electricidad*, and to Gesine Manuwald and Steve Oberhelman, who helped to shepherd that paper into becoming an article in *Helios*. Thanks also to Oxford University Press and *Helios* for permission to reproduce some material from those articles and to all of the photographers who have kindly granted me permission to reproduce their stunning images of the productions here discussed.

John Jay College of Criminal Justice has supported me with travel funding to conferences and a sabbatical year that allowed me the luxury of time to read, think, and write. John Jay's Office for the Advancement of Research and CUNY's union, the Professional Staff Congress, have assisted my research by funding me with generous faculty scholarship grants that have helped to pay for images, indexing, travel, and an outstanding assistant, Shane Breaux, who provided excellent help with preparing the *Works Cited* pages, as well as the copy-editing, proofreading, and indexing. I am deeply grateful for the care and attention he gave to this work. Susy Mendes, Daniel Stageman, and Levon Volpe, in particular, have also all taken great time and care in assisting me with the grants process.

This book has benefited greatly from the expertise of Hilary O'Shea and Charlotte Loveridge at Oxford University Press, the series editors Lorna Hardwick and James Porter, the anonymous reviewers of my book proposal, and Mary-Kay Gamel who anonymously reviewed the final manuscript and later allowed herself to be identified. They have all provided me with notes and suggestions that have immensely helped the development and production of this project. Donald Watt has been a quick and careful copy editor, and Drew Stanley a perceptive proofreader.

Together with Kalpana Sagayanathan, they kept the production process smooth and on schedule. Georgina Leighton at Oxford has also been especially helpful; her informative and professional replies to my many, many emails helped to make the publication process an enjoyable experience.

My parents, as always, have been an unfailing source of support, encouragement, and learning. I have many a childhood memory of sitting with them or my big sister in off-off-Broadway theatres, which is where the real inspiration for this project ultimately began. My deepest gratitude is for Joe and Meli, two people without whom the research and writing would have been a much lonelier process. Thank you for the love and the joy that helped me to create. I dedicate this book to Meli, the world's greatest listener. Thank you for all of your interest in my ideas, which we explored on our many long walks together, rain, snow, or shine.

Contents

List of Figures

*The publisher and the author apologize for any errors or omissions in the
above list. If contacted, they will be pleased to rectify these at the earliest
opportunity.*

Introduction

Although in some areas of the world[1] Greek tragedy has traditionally been associated with colonialism, the canon, the Euro-American elite, and a Eurocentric vision that privileges Greece as the so-called 'cradle of Western civilization',[2] recent scholarship has demonstrated that the genre has also often played a critical role in movements of anti-colonialism and resistance.[3] In nineteenth- and early-twentieth-century America, for example, much of Greek drama was imported through European theatrical companies,[4] but at the same time, as Fiona Macintosh, Justine McConnell, and Patrice D. Rankine have explained:

> Blacks and women read and engaged in the subterranean Classics to craft their values in the New World, those of freedom, equality, literacy, art and so on . . . In the Americas the closeted and those who pass—women, blacks, Latinos, Asians, and so on—take up the classics as their own at an unprecedented rate.[5]

According to Emily Greenwood, 'The discipline of Classics may have been complicit with imperialism, but this is properly a phenomenon of reception—how Greece and Rome have been assimilated to narratives of empire.'[6] Thus, in opposition to the narrative that conflates the study

---

[1] As a reader noted to me, this is not necessarily the case in Asia, especially Japan.

[2] On the misidentification of Greece with Europe, see Emily Greenwood (2009) 2-3. On the 'democratic turn' in Classics, see Hardwick and Harrison (2013). On Classics and postcolonialism, see Goff (2005); Goff and Simpson (2007); Hardwick and Gillespie (2007); Bradley (2010); Greenwood (2009); Hall and Vasunia (2010); Stephens and Vasunia (2010); Goff (2013a); McConnell (2013); Rankine (2013).

[3] On the role of Classics in challenging colonialism, see Goff (2005) 1-24. On the changing role of the study of Classics in English schools, from being the mark of an elite education to an arcane academic subject, see Christopher Stray (1998).

[4] Macintosh, McConnell, and Rankine (2015) 14.

[5] Macintosh, McConnell, and Rankine (2015) 11-12.

[6] Greenwood (2009) 2-3.

of Classics with an elite, white, imperialist agenda, the historical record demonstrates an alternative perspective, namely that in nineteenth and early-twentieth-century America, 'the artefacts that could reify freedom and equality were, for blacks as well as women, just beneath the surface and very often ancient Greek in their provenance.'[7]

Following in this tradition, a variety of contemporary US theatre artists have been 'resignifying'[8] Greek tragedy and its assumed connection to the colonial past. Their productions have worked to rupture the archive in ways that negate the elitist associations with the genre to address instead cultural, sexual, and racial formations in diverse communities from the Boyle Heights cholxs to disabled veterans. The historical-mythological content combination provided by tragedy especially aids this process, for in the ancient world, mythological narratives functioned to create and preserve cultural identity and history, individual and communal. Theatre artists today exploit this function in revising the drama that served as the hallmark of Athenian democracy to develop a new syncretic, mythological mix that reflects the needs, concerns, and anxieties of a democracy in the present.

At times in this book, I refer to this process of revising Greek tragedy as 'reclaiming', a term which Harvey Young has used to discuss the transformative potential of performance. '*Re*-claiming', he explains, 'does not require that we erase the past and script a new one . . . It is to remain aware of its previous "claims" even as you articulate your own. It is to know the past in the present as you work toward creating a future.'[9] The theatrical medium is especially conducive to this process of recycling, reimagining, and 'reclaiming', because, in Marvin Carlson's words, 'There clearly seems to be something in the nature of dramatic presentation that makes it a particularly attractive repository for the storage and

---

[7] Macintosh, McConnell, and Rankine (2015) 11.

[8] 'Signifying', a term drawn from Henry Louis Gates, Jr (1988), refers to one view of an African American, self-conscious relationship to tradition. Kevin Wetmore (2015) has explained that 'the trope of signifyin(g) is the trope of the talking book—the "double voiced text that talks to other texts"' (Gates, Jr 1988: xxv, quoted in Wetmore 2015: 545). 'The impetus of African-American signifying', states James R. Andreas, Sr. (1998), 'is the search for the "black voice" in the "white written text"' (Andreas, Sr 1998: 105, quoted in Wetmore 2015: 545).

[9] Young (2010) 135. 'Reclaiming' is another term that refers to a self-conscious relationship to tradition.

mechanism of the continued recirculation of cultural memory.'[10] The artists discussed here have exploited this function of theatre as 'memory machine' to challenge stereotypical cultural representations of African Americans, Latinxs, women, LGBTQs, and veterans.

Some of the artists whose work I examine are Take Wing and Soar Productions, the Classical Theatre of Harlem, Luis Alfaro, Split Britches, the Faux-Real Theatre Company, Aaron Mark, Tim O'Leary, Allain Rochel, Aquila Theatre, and Outside the Wire. I have focused on their work in particular because, in the service of my methodological lens of performance, I have chosen to limit my discussion to professional productions that I have seen live in the theatre.[11] For over a period of ten years, from the time I first saw Luis Alfaro's *Electricidad* in 2005 to the time I saw his *Oedipus El Rey* in 2015, I have seen a trajectory of performances of Greek drama produced by or for under-represented communities. In fact, with the exception of one show, Split Britches' *Honey I'm Home: The Alcestis Story* (which I have included because of its historical significance and to include a lesbian voice in my chapter on women), I have seen all of the productions in this book live and not recorded.[12]

Due to this focus on live theatre, which I have experienced first-hand, my study is not a comprehensive account of productions of Greek drama by or for US minority populations. That study has yet to be done and could include many key performances that I do not discuss. Such a work might, for example, examine productions by communities that are here absent, such as the National Asian American Theatre Company's *Antigone*, performed in New York in 2014; Rhodessa Jones' ongoing San Francisco-based programme *The Medea Project: Theatre for Incarcerated Women*; the Alaskan *Yup'ik Antigone* that toured Europe in 1985;[13] and

---

[10] Carlson (2001) 8.

[11] Because it would be a topic in its own right, I do not include, apart from *Honey I'm Home*, a discussion of non-professional and college productions, such as the inspiring works of Mary-Kay Gamel at University of California, Santa Cruz.

[12] For a discussion of the current interest in recording productions, the increased availability of such recordings, and the attendant problems in using such recordings as documents of live performance, see Bratton and Peterson (2013). On the study of live events, see Kershaw (2008).

[13] Foley (1999) 2 explains that the show 'included a shaman Tiresias and tribal masks and music that enhanced the heroine's stirring defense of Inuit mores'. As Foley notes, the work is available on video from KYUK-TV Productions, Pouch 68, Bethel, Alaska, AK, 99559. See also Hunsaker (1987) and Fienup-Riordan (1990) 126–7.

the Native American playwright Terry Gomez's adaptations of Sophocles' *Antigone* (2004),[14] and Euripides' *Trojan Women Numunu Waiipunu: The Comanche Women* (2008),[15] both produced in New Mexico. Also included may be other key productions by communities that I have here discussed, such as Theater for the Blind's *Oedipus*, performed in New York in 2005, Five Lesbian Brothers' *Oedipus at Palm Springs*, New York, 2005, John Fisher's *Medea: The Musical*, San Francisco, 1994, and the African-American Shakespeare Company's *Medea*, San Francisco, 2014. These works might all be included in the 'genealogy'[16] of performances that I here explore, but because I have not been able to see them live or recorded, I have not included a discussion of them.

All of the works I study are tragedies apart from Douglas Carter Beane and Lewis Flynn's *Lysistrata Jones*. I have included this production because it is a well-known Broadway show that took place during the time frame on which I focus and its representation of women serves as a significant contrast to the two avant-garde productions also discussed in Chapter 3. This focus on tragedy in part has been determined because of my interest in writing about live productions that I have seen, but primarily reflects the choices of the artists.

I use the term 'minority' in terms of representation and status within the larger culture. Such a perspective has led me to include, for example, a discussion of women, who make up about 50% of the population, and veterans, who compose 0.5 per cent of the population. Moreover, by including disabled veterans as part of my discussion in Chapter 5, I address disability not as an 'isolated, individual medical pathology but instead as a key defining social category on par with race, class, and gender'.[17]

I realize that my coverage of such communities is not without risk, for some members of the disabled community, for example, have issued the

---

[14] The play tells the story of 'a corrupt tribal chairman who attempts to totally control his family with tragic results', https://newmexicodramatists.org/2014/02/21/profile-terry-gomez/, accessed 19 September 2016.

[15] The play is a 'historical retelling of the survival of a group of Comanche women interwoven with a contemporary story', https://newmexicodramatists.org/2014/02/21/profile-terry-gomez/, accessed 19 September 2016.

[16] I borrow the term 'genealogy' from Joseph Roach. He argues that 'Genealogies of performance also attend to "counter-memories", or the disparities between history as it is discursively transmitted and memory as it is publicly enacted by the bodies that bear its consequences.' (1996) 25–6.

[17] Kudlick (2003) 764, quoted in Johnston (2016) 4.

guideline of 'nothing about us, without us'. Despite such requests, I have approached the issues affecting such communities not necessarily as a member of them (even those I belong to)[18] nor as an expert in each respective subject, but as a researcher of classical theatre, historiography, and Performance Studies. I have synthesized these fields to identify, interpret, and explain a trajectory of the performance of Greek tragedy that US artists have been creating to comment on the stereotypes and discrimination that not only afflict each respective community, but also infect the culture at large. However, while I am not a member of each of the communities here discussed, all of the performances I cover have been written or produced primarily by members of the respective community discussed in each given chapter, with the exception of the Classical Theatre of Harlem's *Trojan Women* (which was written by a Euro-American but performed by a primarily African American cast), *Lysistrata Jones* and *Oedipus Rex XX/XY* (which I discuss in my chapter on women but which were written and conceived by men), and Outside the Wire's *Ajax* (Bryan Doerries and most of his actors are not veterans).

In discussing these various productions, I realize, like Jill Dolan, whom a feminist group once chided for her depiction of their work, that my assessments may not always please the artists whom I have discussed. However, I agree with Dolan that as a critic and theorist my primary responsibility does not necessarily lie 'in faithfully reporting the authorial intentions of feminist [or other] theatre groups and squelching my own response as a feminist spectator'.[19] Instead, I see my responsibility as resting 'in attempting to place the work in a larger cultural, theoretical, and ideological context, in which it becomes part of a movement of ideas'.[20] I realize that, in taking this approach, I too may have risked alienating myself from those whose work I respect and admire, but, like Dolan, I do not equate the process of being a critic and spectator with being a nurturer of artists, even those whom I admire and see as doing beneficial work.[21]

---

[18] My identity has, of course, influenced my perspective and writing; however, my point here is that I have not taken an approach that highlights the personal.

[19] Dolan (1988) 122.

[20] Dolan (1988) 122.

[21] I made a concerted effort to contact all of the artists whose work I cover to offer them the chance to respond to my discussion. Some, such as Debra Ann Byrd and Bryan Doerries, were not able to read and comment; others, such as Aaron Mark and Tim

I use the word artists to refer to theatre directors, librettists, playwrights, actors, dancers, lighting, set and costume designers, and so forth—basically, any and everyone involved in the creation of the theatrical work which is produced through their collective effort. I replace the traditional usage of Latino/a with the gender neutral Latinx, which is in common use. Although I primarily employ the more specific term US, I reserve the term 'American' for people in the United States. In accordance with this book's focus on reception, I use the popular term 'Greek drama', despite its association with the literary study of the genre, but to highlight my focus on live theatre, I often break the text of my writing to cite the names of actors to emphasize the distinction between actor and character that is essential to studies of performance.

I eschew any discussion of 'authenticity', which is inevitably impossible given the use of translation and scholars' limited understanding of ancient production and the historical conditions in which the texts participated.[22] Instead, I give equal attention to productions that use translations of the ancient plays and those that are adaptations[23] and new versions.[24] I look at each work, regardless of its approach or affect, as a creation in its own right rather than as new cultural products that 'send up'[25] the original'[26] or 'go down easy'.[27] In this respect, I agree with Helene P. Foley that 'Experimental versions that some viewers might view or have viewed as travesties of the original plays—not "Greek" or "failures"—perform this cultural work differently from but as significantly as those that aim to reinvigorate "high culture" with them.'[28]

Because of my emphasis on the US, I have chosen not to discuss overseas productions that have travelled to the states, such as Satoshi

O'Leary, generously discussed their work at length with me and provided helpful comments on a draft; and others, such as Lisa Petersen, Kevin Moriarty, and Douglas Carter Beane, I was unable to contact.

[22] On the historical conditions of Athenian performance, see Powers (2014). On 'authenticity', see Gamel (2010).

[23] On 'adaptation' from a literary standpoint, see Julie Sanders (2006) and Linda Hutcheon (2006). For performance-based approaches to adaptation, see Tompkins (2014).

[24] Katja Krebs (2013 47) has defined 'versions' as 'a term used by rewriters who have no access to the source text's language yet claim to have been "faithful" to their source'.

[25] As Rush Rehm (2003 39) refers to John Fisher's musical comedy *Medea: The Musical.*

[26] Rehm (2003) 39.

[27] As Rehm (2003 39) refers to Charles Mee's *Big Love,* a version of Aeschylus' *Supplices.*

[28] Foley (2012b) xiii.

Miyagi's *Medea* at New York's Japan Society in 2011, the Peruvian Grupo Yuyachkani's *Antígona* in 2008 at the Getty Villa, Los Angeles, and the Italian Teatro Patologico's *Medea*, performed at La MaMa E.T.C. in 2011 and 2015. Productions such as these are surely significant and a topic in their own right. However, they do not appropriately fit within the limits of my study.

Remaining focused on US-produced works is important to my discussion of cultural identities and stereotypes. As Juana María Rodríguez has explained, identities are related to space and motion and are developed through encounters with language, law, culture, and public policy. 'Identity is about situatedness in motion: embodiment and spatiality... It is about a self that is constituted through and against other selves in contexts that serve to establish the relationship between the self and the other.'[29]

While such discussions of identity formation are complex and multifaceted, I narrow my discussion of the subject by exploring one aspect of these topics in particular. I focus on the ways in which artists situated in the United States have been using Greek tragedy as a framework through which to exercise identity practices that aim to take back, revise, challenge, 'resignify', 'reclaim', or 'execute'[30] stereotypical representations, but also how, in the process, some artists may inadvertently reinforce the very stereotypes they aim to destroy, thus demonstrating that Greek drama can be both a powerful and dangerous tool.

Because the idea of stereotypes factors into all of my discussions, it is important for me to define the term carefully here. Brian Eugenio Herrera has given an excellent account of the genealogy of this term. He traces its use beginning with American essayist and newspaper reporter Walter Lippmann, who in 1922 first used the term metaphorically in his *Public Opinion* to refer to 'a preconceived and oversimplified idea of the characteristics which typify a person, situation, etc.; an attitude based on such a preconception. Also, a person who appears to conform closely to the idea of a type'.[31] Following Lippmann, Gordon W. Allport, in his 1948 pamphlet *ABC's of Scapegoating*, saw stereotypes

---

[29] Rodríguez (2003) 5.
[30] For a discussion of Herrera's (2015) term 'executing the stereotype', see Chapter 2.
[31] http://www.oed.com.ez.lib.jjay.cuny.edu/view/Entry/189956?rskey=ED0hZy&result=1#eid, accessed 19 September 2016.

as 'reducing people, groups, and events to "a few clear cut traits"'. Allport's work applied the term to 'feelings of difference between social groups'.[32] It built on 'Lippmann's idea that stereotypes resolved the gap between "the world outside and pictures in our heads" . . . especially with regard to racial and ethnic distinctions'.[33] He also recognized 'as early as 1948 that . . . "when the same type of emphasis is found repeatedly, the screen can become a powerful tool in the formation of stereotypes"'.[34]

Continuing his overview of such scholarship, Herrera has explained the social scientific discourse of stereotype that emerged in the 1960s and 1970s in key works such as Donald Bogle's *Toms, Coons, Mulattoes, Mammies, and Bucks: An Interpretive History of Blacks in American Film* (1973); Raymond William Stedman's *Shadows of the Indian: Stereotypes in American Culture* (1982); Molly Haskell's *From Reverence to Rape: The Treatment of Women in the Movies* (1974); and Vito Russo's *The Celluloid Closet: Homosexuality in the Movies* (1981). According to Herrera, these foundational works identify stereotypes as vehicles of bias inscribed by and legitimated by the US entertainment industry.[35] This viewpoint is in accordance with what, in 1972, the 'Chinese American author, activist, and playwright Frank Chin (with Jeffery Paul Chan) wrote, "The ideal racial stereotype is a low maintenance engine of white supremacy whose efficiency increases with age, as it [becomes] 'authenticated' and 'verified'."'[36]

Herrera also accounts for Richard Dyer's, Stuart Hall's, and Homi Bhabha's work on stereotypes and summarizes their perspectives as 'taken together, these thinkers open questions about whether stereotypes tell a story (Dyer), enforce power relations (Hall), or tell the story of power (Bhabha)'.[37] He then concludes that:

throughout the work of all the contributors to the discourse of stereotype— Lippmann, Allport, Chin and Chan, Dyer, Hall, and Bhabha, among others—a curious continuity emerges. The stereotype itself remains an indefatigable obstacle, an unyielding antagonist in a sustained battle over the discursive features of

---

[32] Allport (1948) 33, quoted in Herrera (2015) 135.
[33] Lippmann (1997) 60–1, quoted in Herrera (2015) 135.
[34] Allport (1948) 35, quoted in Herrera (2015) 136.
[35] Herrera (2015) 136.
[36] Herrera (2015) 137; Chin and Chan (1972) quoted in Herrera (2015) 137.
[37] Herrera (2015) 137.

representational truth... Put simply, stereotypes seem to be impervious to all efforts to extinguish them—always winning, somehow surviving, ever ready to manifest another day.[38]

Perhaps because of its ubiquity, the problem of the stereotype is addressed in distinct ways by a number of Performance Studies theorists, whose work has benefited this study. Harvey Young's theory of 'the black body', Brenda Dixon Gottschild's 'Africanist presence', José Esteban Muñoz's 'disidentification', and Herrera's 'executing the stereotype' have been particularly influential. These ideas relate to the contemporary communities whose productions I feature and have been the focus of key studies in the field of performance, thus allowing me to engage in a critical dialogue about identity already taking place in the field.

I have also learned from many previous studies on the reception of Greek drama in the US, such as Marianne McDonald's pioneering *Ancient Sun, Modern Light* (1991), Amy Green's *The Revisionist Stage* (1994), Karelisa Hartigan's *Greek Tragedy on the American Stage* (1995), Kevin Wetmore's *Black Dionysus* (2003), E. Teresa Choate's *Electra USA* (2009), Helene P. Foley's *Reimagining Greek Tragedy on the American Stage* (2012b), Emily Klein's *Sex and War on the American Stage: Lysistrata in Performance 1930–2012* (2014), and *The Oxford Handbook to Greek Drama in the Americas* (2015).[39]

Drawing on such works, I have attempted to ground my study in some of the latest research in performance and reception, as I aim to negotiate distinct reading audiences in the fields of Classics and Theatre and Performance Studies. In doing so, I have had to make various choices and compromises in approaching my subject. I have chosen, for example, not to offer an in-depth discussion of the Greek dramas in their historical context. Attempting such a study could only be superficial, since any diligent effort would constitute a book in its own right

---

[38] Herrera (2015) 138.

[39] Another work that addresses US productions is McDonald (2003). Some articles that engage with diverse productions of Greek drama on the US stage include Blair (1993); D'Aponte (1991); Foley (2004); Fraden (2001); Moritz (2008); and Rabkin (1984). Some other important studies on reception are Hall, Macintosh, and Taplin (2000); Macintosh, Michelakis, Hall, and Taplin (2005); Riley (2008); Hall (2012); Hall and Wrigley (2007); Hardwick and Gillespie (2007); Greenwood (2009). For production history on the world stage, the UK, and Europe, see, e.g., Foley and Mee (2011); Hall and Macintosh (2005); and Wrigley (2011).

and thus detract from my primary aim of examining contemporary performances and the ways in which they speak to issues of identity in the US. I have, instead, focused my efforts on pointing out only those aspects of the historical conditions of the ancient plays that are specifically relevant to my analysis of the modern reinterpretations I discuss. Many of these points can be studied and analysed in detail, but rather than digress from my primary focus on the contemporary performances by engaging in scholarly debates about the classical dramas, I have instead referred readers interested in such topics to some excellent scholarship on each Greek play. I have also chosen not to offer a documentary history of each of the contemporary performances. For those readers who are interested in a documentary of each production, I plan to produce soon an anthology of many of the play scripts here discussed. In the meantime, I have provided references to relevant articles and reviews and as many images of the performances as possible, with references to those who own copyright of the fuller catalogues. My aim for the present is to frame my documentation of each production in a way that illustrates the questions that surfaced in my research about the representation of under-represented communities in contemporary performances of Greek drama—a subject of interest shared by scholars of both performance and classical reception.

Focusing on this topic, I offer an analysis of a cross section of socially engaged US productions of Greek tragedy created by multiple US communities over the course of about ten years from 2005 to 2016. My methodological interest in live performance has in part influenced the selection of this time period, for I have seen the majority of performances[40] that I discuss live in the theatre during this time, a period that, as of the publication of this book, can be defined as contemporary.[41] One day, of course, these productions will be outmoded, not contemporary. I hope at that time they may serve as a snapshot of a critical cultural and historical moment in US history during the ongoing struggle over the appropriate representation of under-represented groups.

For the time period on which I focus is one in which the US has seen its first African American president, Barack Obama, and its first woman nominee for president by a major party, Hillary Clinton, at the same time

---

[40] As discussed elsewhere, the one exception is Split Britches' *Honey I'm Home*.
[41] On theorizing the contemporary, see Román (2005).

that it has seen Clinton's 2016 opponent, now President Donald J. Trump, inspire protests and make headlines such as 'Is Donald Trump Racist?'[42] and 'What Do People Mean When They Say Donald Trump Is Racist?'[43] With contentious debates over immigration, sexual harassment, racial and ethnic profiling, not to mention who can use a public toilet, issues of identity are playing a central and important role in American life and politics.

Mindful of these cultural dynamics, each chapter situates my case studies within the context of key political or social events that exhibit a certain popularized discourse about a particular community within a given historical moment. For example, in Chapter 1, which discusses three performances produced by two black theatre companies in Harlem in 2008 and 2010, I contextualize the case studies within the discourse surrounding the presidential campaign and election of Barack Obama. In Chapter 5 on veterans, I discuss the work of Aquila Theatre and Outside the Wire within the context of popular discourse about veterans generated by Hollywood films such as *The Hurt Locker*, *Zero Dark Thirty*, and *American Sniper*. This type of 'popular performance', according to Herrera, 'is often where such ideas about race, ethnicity and nation stir to life',[44] so I mention such mass media events, because they can be instrumental in reflecting and affecting ideas and attitudes in the culture at large, ideas that the various, small-venue theatrical performances discussed in this book often counter.

Thus, my methodology is not an empirical approach that attempts to discern what a given audience has said about a given production. Rather, integrating the fields of performance, cultural studies, historiography, and theatre criticism, I work like a cultural historian, examining the corporeal signifiers of each performance as if they were artefacts. Theatrical space, audience, performance style, and costumes are the material that I document and situate within specific historical moments to build my arguments.

In the process, my use of the first person often reflects my method of investigation; each source is not simply a performance but rather a 'theatrical event', i.e. Wilmar Sauter's term for the joint creation of meaning from the actions and reactions of both performers and spectators.

---

[42] Kristof (2016).   [43] Sanneh (2016).   [44] Herrera (2015) 17.

The 'theatrical event' arises from the dynamic connection between performance and spectators that through my presence in the audience[45] I helped to create.[46] Erika Fischer-Lichte has referred to this interaction as the 'feedback loop'. Artists have the ability to 'force new behavior patterns onto the audience, often plunge them into a crisis, thus denying the spectators the position of distanced, uninvolved observers . . . Through their actions and behavior, the actors and spectators constitute elements of the feedback loop, which in turn generates the performance itself.'[47] In other words, the performances transformed me, just as I transformed them. Thus, my descriptions of the performances not only serve a documentary purpose but are integral to my analysis, which reflects my own identity as it connects with those of the performers on stage and the various student and academic audiences with whom I have shared and formulated my ideas.

In this way, I examine the function of performance in transmitting social knowledge not by attempting to discern what a given audience or critic may have said about a production, or what the production has said to or about them, but instead by looking to the 'embedded logic expressed by the performance work itself'.[48] In other words, I am interested in the give and take between a performance and its cultural and historical environment, the embedded logic within the production that the artists and audience create. I focus not on any individual intention or response but rather on the cultural and historical forces that shape ideas, individual and communal, and influence responses to them. In this way, I work as a critic and historian of contemporary, live performance and its role in creating and reflecting social, cultural, and historical contexts, while articulating questions related to US identities.

Like David Román, I reject the charge of 'presentism' against those who study the contemporary.[49] Instead, I aim to demonstrate that contemporary productions can be interpreted in historical and political

---

[45] Except in the case of the Split Britches video I discuss.

[46] For a discussion of this term, see Sauter (2000) especially pp. 2–9.

[47] Fischer-Lichte (2008) 50.

[48] Herrera (2015) 10. Like Herrera, in assessing these performance choices, I seek 'to divine neither the creative collaborators' intentions nor the audience's response but rather to discern some instructive cues as to why certain choices "made sense" in given historical moments' (10).

[49] Román (2005) 12.

terms. In the process, I seek to document and explain the embodied discourse of each production and its ability at some times to challenge, at others to reinforce, stereotypes of under-represented communities within the majoritarian sphere.

To achieve this end, I have divided the work into five chapters: 'The Black Body' in TWAS' *MEDEA* and *Pecong* and CTH's *Trojan Women*; 'Executing Stereotypes' in Luis Alfaro's *Electricidad*, *Oedipus El Rey*, and *Mojada*; Representing 'Woman' in Split Britches' *Honey I'm Home*, the F-RTC's *Oedipus Rex XX/XY*, and Douglas Carter Beane and Lewis Flynn's *Lysistrata Jones*; 'Disidentification' in Allain Rochel's *Bacchae*, Tim O'Leary's *The Wrath of Aphrodite*, and Aaron Mark's *Another Medea*; Challenging the Stereotype of the 'Disabled Veteran' in Aquila's *A Female Philoctetes* and Outside the Wire's *Ajax*. Each of these chapters features two or three performances that serve as case studies, a cross section of productions through which I have studied the construction of identity and identification through the corporeal signifiers of US theatrical performances.

Chapter 1 explores issues of identity through a discussion of three Harlem-based productions of Greek dramas that have challenged cultural stereotypes of African Americans: Take Wing and Soar's *MEDEA* (2008) and *Pecong* (2010), and the Classical Theatre of Harlem's *Trojan Women* (2008). I argue that these three productions work against what performance theorist Harvey Young has referred to as 'the black body', i.e. the 'societal assumptions, the myths, of the black body'[50] that occur 'when popular connotations of blackness are mapped across or internalized within black people'. Chapter 2 examines the difficult process of 'executing stereotypes'[51] and the risks of inadvertently reinforcing them, with respect to the Latinx subcultures represented in MacArthur award fellow Luis Alfaro's productions of *Electricidad* at the Mark Taper Forum, Los Angeles (2005), *Oedipus El Rey* at the Dallas Theater Center (2014), and *Mojada* at the Getty Center, Los Angeles (2015), revisions of Sophocles' *Electra* and *Oedipus Tyrannus*, and Euripides' *Medea* respectively. Chapter 3 uses case studies from both comedy and tragedy,[52] including Split Britches' *Honey I'm Home: The Alcestis Story* (1989), the Faux-Real

---

[50] Young (2010) 7.

[51] Herrera's (2015) term for 'resignifying' stereotypes in Latinx culture.

[52] As I discuss further in Chapter 3, I recognize that some scholars question *Alcestis*' classification as a tragedy.

Theatre Company's *Oedipus Rex XX/XY* (2012), and Douglas Carter Beane and Lewis Flynn's *Lysistrata Jones* (2011), to explore the extent to which casting choices may reinforce or challenge some of the negative depictions of women that already exist in ancient drama. Chapter 4 discusses Allain Rochel's *Bacchae* (2007), Tim O'Leary's *The Wrath of Aphrodite* (2008), and Aaron Mark's *Another Medea* (2013), based on Euripides' *Bacchae*, *Hippolytus*, and *Medea* respectively. I argue that through the process of 'disidentification'[53] these productions demonstrate the operation of queer performative counter-discourses that challenge popular representations of gay men, and the gay suicide trope in particular.

Whereas these first four chapters address cultures that have been marginalized by the association of classical theatre with the Euro-American elite, Chapter 5 considers US veterans. Although veterans today, particularly those who are disabled, are a minority population that comprises less than 1 per cent of the total population, in ancient Athens, veterans had a direct connection to ancient Greek drama, and the majority of the ancient playwrights and the audience would have had first-hand experience of combat. As Jonathan Shay has famously stated, Greek drama was a 'theater of combat veterans, by combat veterans, and for combat veterans'.[54] By focusing on Aquila Theatre's *A Female Philoctetes* and Outside the Wire's *Ajax*, I explore the ways in which Greek tragedy can function to challenge the stereotype of the 'disabled veteran', but can also inadvertently reinforce stereotypes about members of this community.

According to Foley, the history of the 'democratic turn'[55] in which all of these productions participate begins in the late 1960s and 1970s when artists such as Judith Malina, Julian Beck, Richard Schechner, and Peter Sellars began to politicize Greek drama. The growth of the movement

---

[53] José Esteban Muñoz's term for 'the survival strategies the minority subject practices in order to negotiate a phobic majoritarian public sphere that continuously elides or punishes subjects who fail to conform to normative culture'. Muñoz (1999) 4.

[54] Shay (2002) 153.

[55] On the 'democratic turn' in Classics, see Hardwick and Harrison (2013), especially p. 16, where Hardwick defines the term and associates it with the increased use of Greek material in the last thirty or forty years with 'more "liberal" and even "democratic" causes as well as with broader-based access that crosses boundaries of gender, class, ethnicity, place, and language'. Foley has commented that since the 1990s new productions have also 'often demonstrated a new self-consciousness and range of doubts about the country's global activities and its international reputation' (2012a: 321).

may have also been encouraged by practical factors such as the greater availability of accessible translations and a built-in audience that makes the work marketable for theatre companies which need to generate more and more revenue from ticket sales. In any case, the trend extended into the 1980s, when, as Foley states, 'identity politics concerning gender, race, and nationality played an increasingly central role in American theatre. U.S. society came to be viewed as a "mosaic" rather than a melting pot.'[56]

In addition to such reasons for the growing interest, another that may attract under-represented communities to the subject is the insight that tragedy in particular gives to the inadequacies and failures of the justice system. Foley has suggested that Greek tragedy is incompatible with America's belief in downplaying 'history and the forces of social determinism in favour of optimistic stories of hard work and struggle leading to success'.[57] Members of communities who have been traditionally excluded from power or, in the case of veterans, abandoned by it have often approached the Horatio Alger myth, the classic American rags to riches success story, with great scepticism. This scepticism—this appreciation for and understanding of the ways in which fate can intervene or, in this case, the ways in which unfavourable social circumstances can limit opportunity and equal justice—is in part what the artists in this book have expressed in connecting Greek tragedy to their respective communities.[58]

But perhaps another answer to the question of why these artists are attracted to Greek drama is the simplest: why not? In other words, perhaps, as David Román has suggested, instead of fetishizing these 'works by minority artists—as exceptional..., why not, as [Suzan-Lori] Parks suggests, "Just watch. Just look. Just take it in?"'[59] Whatever the

---

[56] Foley (2012b) 9.

[57] Foley (2012b) 123. Foley (2012b) 3 states that her book:

> will argue that America particularly favors Greek tragedies that permit an exploration of the struggle to establish a self in a world that can appear to encourage and allow self-determination but can finally betray that effort in different ways... Moreover, when the plays do address controversial cultural and political issues relating to national identity, directors have needed to negotiate productions carefully to be heard.

[58] Such as Luis Alfaro's connection of the ancient system of vendetta justice to the system of justice in the underserved communities in Los Angeles.

[59] Román (2005) 48.

implicit or explicit reasons for their interest may be, the contemporary artists discussed in this book have been using Greek tragedy in ways that present powerful, oppositional voices to combat pernicious stereotypes that contribute to inequality within the social and legal systems of justice.

1

'The Black Body' in TWAS' *MEDEA* and *Pecong* and CTH's *Trojan Women*

Although the relationship between Greek drama and African Americans in Harlem dates back at least to Countee Cullen's 1935 translation of Euripides' *Medea*,[1] the popular view of classical drama's association with an elite, white, Eurocentric vision has continued to influence the subject's reception from Cullen's time into the present. In Cullen's time, for example, white critics condescendingly focused on a black man's ability to translate Greek drama successfully,[2] but during the time of the Civil Rights Movement, the criticism reversed direction. Black writers began to question the need to work with Greek or white European drama at all. While black colleges often staged Greek dramas prior to the 1960s,[3] political developments in the African American community began to change its perspective on classical works. The Black Arts Movement of the late 1960s,

---

[1] The work, published as *Medea and Some Poems*, was the first major attempt by a twentieth-century black American poet to translate Greek drama. Since the early 1900s, the population in Harlem was developing, and by the 1920s a cultural renaissance blossomed of which Cullen, together with writers such as Langston Hughes, Claude McCay, and Zora Neale Hurston, was a leading figure. For a discussion of this important work, see Lillian Corti (1998); Helene P. Foley (2012b); and Daniel Banks (2015).

[2] Citing several reviews, Corti describes them as ranging from 'liberal enthusiasm to racist condescension' (1998: 621). For recent studies on nineteenth- and early-twentieth-century engagements with the Classics by African Americans, see Curtis (2015) on the Frogs organization, and Hill (2015). See also Cook and Tatum (2010). On antiquity and race on the nineteenth-century stage, see Davis (2015).

[3] Artists such as Glenda E. Gill (2005), while recognizing that many of these performances took place through a lack of racial awareness and access to plays by African American playwrights, still reflect positively on the learning that took place despite the racial consequences.

which went hand in hand with the Civil Rights Movement, criticized the performance of classical drama, as black writers such as Lorraine Hansbury were increasing racial awareness and producing African American alternatives to the so-called white classic and classical plays.[4]

This shift of focus may have limited individuals who still wished to perform ancient drama, but opportunities did exist, such as the Mobile Theatre's 1969 production in New York's Washington Square Park of Sophocles' *Electra*, which featured an African American cast and African-inspired costumes. According to Karelisa Hartigan, 'The production was among the first to suggest the non-Western appeal of the Greek texts'[5] so even though some individuals resisted classical theatre, the Civil Rights Movement and American feminism may have actually provoked, as Helene P. Foley has argued, 'a rash of new Medeas in the late 1970s'.[6] Whatever the cause, interest in classical theatre has persisted.

This chapter considers two contemporary Harlem-based theatre companies that have negotiated this problematic history between artists of colour and ancient drama. From their casts and audiences to their intercultural scripts, Take Wing and Soar Productions (TWAS) and the Classical Theatre of Harlem (CTH) represent a plurality of perspectives. Drawing on an African American performance tradition of stylizing 'alternative forms of cultural expression that cut across the grain of conventional social and political ideologies',[7] the companies performed Euripides' *Medea* and *Trojan Women* in 2008 and Steve Carter's *Pecong* (an adaptation of *Medea*) in 2010, before primarily African American audiences in an ever more gentrified Harlem.

I will focus in particular on the role of what performance theorist Harvey Young has termed 'the black body', i.e. the imagined, stereotypical, social idea of 'the black body' that supersedes flesh and blood bodies and can become a target of violence.[8] 'When popular connotations of

---

[4] For a discussion of African American writers and Classics, see Cook and Tatum (2010) and Rankine (2006) and (2013).

[5] Hartigan (1995) 33.   [6] Foley (2012b) 210.

[7] Brooks (2006) 4. Brooks discusses this performance technique in relation to mid-nineteenth- to early-twentieth-century performances by black transatlantic artists who experimented with what she calls 'Afro-alienation acts', i.e. when the 'condition of alterity converts into cultural expressiveness and a specific strategy of cultural performance...we can consider these historical figures as critically defamiliarizing their own bodies by way of performance in order to yield alternative gender and racial epistemologies' (4).

[8] Young (2010) 7.

blackness are mapped across or internalized within black people', states Young, '. . . it is the black body and not a particular flesh-and-blood body that is the target of a racializing projection.'[9] Since Young published his book, the nationwide protests in 2014 over the death of Michael Brown, among many other unarmed black men who have been shot and killed, have brought 'the black body' into the current media spotlight. My interest here lies in the performance strategies used by TWAS and CTH to speak to and against such popular media discourses as the companies negotiate cultural ideas of 'hybridity' with those of 'the black body'.

TWAS and CTH in Context

Both TWAS and CTH are theatre companies specifically dedicated to classic and classical theatrical works, but they have distinct philosophies and approaches to the subject. Take Wing and Soar was founded by Debra Ann Byrd, an African American woman who aimed to provide opportunities for artists of colour in classical theatre by supporting 'emerging and professional classical artists of colour, by fostering their artistic achievement and personal growth, by providing opportunities for career development, and by developing creative programming that fosters diversity in classical theatre'.[10] The company has a limited budget, charges approximately eighteen dollars per ticket, and primarily attracts a local audience from Harlem. Since their inception, they have been hosted by the National Black Theatre,[11] which is the first black theatre

---

[9] Young (2010) 7. As Nicole R. Fleetwood has argued, 'the visible black body is always already troubling to the dominant visual field . . . [for] racialized heteronormativity structures the gaze and the field of vision' (2011: 6).

[10] TWAS website, www.twasinc.xbuild.com, accessed 16 September 2016.

[11] For more information on the National Black Theatre, see http://www.national-blacktheatre.org/about.htm, accessed 3 March 2015. The website states:

> Dr. Barbara Ann Teer's National Black Theatre Institute of Action Arts operates from an African context of a spirit culture. The National Black Theatre (NBT) began in 1968 as a non-profit organization and center for research & development known as the National Black Theatre Workshop Incorporated. NBT has since grown into an institution providing an alternative learning environment offering organizations and individuals, specifically those of African descent born in America, a space to discover, explore, nurture, articulate, address and heal the negative attitudes and emotions blocking freedom of expression.

arts revenue-generating institution in the country. For the last five years, TWAS has been the company in residence there. Since 2003, the company has primarily produced a variety of works by Shakespeare; *MEDEA* is the only full production of an ancient Greek play.[12] However, TWAS has also produced two adaptations of ancient Greek drama, including Stephen Carter's *Pecong*, an adaptation of *Medea*, which I will discuss later in this chapter, and Rita Dove's *The Darker Face of the Earth*,[13] an adaptation of Sophocles' *Oedipus Tyrannus*, performed in 2006. Through staging such works, TWAS 'has served over 400 classically trained artists, directors, designers, technicians and young entrepreneurial artists', and the company, as of May 2014, has been nominated for nineteen AUDELCO[14] awards for Excellence in Black Theatre and won five.[15]

With a different mission from that of TWAS, two Euro-Americans Alfred Preisser and Christopher McElroen founded the Classical Theatre of Harlem in 1999, in order to return Harlem theatre to the days of its renaissance. The company, of which Preisser and McElroen are no longer members,[16] enjoys a high production quality, the historic landmark of the Harlem Stage Gatehouse theatre, which used to be an old pumping station, reviews in the major newspapers, and audiences who pay forty dollars per ticket (although the company announced a plan to offer free tickets to the housing community being served under their Project Classics mission). According to its website, CTH's mission is:

To maintain a professional theatre company dedicated to presenting the 'classics' in Harlem ... [and] to create the next great American theatre company ... that is

---

[12] In addition to the 2008 production, TWAS also produced a reading of *MEDEA* with Trezana Beverley in 2006.

[13] For further reading on this work, see Carlisle (2000); Pereira (2002); Goff and Simpson (2007) 135–77; Sexton (2008); Rankine (2013); and Rabinowitz (2015).

[14] AUDELCO [Audience Development Committee] was:

Established and incorporated in 1973 by the late Vivian Robinson, to stimulate interest in, and support of performing arts in black communities. AUDELCO coordinates an average of one to two theatre events monthly, bringing approximately 50–75 people to each event ... The annual Vivian Robinson/AUDELCO Recognition, 'The VIV' Awards are the only formally established awards presented to the black theatre community. Every third Monday in November the nominees are awarded in various categories.

http://www.audelco.net/aboutus.html, accessed 12 March 2014.

[15] http://twasinc.xbuild.com/#/company-history/4527929172, accessed 12 March 2014.

[16] Preisser and McElroen have left the company. On this issue, see Propst (2009).

engaged in producing theatre that has the capacity to change lives and truly reflects the diversity of ideas and racial tapestry that is America.[17]

Since its founding, the company has provided opportunities for artists in over forty productions by authors such as Anton Chekhov, Samuel Beckett, Jean Genet, Langston Hughes, Adrienne Kennedy, William Shakespeare, Derek Walcott, and August Wilson, as well as Euripides.

In 2008, when TWAS and CTH presented *MEDEA*[18] and *Trojan Women*,[19] the issue of racial identity was in the spotlight. At that time, the media was fixated on the identity politics surrounding then Presidential candidate Barack Obama, who had begun the campaign that led to his eventual election as president. Ta-Nehisi Paul Coates' 2007 *Time* magazine article titled 'Is Obama Black Enough?', for example, argued that, 'Ever since Barack Obama first ascended the national stage at the 2004 Democratic convention, pundits have been tripping over themselves to point out the difference between him and the average Joe from

---

[17] http://www.classicaltheatreofharlem.org/about.html, accessed 12 March 2014.

[18] Euripides' *Medea*, produced in 431 BCE, dramatizes the story of the Greek hero Jason's abandonment of his two children and their mother Medea, a non-Greek woman from Colchis (a region on the Black Sea) who had helped him steal the mythical Golden Fleece and betrayed her family in the process. Hoping to advance his status, Jason wants to marry Glauce, the daughter of Creon, ruler of Corinth. Because Medea is not only a woman, but also a foreigner with no family to support her, she has no recourse to justice. Distraught and angered by Jason's selfish justification for his actions, Medea plans a cruel revenge. She convinces Creon to let her stay in Corinth for one more day. She secures a new home for herself by helping Aegeus, the ruler of Athens, cure his infertility. She then pretends to sympathize with Jason and offers Glauce gifts, but the gifts are poisoned. Glauce dies. Medea then murders her children and departs *ex machina* on the dragon-led chariot of her grandfather Helios. With no bride and no children, Jason is distraught.

[19] Euripides' *Trojan Women*, produced in 415 BCE, takes place immediately following the Greeks' defeat of Troy in the infamous Trojan War, which began over the beautiful Helen's leaving her Greek husband Menelaus for the Trojan prince Paris. The play opens with the god Poseidon lamenting his city's defeat. He is joined by Athena, who is outraged by the degradation of her sanctuary, where the Trojan princess Cassandra was raped. Angered at the Greeks, the two gods conspire to punish them. The plot focuses on the woeful fate of Hecuba, queen of Troy, who has been told that she will become a slave to the Greek hero Odysseus. Her husband and son have died, her youngest daughter Polyxena has been murdered as a sacrifice at the tomb of the hero Achilles, her daughter Cassandra will become the general Agamemnon's sex slave, her daughter-in-law Andromache will become the sex slave of Achilles' son Neoptolemus, and her baby grandson Astyanax will be hurled from the walls of Troy. Although it is the men who have caused all the destruction, Hecuba curses Helen. When Menelaus arrives, Hecuba warns him of Helen's wiles, but Menelaus refuses to murder or even punish his wife. At the end of the play, the body of Astyanax is mourned, and Hecuba is taken away with her daughters to the Greek ships.

the South Side.'[20] In his speech on race in Philadelphia, Obama himself stated, 'At various stages in the campaign, some commentators have deemed me as either "too black" or "not black enough".'[21] Even after his election, the debates over Obama's race continued. In 2010, for example, when TWAS' *Pecong* was produced, several newspapers reported on the President's census form, where he ticked 'black' as his race,[22] and books began to report on the subject.[23] As Tavia Nyong'o has explained, 'Obama embodied precisely the cosmopolitan hybridity against which an obdurate blackness has so often been invidiously contrasted. To the extent that postnational, postcolonial mulattos like Obama were welcomed by a predominantly white American public, they threatened to displace the authentically black in the national imaginary.'[24] This question of the 'authentically black', which has been endemic to the Obama campaign, is also relevant to studies of Black Theatre.

'The Black Body' and a 'Theater of Civil Disobedience'

Harvey Young, for example, began his introduction to the December 2009 *Theatre Topics*, an issue devoted to the subject of teaching African American theatre, with the questions 'What is black theater? What is a black play?'; and in the December 2005 special issue on Black Theatre in *Theatre Journal*, several artists and scholars addressed the question 'What is a black play and what is playing black?'

In his *Aristotle and Black Drama*, classical scholar Patrice D. Rankine has identified two types of black theatre. He states that, 'Artistic works can reflect more revolutionary political messages, as is the case with some of the plays of Amiri Baraka'; or playwrights, such as Adrienne Kennedy, Rita Dove, and Suzan-Lori Parks, can 'offer deeply self-conscious challenges to classical theater from within, and by doing so they perform a theater of civil disobedience'.[25] 'The theater of civil disobedience', he argues, 'encapsulates how dramatic writers resist traditional aspects of theater in order to infuse it with their moral conscience, through the black body.'[26]

[20] Coates (2007).   [21] Obama (2008).

[22] See, for example, Roberts and Baker (2010); Smith (2010); and Chang (2010).

[23] See Sugrue (2010).   [24] Nyong'o (2009) 3.

[25] Rankine (2013) 24.   [26] Rankine (2013) 20.

TWAS' and CTH's productions have enacted such a 'theater of civil disobedience'. As I will explain later, they have performed a discourse of 'hybridity' that counters the popular discourse of the Obama campaign when it argued (in response to media debates over whether Obama is 'black enough') that Obama's biracial, binational heritage was representative of America herself. According to Nyong'o, such an idea of racial transcendence, propagated by the campaign, has risked working as a 'depoliticizing catchall, pre-empting a more critical engagement with the traumas of the American past'.[27] He explains that:

The rising multiracial movement, as well as its academic interlocutor, critical mixed-race studies, has tended to ... [claim] hybridity both as the biopolitical overcoming of centuries of racial domination in the United States and, simultaneously, as the culmination of American integrationist values. Americanism, that is to say, becomes its own remedy. But such a position is helplessly in thrall to the empty tautologies of the national Thing.[28] It accommodates hybridity to an official teleology that is forever reducing the many to the one. Such a politics hardly inspires hope for hybridity's subversive potential.[29]

In contrast to this popularized notion of hybridity, TWAS' and CTH's performances of hybridity actively acknowledge the problems of racism and segregation that have denied opportunities to artists of colour. Their productions have thus avoided the traps of the Obama campaign's reduction of hybridity to the 'official teleology that is forever reducing the many to the one'. Instead, the companies work to negotiate the distinction between the 'lures and the loathing of hybridity'[30]—the lures of hybridity as a way forward and the loathing of the term's ability to obscure racial inequality.

This negotiation of the lure and loathing of hybridity is apparent in the ways that TWAS' and CTH's performances of MEDEA, Pecong, and

---

[27] Nyong'o (2009) 5.

[28] Nyong'o borrows this term 'the national Thing' from Slavoj Žižek. He describes it as follows:

More than just a love of country, the national Thing is a powerful force shaping the nation as the source of our enjoyment. The national Thing 'appears as what gives plenitude and vivacity to our life', Slavoj Žižek writes, and yet the only way we can determine it is by resorting to different versions of the same empty tautology.

Nyong'o (2009) 3, quoting Žižek (1993) 201.

[29] Nyong'o (2009) 5.   [30] Nyong'o (2009) 32.

Trojan Women challenge the idea of 'the black body', i.e. the imagined, societal idea of 'the black body' that often supersedes the recognition of any individual body.[31] On the one hand, by challenging ideas of 'the black body' and the ways in which it denies opportunities to artists of colour, TWAS and CTH demonstrate the lure of hybridity. In this way, they look toward the future. On the other hand, their mission statements acknowledge and engage with a segregationist past the effects of which continue to deny opportunities to artists of colour and their ability to have equal access to the representation of characters in classical theatre. In other words, the companies work to strike a balance between 'trying to live in the "world of the play" while performing in the world of race'.[32] They resist the idea that a utopian hybrid America currently exists by acknowledging the history of racial segregation that has contributed to the creation of 'the black body'.

The 'Africanist Presence' in TWAS' *MEDEA*

Debra Ann Byrd,[33] a classically trained artist with a passion for performing Shakespeare and the Greeks, attended acting school with the intention of pursuing a career in classical theatre, but, in her final year, two professors suggested that she focus on something other than classical acting because she was not traditional. While the meaning of 'traditional' may be ambiguous, it evokes the comments of theatre critics such as John Simon when he

[31] At the same time, the 2016 protests over the Academy of Motion Picture Arts and Sciences' lack of nominations for black actors two years in a row demonstrate the invisibility of African Americans and other minorities in the media. As Tim Gray (2016), the Awards Editor for *Variety*, has explained:

> Some may conclude that the nominations reflect institutional bias against minorities and women within the Academy of Motion Picture Arts & Sciences, but the problem is with Hollywood's major studios and agencies. There were 305 films eligible this year. If hiring reflected the U.S. population, Oscar voters would have weighed 150-plus films directed by women, 45 directed by blacks, 50 by Hispanics, and dozens of movies by directors who are Asian-American, LGBT individuals, people with disabilities and members of other minorities. Of course, the actual tallies were a fraction of those numbers.

[32] Wiles (2000) 170.

[33] Byrd (2009), personal interview. I am most grateful to Deborah Ann Byrd and Petronia Paley (2016) for generously granting me an interview and for providing me with images from their production.

criticized Joseph Papp's casting practices in the New York Shakespeare Festival in the 1960s:

Out of laudable integrationist zeal, Mr. Papp has seen fit to populate his Shakespeare with a high percentage of Negro performers. But the sad fact is that, through no fault of their own, Negro actors often lack even the rudiments of Standard American speech . . . It is not only aurally that Negro actors present a problem; they do not look right in parts that historically demand white performers.[34]

Simon's comments were written in the 1960s, but they are indicative of a prejudice that continues to exclude actors of colour from performing in classical theatre.

In response to such assumptions as well as to the proponents of 'traditional' casting practices, Ms Byrd founded Take Wing and Soar to create a venue for artists of colour to play classical roles at the professional level. Although new playwrights searching for the same opportunities as TWAS' performers might criticize their exclusion from the theatre and its success, other venues exist for playwrights. TWAS exists for performers and audiences, many of whom are experiencing classical theatre for the first time.

Yet, while TWAS provides opportunities for artists of colour, race was not a factor in the casting choices for *MEDEA*. Instead, the casting practice is something similar to what the Actors' Equity Association calls 'non-traditional casting', also referred to as 'colour-blind casting', which is 'designed to increase artistic options by expanding casting opportunities for women, actors of color, seniors and actors with disabilities in roles where race, gender, age or the presence or absence of a disability is not germane'.[35] Thus, while Ms Byrd founded TWAS to create opportunities for artists of colour, the company does not exclude anyone from its stage.

Competition for roles, however, is fierce. Many of TWAS' artists are award-winning professionals who continue to return to the small off-off-Broadway venue to perform in the classics. One such artist is Trezana Beverley, who in 1976 won the Tony award for her role in *for colored girls who have considered suicide/when the rainbow is enuf*. Ms Beverley

[34] John Simon, quoted in Catanese (2011) 15. Catanese, quoting from Epstein (1994) 291.
[35] Actors' Equity, http://www.actorsequity.org/theatrenews/archive/non-traditional_06-10-2003.html, accessed 10 August, 2014. For a discussion of non-traditional casting, see Catanese (2011), especially 9–19.

led the *MEDEA* cast, primarily composed of actors of colour, with the exception of the role of Aegeus, which was played by Ian Stewart. Her AUDELCO-nominated performance captured the anger, sadness, and confusion of the title character but also offered comic relief through her interpretation of Medea's gripes about the limitations imposed on her gender. However, despite her reputation and the brilliance of her performance, the production attracted only one reviewer.[36]

As I discuss in the next section, this absence of coverage may have been due to Petronia Paley's directorial choice of staging *MEDEA* without translocating the play into a distinctly African American or African context. In other words, despite the identity of TWAS' actors, the performance did not attempt to resituate the play in any specific African American context, or any context for that matter. As the reviewer Kat Chamberlain has described, the production presented a 'full-volume yet unvaried rendering of the text'.[37] Paley used Nicholas Rudall's translation,[38] which Chamberlain has described as 'very straightforward language',[39] to present the fifth-century BCE tragedy about the 'barbarian' woman from Colchis who murders her children to avenge her Greek husband Jason for leaving her to marry a young Greek princess.

Instead of translocating the play into a distinctly African American context, as many other artists have done,[40] the production design presents a time-out-of-time aesthetic with Pavlo Bosyy's minimalist set, in the approximately 150-seat theatre. The simple and sparse design consists of two benches and two pillars, made of sculpted fabric on wires, which frame the *skēnē* door. It suggests a setting in the not too distant past and shows great style despite the production's limited budget.

The costumes also evoke this time-out-of-time aesthetic. Apart from the 1950s inflection of Medea's suit, which she wears for the final scene of the play, and the Nurse's maid's uniform, which consists of a black dress with a white apron and a white lace collar, the costume design, by Ali Turns, is not specific to any historical time period. Instead, the majority of the male characters wear black suits or dinner suits, which have

---

[36] Chamberlain (2008a).   [37] Chamberlain (2008a).
[38] Ms Byrd has explained that she chose this translation for its readability on the stage.
[39] Chamberlain (2008a).
[40] See Foley (2012b) 190–228 and Wetmore (2013) on such productions.

Figure 1.1 Jason in Take Wing and Soar Productions' *MEDEA*, directed by Petronia Paley, starring Trezana Beverley. 2008.

Photo 2008 Renaldo Davidson.

different styles of ties or accessories (waistcoats, buttonholes, jewellery, watch chains, braces, and handkerchiefs). Such details help to differentiate each character from the others. Dathan B. Williams' Jason, for example, arrives in a crisp dinner suit and bow tie with a watch chain accenting his pocket (Figure 1.1). His booming voice, cigar, and

Figure 1.2 Medea in Take Wing and Soar Productions' *MEDEA*, directed by Petronia Paley, starring Trezana Beverley. 2008.

Photo 2008 Renaldo Davidson.

gelled-back hair further characterize him. The children wear school uniforms with crisp white shirts, and Aegeus wears a panama hat, as well as the performance's only white suit, which helps to indicate that he is from Athens not Corinth. The chorus, performed by Mary Hodges, Marishka Phillips, Beverley Prentice, Natasha Yannacañedo, and Ma'at Zachary, wear long, flowing, black dresses with tight-fitting bodices. Some have colourful headscarves or long necklaces.

In accord with this time-out-of-time aesthetic is Medea's costume (Figure 1.2). She wears a long, flowing, black dress with a tight bustier and a long black cape with gold sparkles, which highlight her gold choker, bracelet, and earrings. Her short, loosely curled hair has a reddish tint that gives it a snake-like quality, which perhaps alludes to Medea's supernatural powers. This costume designates Medea as Medea, but later when she appears *ex machina*, with a chauffeur in lieu of the Euripidean chariot, she wears, not any goddess-like apparel, but a red suit, fur stole, clutch bag, and high heels.

Thus, the production indicates Medea's otherness (i.e. her status as a foreign woman as opposed to a Greek male), not by the colour of her skin, but rather by contrasting the style of her costume with those of the other characters. Medea's gender makes her status 'other', and perhaps her age (since Trezana Beverley appears to be somewhat older than the actor playing Jason), but not her race.

This casting approach contrasts with contemporary productions of *Medea* that cast a black Medea opposite a white Jason in order to connect Medea's foreign status in the ancient play with an African American identity so that race becomes associated with the inferior status of a foreigner in ancient Greece.[41] These black Medeas have become so common that George C. Wolfe in his play *The Colored Museum* has parodied productions that take this casting approach:

MEDEA: I beseech thee, forgo thine anger and leave wrath to the gods!

SON: Girl, what has gotten into you?

MEDEA: Juilliard, good brother. For I am no longer bound by rhythms of race or region. Oh, no. My speech, like my pain and suffering, have become classical and therefore universal.

LADY: I didn't understand a damn thing she said, but girl you usin' them words.

(*Lady in Plaid crosses and gives Medea the award and everyone applauds.*)[42]

---

[41] Van Zyl Smit (2014) 157.   [42] Wolfe (1988) 28.

Explaining this scene in terms of Wolfe's satire of several theatre conventions, Kevin Wetmore has stated that:

First, ... the scene is a satire of black Medeas, Medea being the tragic figure most identified with women of color. Second, the scene is a parody of 'Black Orpheus'[43] productions that dismiss difference by universalizing—black suffering as the suffering of all. Medea Jones is a self aware stereotype of sorts who mocks that which she praises.[44]

Thus, while casting black Medeas aims to challenge the marginalization of black women, doing so may inevitably risk reinforcing the paradigm of not only 'black suffering as the suffering of all', as Wetmore/Wolfe suggest, but also of black women as 'other'.

This dilemma is, of course, endemic to the play itself. Feminists continue to debate the degree to which *Medea* challenges or reinforces stereotypes about women as 'other', conniving, obsessive creatures who need to be controlled.[45] For, despite Medea's being the most intelligent and heroic[46] character in the play, she is nevertheless a sorceress of sorts with magical powers that she uses to commit horrible acts. Moreover, while her cleverness and strength are something that feminists applaud, those same attributes would have evoked vitriol from the average fifth-century

---

[43] Wetmore (2003) 14–15 has proposed three models for understanding the relationship between ancient Greek works and their reception in the African diaspora: 'Black Orpheus'-, 'Black Athena'-, and 'Black Dionysus'-style productions. He explains that 'Black Orpheus' productions are:

> 'straightforward' adaptations with direct, one-to-one correspondences, or not even adaptations, but referential works, pieces that use Greek culture as a metaphor for African culture. 'Black Orpheus' is a model of equation; the African material is the equivalent of this aspect of Greek culture. The second model, 'Black Athena' is a reappropriation of material that is already African in origin. Under this model, the Greeks received their myths, their religion, their culture, etc. from the Egyptians. Therefore, all Greek material is really all African in the first place. The use of Greek material is not cultural colonialism and an expression of western superiority, but rather a corrective, returning the culture to its rightful African context. The third paradigm is 'Black Dionysus', which considers adaptation of Greek tragedy within the context of the African diaspora as a creative and constructive system of complex intertexuality designed to critique the very cultures that prioritize ancient Greek culture. It seeks to uncover the historical reality behind both Greek and African cultures, respecting both within their own context.

[44] Wetmore (2003) 149.

[45] For a recent discussion of this question, see Cairns (2014).

[46] On Medea's desire for *kleos* (heroic glory), see Foley (1989).

Athenian male who believed a woman's place was in the home.[47] In fact, because no Greek woman should or, to the Greeks' mind, could be like Medea, Euripides had to make her a foreigner.

Accordingly, if Douglas Cairns is correct and the ancient production of *Medea* suggested 'that chaos and destruction would result should women ever act like men, demand equality, and throw off the constraints that their society places on them',[48] then the use of an actor's racial identity as a signifier for the character's foreign status might reinforce a stereotype already inscribed in the ancient play by suggesting that not only women but particularly women of colour are destructive forces in need of control. Such a use of conceptual casting, or casting an ethnic, female, or disabled actor in a role in order to give the play greater resonance,[49] according to Brandi Wilkins Catanese, is the most 'oxymoronic [of casting choices] for its simultaneous reliance upon and denial of the significance of race'.[50] Thus, employing this casting choice in the case of *Medea* could in fact result in a reinforcement of the self/other paradigm of a white and black America rather than a challenge to it.[51]

Instead of using this approach or translocating the play, *MEDEA*'s production design (the time-out-of-time setting and the minimalist costume design), together with the identities of the performers and audience, works symbiotically with the text to make manifest the 'Africanist presence', a term which Brenda Dixon Gottschild has used to describe the often ignored fusions of African-based cultures with European and American ones:[52]

When we are able to see the African reflection as the image of our culture, then finally we will behold ourselves fully as Americans—in the mirror. At that point it will be silly to talk about Africanist presences as 'the Africanist contribution'. That is the outdated language of disenfranchisement, the mindset that implies that European is something bigger or better into which the African—the Other— is subsumed. But there is no Other, *we are it.*[53]

Recognizing the Africanist presence is recognizing the African *in* the American, not seeing it as something adjacent to it. For, according to

---

[47] On *Medea* in context, see Stuttard (2014). On women in tragedy, see Foley (2001).
[48] Cairns (2014) 137.   [49] Catanese (2011) 12.   [50] Catanese (2011) 13.
[51] See Wetmore (2003) 144–9 for a discussion of Medeas played by women of colour. See also Foley (2012b) on 'Medea as Ethnic Other from the 1970s to the Present', 210–24.
[52] Gottschild (1996) 2.   [53] Gottschild (1996) 78.

Gottschild, 'In spite of the politics of exclusion, Africanisms are inextricably dreadlocked into the weave of the American fabric and, like that hairdo, cannot be undone without cutting off both black and white strands at the root and diminishing the potential quality of life for us all.'[54] It is these dreadlocked Africanisms that *MEDEA*'s casting choices and straightforward production style reflect.

TWAS' production does not use the self/other, foreigner/Greek binary inscribed in the Euripides to reinforce the paradigm of black and white America by opposing a black Medea to a white Jason. Nor does *MEDEA* translocate the setting to a distinctly African or African American context. In this way, the actors of colour can perform an affinity with the material, rather than a distance from it. They show that their bodies of colour have equal access to the performance of classical drama and that white and black America are intertwined, not separate. In the process, the production underscores the 'Africanist presence' in American culture.

At the same time, Greek drama itself already contains Africanisms. One need not accept Martin Bernal's controversial thesis about the Afro-Asiatic roots of ancient Greek civilization to acknowledge the commonalities between ancient Greek and African theatre.[55] The use of mask, choral performance, call and response between actors and chorus, and repetition and revision of song, such as that between the choral strophe and antistrophe, are all characteristics of African performance. As Wole Soyinka has discussed in his 'The Fourth Stage: *Through the Mysteries of Ogun* to the Origin of Yoruba Tragedy', the Yoruban culture of Nigeria has distinct views of time, ritual, ancestors, and deities that distinguish it from European culture but overlap in some ways with ancient Greek culture.[56] These similarities between the cultures may or may not account for the similarities in their performance traditions. Regardless, contemporary audiences associate theatrical conventions, such as the mask, with Africa, because African performance traditions, unlike European ones, still regularly practise them as a part of a continued—as opposed to revived—tradition. Africanisms are thus inherent in Greek drama, so the performers of colour also reclaim Greek drama in that the genre is

---

[54] Gottschild (1996) 9–10.   [55] Bernal (1987), (2001), and (2006).
[56] Soyinka (1976) 140–60. For example, he discusses the connection between Dionysus and the Yoruban god Ogun, a connection which he further explores in his adaptation of Euripides' *Bacchae*.

not distinctly European but rather fuses performance traditions typically associated with both Europe and Africa.

Moreover, by making manifest the inextricable dreadlockings of so-called European and African performance traditions in the US, TWAS has also presented a *Medea* in which artists of colour have the opportunity to be just artists. This company of artists for whom race is always an issue has avoided depicting the self/other binary of Jason versus Medea through casting a white actor opposite a black one. Instead, gender, costume, and possibly age play out the self/other binary inscribed in the play. In this way, the production is conscious of racial identity without necessarily performing it, thus presenting a powerful cultural critique that paradoxically rests in the absence of one.

The production is not an Afro-centric revision, nor does it use Greek drama as a metaphor for Africa. Unlike productions such as Lee Breuer and Bob Telson's *The Gospel at Colonus*,[57] Paley has not performed the identity of her artists. She has not emphasized any distinct features of African American culture or identity by translocating the play. Nor has she situated her actors in a distinctly African American context or offered any overt cultural or political critique. Perhaps because of the primarily middle-class African American audience, her artists have had a better chance at being 'ordinary', for, as Kobena Mercer has argued, 'Black artists are never allowed to be ordinary...but have to visibly embody a prescribed difference.'[58]

In other words, Paley makes race *the* factor in the production; yet, in doing so, she succeeds in taking race out of the equation. She thus challenges the idea of 'the black body' by trying, as far as possible, to provide a space where bodies can perform as bodies without social stigmas, stereotypes, and prejudices attached to them. In the process, *MEDEA* speaks not to a black/white America but a hybrid one, for the play does not equate the character's foreign status with the title actor's racial identity but instead demonstrates the hybrid characteristics of both ancient Greek theatre and its reception on the US stage. At the same time, the production avoids the problem of suggesting a post-racial US because the company's mission underscores the history of division that has denied opportunities to artists of colour.

---

[57] For a recent discussion of this production, see McConnell (2015).

[58] Mercer (1997) 33, 37, quoted in Wetmore (2003) 43.

TWAS' *Pecong*: Translocating Classical Drama

Following these same principles, in March 2010 at the National Black Theatre, Deborah Ann Byrd and Jacqueline Jeffries of TWAS produced Steve Carter's *Pecong*,[59] which premiered in 1990 at the Victory Gardens Theatre, Chicago, with subsequent productions performed in Newark (1992), San Francisco (1993), and London and New York (2009).[60] The play is an adaptation of Euripides' *Medea* set on the imaginary Caribbean islands of Trankey (also referred to as 'Île Tranquille') and Miedo Wood (known as the Island of Darkness). Driven by the spirit of her recently deceased grandmother, Granny Root, played with relish by Phyllis Yvonne Stickney, Mediyah (Lorna Haughton) is the daughter of Damballah, a loa (god) in the voodoo religion (Figure 1.3). She uses her magic to help her beloved Jason Allcock, or Jason the Ram, played by the AUDELCO-nominated David Heron,[61] to defeat her brother Cedric (Albert G. Eggelston III) in the 'pecong'[62] of carnival (Figure 1.4). Yet, after winning the contest, Jason abandons Mediyah and her twin boys for the silent, light-skinned Sweet Bella, played by Lily Robinson, the daughter

---

[59] For an extensive discussion of Carter's play, see Wetmore (2003) 175–83. See also Foley (2012b) 212.

[60] Foley (2012b) 212. According to the *Chicago Tribune*, the premiere was 'an impressive and exciting accomplishment', even though the text was 'in need of some judicious trimming' (Christiansen 1990).

[61] According to Gooch (2010):

> David Heron brings his superior acting skills to the role of Mediyah's lover and foil. While some in the cast get weighted down with the West Indian patois, Heron was able to clearly articulate the dialectical rhythms and patterns and not get lost in the singsong banter of Carter's dialogue. Heron's Jason is cocky, arrogant and has coloration issues, all of which result from his upbringing. Yet, at the same time, Heron is able to show Jason's truthfulness and vulnerability in a way that makes his character likeable and relatable.

[62] Kevin Wetmore (2003) has described the 'pecong' as 'a contest of manhood, bravery, and creativity in which men duel with insults, not unlike the song duels of the Inuit, or "playing the dozens" in the African-American community, also known as "sounding", "woofing", or "signifying"' (2003: 178). Staging this critical scene, a crowd of ten actors quickly surrounded Jason and Cedric. With the rumble of bongos beneath their raps, the two men sparred for their manhood. Cedric, donning a bird hat and waggling his hips, moved like a cock in his high-waisted white trousers and high black boots, while Jason, with equal swag, sported a gold mask over his eyes. As Saltz (2010) has observed about TWAS' production, 'The director stages the contest with relish, and Mr. Heron and Mr. Eggelston make it clear that these men are most alive when they are performing.' Moreover, Deardra Shuler (2010) enjoyed Eggelston's performance of the pecong, 'by way of amusing posterior and pelvic gyrations that provided endless belly laughs. As they tossed insults back and forth over everything from their mothers' sex life [lives] to the length of their penises, Cedric started to falter.'

Figure 1.3 Mediyah in Take Wing and Soar's 2010 Mainstage Production of *Pecong*.

Photo Hubert Williams. Imagez of Us.

Figure 1.4 Mediyah, Jason, Creon, and his daughter Sweet Bella at the pecong competition, in Take Wing and Soar's 2010 Mainstage Production of *Pecong*.

Photo Hubert Williams. Imagez of Us.

of Creon Pandit (Karl O'Brian Williams), the wealthy, class-conscious town magistrate. Avenging this rejection, Mediyah agrees to give up the twins to Jason but instead gives Persis and Faustina (the 'cackling, gossiping hens'[63] who have no equivalent in the Euripides except to serve in the role of a chorus and messengers) a drink that will poison the baby's milk[64] and a nightdress that will poison Sweet Bella.

Kevin Wetmore has explained that 'Carter, by naming his play after the contest and not the heroine [Medea], as nearly every other playwright has, moves the focus from her to the verbal battle of Jason and Creon.'[65] Moreover, 'Because Carter's characters are all Caribbean of African descent . . . the conflict between black and white, present in almost every other [Medea] adaptation, is not present here.'[66] Thus, just as TWAS' MEDEA has avoided reinforcing a black/white binary by casting a black Medea opposite a white Jason, Pecong avoids this binary as well. The play itself calls for characters of Caribbean-African descent, and TWAS' cast consists entirely of actors of colour.

Despite this similarity to TWAS' MEDEA, Pecong's performance is distinct in other ways. In contrast to MEDEA's nondescript, time-out-of-time setting, the performance translocates Medea to the Caribbean, not as the result of a directorial choice, but because Carter's play-text called for it. This contrast in approach is important, for I will argue that Pecong has attracted more critical attention than MEDEA precisely because Pecong sets the Medea story within a distinctly black cultural context. Whereas in MEDEA the actors of colour could assume that 'their performing bodies were as neutrally available to the texts as white actors',[67] Carter's Pecong emphasizes a distance between the actors and classical theatre because the play-text adapts the ancient Greek source text into a distinctly Caribbean context.

Unlike MEDEA, which, despite Tony award-winning Trezana Beverley's performance in the title role, received only one review,[68] Pecong received five,[69] including one by the New York Times. Rachel Saltz concluded that

---

[63] Gooch (2010).

[64] The drink was for Persis and Faustina, whom Mediyah sent off with Jason to be wet nurses for her babies.

[65] Wetmore (2003) 179.   [66] Wetmore (2003) 179.   [67] Catanese (2011) 16.

[68] Chamberlain (2008a). Chamberlain also reviewed CTH's Trojan Women a month previously: see Chamberlain (2008b).

[69] Armstrong (2010); Durrell (2010); Gooch (2010); Saltz (2010); and Shuler (2010).

'if the play's ending doesn't stay with you (sorry, no catharsis) then what comes before surely will'.[70] And Sandi Durrell of *NiteLifeExchange* called Arthur French's direction[71] 'first rate theatricality', David Withrow's costume design 'stunning', and renowned actress Phyllis Yvonne Stickney's AUDELCO-nominated performance as Granny Root 'powerful, cunning, and almost frightening'.[72] Like TWAS' *MEDEA*, the production was nominated for AUDELCO awards (five, in fact, three of which it won for Best Revival, Best Costume Design, and Best Lighting Design); however, unlike *MEDEA*, *Pecong* received critical attention from reviewers. As Saltz stated, 'tragedy, shmagedy. "*Pecong*" . . . has its own charms.'[73] Although the discrepancy in coverage of these two related productions performed by the same theatre company within two years of each other could have been due to greater interest in Carter's play, the Classical Theatre of Harlem's production of Euripides' *Trojan Women*, performed within a month of TWAS' *MEDEA*, also received five critical reviews.[74] This performance, like *Pecong*, emphasized a distance between the actors of colour and classical theatre by translocating the play.[75]

Angela C. Pao has discussed the problems with translocating settings by comparing the National Asian American Theater Company's (NAATC) productions of Eugene O'Neill's *Long Day's Journey into Night* and *Ah! Wilderness*, performed by an all-Asian American cast in 1997, with the Beijing People's Art Theatre's production of Arthur Miller's *Death of a Salesman* by an all-Chinese cast in Beijing in 1983. She has explained that NAATC's staging, unlike BPAT's, did not demonstrate an interest in transposing classic plays into an Asian or Asian American context. One of the founding directors of NAATC, Mia Katigbak, has clarified her reasons for this choice:

When I was first thinking about forming the company, we had an informal reading of *The Glass Menagerie*, and no cultural transformation was necessary. That's why we do these plays as written, rather than assuming that people will only understand them if we reset them in Chinatown. I think that would be a step backward; it just perpetuates racism to make the setting that specific.[76]

---

[70] Saltz (2010).   [71] With associate director Timothy D. Stickney.
[72] Durell (2010).   [73] Saltz (2010).
[74] Chamberlain (2008a); La Rocco (2008); O'Brien (2008); Simmons (2008); Soloski (2008).
[75] I discuss this performance in the next section of this chapter.
[76] Katigbak interviewed in 'East Meets West' (31 October 1997), *In Theater*, 31, 6, quoted in Pao (2010) 130.

While TWAS embraces all styles of production, Katigbak prefers a production style similar to that of TWAS' *MEDEA*, in which Paley, as I have earlier explained, has not attempted to perform or play up any distinct features of African American culture or identity.

Paley has not situated her actors in a distinctly African American context or offered any overt cultural or political critique. In other words, like NAATC's productions, TWAS' *MEDEA* has not demonstrated a 'movement across space'[77] that is predetermined by the race of the actors. The straightforward performance and production design of Euripides' text in translation do not bear the mark of African or African American culture, any more so than any other American identity. As a result, 'Instead of reasserting a static, bounded notion of cultural identity, the cross-cultural casting makes a statement about the changing nature of American cultural identity over time.'[78]

Despite its profound yet subtle statement, TWAS' *MEDEA*, like NAATC's productions of O'Neill's plays, disappointed critics,[79] who, worse than giving it bad reviews, simply ignored it and its Tony award-winning star, despite five reviewers having attended CTH's *Trojan Women* just a month previously.[80] The one reviewer who did cover *MEDEA* made no mention of race or TWAS' mission statement. Instead, Kat Chamberlain focused on a description of the plot and expressed disappointment not with the casting, but with the performances, particularly Beverley's AUDELCO-nominated one.[81] She commented that the production failed to find 'a corresponding supply of subtlety, depth, and complexity of human emotion [to the betrayal, rage, revenge, death, and grief in the original that the production played up]'.[82] In addition, she found herself

---

[77] Pao (2001) 408.   [78] Pao (2001) 408.

[79] Pao (2010) 131, describes the critical response to these productions in which the reviewers express confusion and disappointment with the Asian American cast performing the classic works.

[80] See note 96 for these reviews. CTH's *Trojan Women*, like TWAS' *Pecong* and unlike *MEDEA*, sets the ancient play in an African context.

[81] Chamberlain (2008a). Despite Trezana Beverley's AUDELCO nomination for Best Actress, Chamberlain has commented that her 'no-holds-barred performance ... [is a] valiant effort that unfortunately does not pay off'. The 'workhorse production' does not demonstrate a 'real inner struggle to make Medea not some powerful and magical beast, but a real human being'.

[82] Chamberlain (2008a).

'yearning for shades of quiet grey after being walloped by the blindingly garish portrayal of Medea and her wrath'.[83]

The five reviewers of *Pecong*, however, focused on the cultural transformation of the Medea myth. They described the Medea story as 'sway[ing] to a 19th Century Island Rhythm',[84] the carnival atmosphere as 'colorful',[85] and the classic Greek hero as going 'sepia'.[86] One reviewer even observed that:

There is something very ritualistic about this production done within the setting of the National Black Theatre that for this reviewer, at least on opening night, took on a feel of a temple and a subtle invoking of African gods, especially with the cigar smoking that laid [*sic*] heavy in the air but is a favorite of the God Chango.[87]

Another commented on the play's engagement with issues of racial identity:

The playwright left no stone unturned as he delved into the caste [*sic*] systems and attitudes concerning color. The Caribbean is one of the most diverse islands [*sic*] containing a polyglot of peoples in hues of black, brown, yellow, red and white, made up of Africans, Asian Indians, Indonesian Javanese, Chinese, Aboriginal Indians, Europeans and other mixtures. However, there seemed a thread throughout the play that suggested there was, or is, an institutionalized stratification of race and racial ideas whereby lighter skin tones are seen as more socially and economically acceptable and valued. This is demonstrated via the fair skin of Jason (David Heron) and the darker complexioned Mediyah, whom Jason has no problem bedding or even impregnating but yet would never wed. [While] this play touched upon the injustices, biases and ignorances born of the human experience, it also vetted levity which was so brilliantly brought to the fore by Albert G. Eggelston, III, as Cedric, Mediyah's brother.[88]

At the performance on 21 March, which I attended, the nearly fifty members of the audience (the majority of them people of colour) in the 150-seat theatre appreciated this levity and were often laughing, as during the scene when Persis and Faustina tease each other about their identities.[89] Thus, all of the reviewers' descriptions and comments about

---

[83] Chamberlain (2008a).   [84] Saltz (2010).
[85] Shuler (2010).   [86] Gooch (2010).   [87] Shuler (2010).
[88] Shuler (2010).
[89] Carter (1993) 13–14:

> FAUSTINA: It's all that Chinee, Syrian, and Indian blood mix up in you.
> CREON: You ol' Zulu. I ain't have the first piece of Chinee in me.
> PERSIS: How you know? You daddy keep record of he ramblin'?

racial identity reflect the ambiance of Carter's play and the performance itself, but, at the same time, the play's 'exotic' Caribbean context and commentary on racial identity may have been exactly what attracted the reviewers to the performance in the first place.

Pao has made this point in her discussion of BPAT's production of *Death of a Salesman*. She argues that the production had critical success because its writer and director Arthur Miller reframed or transported the play into a Chinese cultural context and that 'translation and transportation of a play across national boundaries is [*sic*] ultimately an affirmation of those boundaries, regardless of the fact that, as in Miller's case, the objective may be to transcend those boundaries'.[90] In other words, in aiming to challenge stereotypes and cultural mores, the production can inadvertently reinforce those same ideas.

As Catanese has explained, NAATC's productions have been, in part, not as favourably reviewed as BPAT's, because:

All-Asian American casts that perform classics of the American canon performatively produce their equal access to narratives valorized as emblematic of American (theatrical) culture. When they do so in a color-blind way, rather than according to conceptual or cross-cultural conceits, they fail to respect the silent conflation of whiteness with Americanness.[91]

Although TWAS' *Pecong*, unlike BPAT's *Death of a Salesman*, has been performed in English for an American audience in the US and is an adaptation of an ancient Greek drama and not an American classic, I would suggest that the same principle applies here.

Like BPAT's *Death of a Salesman*, *Pecong* has performed a distance from its Euripidean precursor, particularly through the dialectical rhythms of the West Indian patois sing-song banter of Carter's dialogue.[92] Although presenting the ancient drama in these Caribbean terms can be empowering, the cross-cultural approach also cannot avoid the risk of reaffirming, to

---

FAUSTINA: And who you callin' Zulu? We ancestor come here straight from Egypt.
CREON: Strike me blue and Holy shite! Cleopatra think she white!

Wetmore has explained this dialogue as Faustina's demonstration of 'Afrocentric classicism—the manifestation of the "Black Athena" paradigm in this play...Unlike Creon, she does not reject Africa entirely, but she looks to its ancient past for her immediate identity' (Wetmore 2003: 177).

[90] Pao (2001) 408.   [91] Catanese (2011) 16.
[92] As described by Gooch (2010) in his review.

THE BLACK BODY' 41

use Catanese's phrase, the 'silent conflation of whiteness' with classical texts. Thus, for TWAS' core audience, the production's commentary on racial identity may have challenged the 'racialized logic of American society'[93] through its commentary on racial identity, but, at the same time, as Catanese suggests, the production's reception by reviewers indicates a reinforcement of such logic because the translocation of *Medea* to the Caribbean can reaffirm the concept of 'the black body' by putting the actors of colour at a distance from the classical text. Thus, the question of audience is here important, a point which I discuss further in Chapter 2.

CTH's *Trojan Women*: A 'Double-Conscious' Translocation

Another example of a performance that translocates Greek drama into an African context is the Classical Theatre of Harlem's *Trojan Women*.[94] Adapted and directed by Alfred Preisser, *Trojan Women*, performed in January 2008, received mixed reviews.[95] Although it follows the

---

[93] Catanese (2011) 16.

[94] For a study of the Euripidean play in its historical context, as well as its reception in the twentieth century, see Goff (2009). See also Croally (1994). For a brief discussion of Preisser's 2004 production of *Trojan Women*, see Foley (2012a) 317–18.

[95] See for example Claudia La Rocco (2008) who found the chorus to be melodramatic and the artistry of the production lacking. Paulanne Simmons (2008) commented:

> There are many inspired moments, but the attempt to marry the ancient tragedy with modern wars is not always successful. The chorus, especially in the beginning, sounds much more whiney than tragic. The crimes committed during the wars in Sierra Leone and Liberia have been well documented, and their enumeration serves little dramatic purpose.

Kat Chamberlain (2008b) thought the production suffered from 'emotional overdrive'. Maura O'Brien (2008) commented:

> There is a lot that Preisser is trying to do with *Trojan Women*, and the production suffers from its grand, but undefined ambitions. Whereas Euripides moved his play around the central character of Hecuba, this adaptation lacks that kind of central focus, and introduces several different ideas, most of them somewhat obvious criticisms. Euripides' play is an interesting vehicle for a critique of modern society, but the themes and structure of the adaptation could benefit from some tightening and a stronger, narrower focus on the African women's accounts, or a more specific connection to the civil wars in Africa. When the audience looks through the fence at Troy it might be looking into a distant mirror, brought up close and personal, but the production's message is too hazy to inspire critical self-assessment, or change.

Euripidean plot[96] fairly closely, the production, unlike TWAS' *MEDEA*, does not rely on a translation but rather adapts *Trojan Women* to tell the story of the civil war in Sierra Leone, which began in 1991. Preisser asks, 'If there is truth in the Greek concept of tragedy, in which cycles of order are governed by fate, then doesn't it stand to reason that the catastrophic disaster always happening somewhere else will someday happen here?'[97] In this way, the performance, like many of *Trojan Women* on the twentieth-century stage, uses the tragedy as a framework to explore the violence of war and its repercussions for the global community.[98]

The production, like that of *Pecong*, garnered five reviews. It is thus another possible example of New York reviewers' interest in productions that perform a distance between classical plays and performers of colour. However, in this section, I want to illustrate that, despite the risks such productions may pose in reinforcing a racialized logic that separates white and black America, these performances can also simultaneously challenge this very logic through a 'double-conscious' perspective.

Performed at the Harlem Stage Gatehouse theatre, the play follows the plot of the Euripides to focus on the Greek army's victimization of the

---

Alexis Soloski (2008) commented:

> Preisser follows the example of Sartre, who thrust the ravages of colonialism into his version, and Charles L. Mee, who added the testimony of holocaust survivors to his *Trojan Women 2.0*. Preisser's efforts to heighten and contemporize the drama somewhat succeed, though they're undercut by certain directorial choices. He stages the action behind a chain-link fence, which prevents the audience from really seeing the faces of the women, rendering their performances more generic or anonymous than they ought to be. And while both Troy Hourie's setting, which exploits the architecture of the grand Gatehouse theatre, and Kimberley Glennon's silky costumes are striking, they, too, lend the proceedings an air of the placeless and timeless. This makes it easier to separate ourselves from the onstage atrocities. Preisser seems to want us to feel culpable—some lines clearly indict the U.S.—but the action plays out as if at a distance.

[96] For a summary of the play, see note 19.

[97] http://www.classicaltheatreofharlem.org/trojanwomen_07-08.html, accessed 11 December 2015.

[98] *Trojan Women* has often been staged as an anti-war play, at least as far back as the Chicago Little Theatre's touring production of 1915, which coincided with H. Granville Barker's 1915 production that toured the US to make an anti-war statement. See Slater (2015) for a discussion of Barker's production. Other examples of anti-war productions performed in the US are Michael Cacoyannis' 1963 production at Circle in the Square, New York, NY, which criticized the Vietnam War. On these and other productions of *Trojan Women* in America, see Foley (2012b); Goff (2009); and Willis (2005).

women of Troy after its defeat by Greece in the Trojan War. However, Preisser has distanced his production from its fifth-century BCE precursor by intertwining the Euripides with eyewitness accounts of women survivors of the recent civil wars in western Africa. In order to emphasize the idea that the 'catastrophic disaster always happening somewhere else will one day happen here', the play is set in the imagined wreckage of a 'train station like Penn Station'[99] (one of the major train stations of New York City). The play opens with a multiracial chorus of barefoot women costumed in tatters of fine evening gowns designed by Kimberley Glennon. They were at a party celebrating victory but now stand behind Troy Hourie's set consisting of a six-foot-high cyclone fence with an approximately twenty-foot-high scaffolding framing it, and large metal doors that open and shut positioned downstage. Played by Zainab Jah, Helen, the woman whose leaving her Greek husband Menelaus and running away with the Trojan prince Paris incited the men to war, is perched high above the stage on a deconstructed Greek column, which serves as her prison. The chorus stands opposite Helen, as one chorus member sings her harrowing account of the war, to music composed by Kelvyn Bell.

With Tracy Jack's choreography punctuating the poignancy of their speech, the other chorus members join in the song. They recall stories of torture, violence, and death. 'Men walk through church, sprinkle gasoline on us,' they cry.[100] 'The men ran out of ammunition and they turned to axes and machetes. They came and sprinkled gas on the house. Now you know us. Now you know the bitterness of the war.' To which Helen later adds, 'Our bodies are currencies in this war and always will be.' The horrors they recount and their battered faces are juxtaposed with the beauty of their halter-neck evening gowns, one short, some beaded, others sparkling, with long gloves emphasizing their elegance. These are the dresses they were wearing when the soldiers raped them after 'celebrating the victory they thought they had won'.

The men provide an aggressive contrast. Amidst the women's screaming, Michael Early arrives in the role of the Greek herald Talthybius, costumed in a suit with two soldiers at his side. He informs the women of Odysseus' orders concerning Hecuba (Lizan Mitchell), Cassandra

---

[99] Later in this section, I explain this choice of setting and its implications.

[100] This quotation and all those following have been taken from my notes of the production. Alfred Preisser has kindly granted me permission to include them.

(Tryphena Wade), and Astyanax, the child of Andromache and the Trojan warrior Hector. One reviewer has described the character as follows: 'Like a CEO whose lot it is to fire half his staff after a bad year, Talthybius lets the women know that he does not want to pain them, but is determined to carry out his orders.'[101] When the women ask, 'Are we to be slaves?', Talthybius responds, 'Let's say wives.'[102] He finally delivers the news that Cassandra and Astyanax must die, and from that point on, the battle between the sexes escalates.

However, in this battle, both sides agree that Helen is to blame. The men loathe but adore her. The women curse her. Played by Ty Jones, Menelaus, who plans to kill his wife Helen, exclaims, 'I'd have to care about you to hate you . . . I came here to kill you.' But Helen pleads with him to spare her. She claims that the gods made her do it, and she blames Hecuba for the war because she gave birth to Paris. Despite the Trojan women's protests, Helen succeeds in seducing Menelaus, and he concedes: 'All right, so maybe I don't have to kill you, right now.' This moment of comic relief is short-lived before the Greeks murder Andromache's son Astyanax. In the rebellion that follows, the Greek soldiers shoot several women and put others behind bars on a ship positioned upstage. Talthybius arrives with the child's body, which Hecuba receives as she warns the herald, 'Your death ship is coming too.' As the chorus has earlier sung, what has happened to these women can happen anywhere. The havoc that the Greeks have wreaked on the Trojan women will be requited in turn, yet despite the men's violence, the women also blame Helen. As Foley notes of the 2004 production, 'Helen departed remarking to the angry women . . . "The men who write history will say this was all the work of a single woman. But I think you all know those men have been known to lie."'[103]

As the woman who is the 'mirror that reflects a man's desire, contempt, indifference, or self-doubt', Helen serves in the production as a scapegoat for the vanity, greed, and corruption that lead to war and violence against women. While Preisser's adaptation does not overtly link the beauty of Helen to the wealth of natural resources in Africa, the work does present Helen as a metaphor. Desire for Helen is compared to

---

[101] Simmons (2008). See note 102 for the source of the quotation.
[102] Quotation taken from Margo Jefferson's theatre review of an earlier version of this *Trojan Women* produced in 2004.
[103] Foley (2012a) 318.

the desire for profit aroused by diamonds in the African blood diamond trade, for attempts to explain Sierra Leone's civil war have varied from 'bad governance' to 'the history of the post-colonial period' to the 'urge to acquire the country's diamond wealth'.[104] Thus, desire for the beauty, wealth, status, and power associated with diamonds, like the desire for Helen, erupts into the violence initiated in Sierra Leone by the violent Revolutionary United Front.

According to a 2000 article in *The Guardian*:

The PAC [Partnership Africa Canada] report into Sierra Leone concludes that the seven-year war there, in which 75,000 civilians were killed, 2 million people displaced and tens of thousands mutilated, opened the country to a gangster economy based on the diamond trade. Neighboring Liberia has, at an official level, been deeply implicated in the trade, the report concludes.[105]

Yet the cause of this devastation is not simply diamonds, just as the cause of the Trojan War is not Helen herself. Rather it is the men's behaviour over them that results in war.

Thus, what is striking about CTH's *Trojan Women* is that, despite the reference to Helen as a 'mirror that reflects men's desire', the production still echoes its ancient Greek precursor by having the Trojan women blame not just the men but Helen herself for the war. As Barbara Goff has explained about Euripides' *Trojan Women*, 'The chorus join in enthusiastically with the appeal to execute Helen.'[106] Likewise, one reviewer has noted about CTH's production, 'Though the women speak with individual voices, they move as a unit. At first, their combined force is brute and animal-like; they gang up on Helen, screaming at her and calling her names. Their hatred echoes that of the men who terrorize them; a parallel they realize too late.'[107] In this production, the women still blame another woman, and not just the male aggressors, for their city's ruin.

However, while CTH's production may not have included an overt feminist revision to the plot,[108] it has included an explicit postcolonial critique. By incorporating accounts from the civil wars in Sierra Leone

---

[104] Sierra Leone Truth and Reconciliation Commission (2004) 3.
[105] Brittain (2000). [106] Goff (2013b) 70. [107] O'Brien (2008).
[108] An example of such a feminist revision of the plot of *Trojan Women* appears in Jocelyn Clarke's adaptation, performed by Ann Bogart's SITI Company in 2011 at the J. Paul Getty Museum and in 2012 at the Brooklyn Academy of Music. This production replaced the chorus of Trojan women, who blame Helen, with a single Trojan eunuch priest. Moreover, Clarke gives the bereft Andromache agency in killing her child, whereas Euripides' play assigns the murder to the Greeks.

and weaving these events into the plot of an ancient Greek play, the adaptation connects the contemporary African conflict to its British colonial past; for Classics was the hallmark of education during the age of imperialism.[109] In this way, the plot of the ancient Greek *Trojan Women* functions metonymically in the production. It is a reminder of the colonial antecedents to Sierra Leone's conflict, such as the former British colonial government's division of Sierra Leone into two nations, known as the 'Colony' and the 'Protectorate', which have had 'far-reaching implications for issues such as citizenship, land tenure rights and conflict of laws'.[110]

In addition to assigning responsibility to the colonial past, the production also implicates Western consumerism and the diamond markets that have fuelled the blood diamond trade. The politically charged accusation is subtle, for one reviewer, missing the allusion, has asked: 'What did American G.I.s or CEOs have to do with those crimes [in Sierra Leone]? What's more, the play never explains how those wars are related to a destroyed Penn Station.'[111] However, while not exactly explaining these points, the production's setting in a post-apocalyptic New York, or as the programme states somewhere like it, suggests not only that the US's consumer-driven support of the diamond trade has contributed to the violence, but also that, in turn, the US may not be immune from the violence caused by the trade.

For, while the set design need not be Penn Station specifically, it is clear that the location is somewhere in the West, since the image must create a connection between wars in foreign lands and American soil. As Preisser has stated in an email to me, he aimed to suggest 'the ruins of the original Penn Station (a brilliant building destroyed by barbarians) and the violence always taking place somewhere else (hence not quite real) finally taking place here'.[112] Through this image, he explores what he calls the Greek concept of tragedy and the cycles of order by suggesting

---

[109] For further discussion on Classics and imperialism in the British Empire, see Bradley (2010) and Goff (2013a), a work which focuses specifically on Classics in colonial West Africa, including Sierra Leone.

[110] Sierra Leone Truth and Reconciliation Commission (2004) 5.

[111] Simmons (2008).

[112] Preisser (2017). Preisser's comment references the 1963 demolition of the original Penn Station, an exquisite landmark demolished to build a new station with office space and a sports complex over it. His comment, like his adaptation, suggests his antipathy to the destruction of heritage in the interest of capitalist exploits.

the violence in the present and the violence of the colonial past have had repercussions not only for Africa but for the US as well.

In this way, the production engages with the Euripidean *Trojan Women* through the double-conscious lens of the 'Black Atlantic', a term which Paul Gilroy has used to refer to a black identity that is not distinctly African, American, Caribbean, or British, but a conglomeration of these cultures. In his *Black Atlantic: Modernity and Double Consciousness*, Gilroy has expanded on W. E. B. Du Bois' notion of 'double consciousness', which refers to:

a world which yields him [an African American] no true self-consciousness, but only lets him see himself through the revelation of the other world. It is a peculiar sensation, this double-consciousness, this sense of always looking at one's self through the eyes of others, of measuring one's soul by the tape of a world that looks on in amused contempt and pity.[113]

Gilroy has drawn on the concept of double consciousness to extend his 'implicit argument that the cultures of diaspora blacks can be profitably interpreted as expressions of and commentaries upon ambivalences generated by modernity and their locations within it'.[114] By using an ancient Greek tragedy and gesturing toward its implicit associations with the colonial past, the production has engaged with such a double-conscious perspective.

CTH's *Trojan Women* operates as a tool to dismantle the ideas and effects of colonialism, for the production's 'gestures [of anteriority as anti-modernity] articulate a memory of pre-slave history that can, in turn, operate as a mechanism to distil and focus the counter-power of those held in bondage and their descendants'.[115] Through a 'double-conscious'[116] lens, the performance reimagines a classical Greek drama to suggest the implication of the West in the suffering of the Black Atlantic. Accordingly, the production uses the Greek to reflect not only on the impact of colonialism on Africa but also on colonialism's repercussions in the network of all global nations.[117]

---

[113] Du Bois (2007) 2.   [114] Gilroy (1993) 117.   [115] Gilroy (1993) 57–9.
[116] On double consciousness, see also Gilroy (1993) 127.
[117] For further reading on revisions of Greek drama that comment on colonialism, see Bradley (2010); Goff (2005); Goff and Simpson (2007); and Hardwick (2010).

Conclusion

In conclusion, these three Harlem productions, performed within two years of one another, illuminate the complexities of the idea of 'hybridity'. Their hybrid characteristics, from their casts to their scripts to their audiences, look to the future, while the companies' mission statements recall a racist past and history of division. Poised between future and past, they attempted to negotiate the present, and they have done so within a cultural climate where the question of race and what constitutes it was increasingly under the microscope due in part to the candidacy and later election of Barack Obama as president.

Yet, in the midst of the Obama campaign's appropriation of the notion of 'hybridity' and reduction of it to the 'official teleology that is forever reducing the many to the one',[118] these three productions reclaimed the subversive potential of 'hybridity' and demonstrated its power through a 'theater of civil disobedience'. Because the primarily African American cast did not use racial identity to translate the Euripidean Medea's status as a foreigner, TWAS' *MEDEA* allowed its actors of colour to be 'ordinary', so to speak. Through its casting choices and the absence of translocation, *MEDEA* demonstrated, to use Catanese's words, that the 'performing bodies were as available to the [classical] texts as white actors'.[119] TWAS took a different approach with *Pecong*, a play that adapts 'the Greek material to a setting within the African diaspora, [while the] characters also voice the opinion that classical culture is African in origin'.[120] While this use of translocation may have been empowering to the company's core audience, the production, through no fault of its own, may have also had inadvertent negative effects; for the discrepancy in coverage of TWAS' *MEDEA* and that of *Pecong* suggests that reviewers prefer productions in which artists of colour perform a presumed distance between their bodies and those of the classical characters. CTH's *Trojan Women* risked playing into these expectations as well, but I have used that production to demonstrate the ways in which performances can challenge these expectations through a 'double-conscious' perspective.

[118] Nyong'o (2009) 7.   [119] Catanese (2011) 16.
[120] Wetmore (2003) 175.

Thus, in distinct ways, each production aimed to dismantle the image of 'the black body' by confronting the gaze that seeks to impose the image upon them. In this way, they demonstrated what Nyong'o has referred to as the 'hybrid future' and the 'mongrel past' working in tandem with each other.[121] They aimed to create a better future, while remembering a racist past persists.[122]

---

[121] Nyong'o (2009) 7.

[122] Portions of this chapter appear in *The Oxford Handbook of Greek Drama in the Americas*. See Powers (2015). I am grateful to Oxford University Press for granting permission to reuse this material.

2

'Executing Stereotypes' in Luis Alfaro's *Electricidad, Oedipus El Rey*, and *Mojada*

While the reception of Greek drama in the Spanish-speaking world has a rich history[1] and is a topic in its own right, the reception of Greek drama among US Latinxs is relatively limited in range. A few productions in recent years are Culture Clash's (2009) *Peace* and (2018) *Sapo* at the Getty Villa,[2] Los Angeles, Marisela Treviño Orta's (2016) *Woman on Fire*, with Camino Real, Albuquerque, NM, Guacamolink's (2014) *Oedipus* on Theatre Row in New York City,[3] Cherríe Moraga's (1994) *The Hungry Woman: A Mexican Medea*,[4] at The Public Theater, NYC, and the adaptations by Caridad Svich,[5] including her (2004) *Iphigenia Crash Land Falls on the Neon Shell that Was Once Her Heart (A Rave Fable)*, which premiered at 7 Stages in Atlanta, Georgia.[6] Thus, unlike African Americans, US Latinxs do not have an extensive historical relationship with the genre. However, this chapter discusses a playwright who may alter that trend through his

---

[1] See Bosher et al. (2015) 252–70, 333–60, 361–79, 380–99, 400–16, 417–33, 434–56, 556–74, 611–27, 708–25, and 726–30.

[2] Culture Clash also produced *Birds* in 1998 at South Coast Rep and Berkeley Rep, http://www.playbill.com/news/article/cas-south-coast-rep-flies-with-updated-version-of-the-birds-jan.-23-73019; http://www.playbill.com/news/article/last-chance-culture-clash-birds-to-fly-away-from-berkeley-apr.-25-74880; http://articles.latimes.com/1998/jan/23/entertainment/ca-11154, accessed 23 April 2017.

[3] Directed by Adelina Anthony, http://guacamolink.com/oedipus/, accessed 23 April 2017.

[4] For a review of a later production, see Eschen (2006).

[5] For a collection of five of her plays that radically reimagine Greek tragedy, see Svich (2012).

[6] Svich's adaptations are not set in distinctly Latinx contexts.

demonstration of the strong connection between the world of Greek drama and the life of inner-city Latinxs.

With his *Electricidad*,[7] *Oedipus El Rey*,[8] and *Mojada*,[9] MacArthur 'genius grant' Fellow, Kennedy Center Fund recipient, Ford Foundation Art of Change Fellow, Emmy Award nominee, poet, journalist, short story writer, solo performer, and professor Luis Alfaro[10] has adapted to critical acclaim Sophocles' *Electra*[11] and *Oedipus Tyrannus*,[12] and

[7] Portions of my discussion of Luis Alfaro's *Electricidad* also appear in *Helios* 38/2 (2011). I am grateful to the journal for granting permission to reuse this material. The production premiered at Tucson, Arizona's Borderlands in 2003 and was directed by Barclay Goldsmith. http://www.gvnews.com/news/world-premiere-of-electricidad-in-tucson/article_f8029f0f-1894-5a46-b980-c5bdfd448158.html, accessed 23 April 2017. The work was subsequently produced at theatres such as the Mark Taper Forum, Los Angeles, Chicago's Goodman Theatre, and the Sacramento Theatre Company.

[8] The production premiered at San Francisco's Magic Theatre in February 2010 and was directed by Loretta Greco. Receiving positive reviews and winning the prestigious Will Glickman Award for the best new play to premiere in the Bay area, the work was subsequently produced at Pasadena's Theatre@Boston Court, DC's Woolly Mammoth Theatre Company, Chicago's Victory Gardens, San Diego Repertory, the Dallas Theater Center, and The Public Theater.

[9] The production premiered at Chicago's Victory Gardens Theater in 2013 and was directed by Chay Yew. However, the play was originally titled *Bruja* (Witch) and premiered at San Francisco's Magic Theatre in 2012, directed by Loretta Greco. In this chapter, I discuss a subsequent production produced at the Barbara and Lawrence Fleischman Theater at the Getty Villa, Los Angeles, CA, in 2015. The title *Mojada* or 'Wetback' is a derogatory term defined in the *Oxford English Dictionary* as an 'illegal immigrant who has crossed the Rio Grande from Mexico to the United States'; it cites a number of journal articles from the 1970s that refer to its use as a derogatory term, http://www.oed.com.ez.lib.jjay.cuny.edu/view/Entry/227970?redirectedFrom=wetback#eid14656300, accessed 23 April 2017.

[10] Luis Alfaro is a professor at University of Southern California's School of Dramatic Arts and former Artistic Director at the Mark Taper Forum, Los Angeles. He is the recipient of multiple fellowships and awards and is well known for his work as a solo performer, in productions such as *Downtown* (1994), and for his Emmy-nominated short film *Chicanismo* (1996). In his essay on Alfaro's *Cuerpo Politizado*, José Esteban Muñoz describes the solo performer's work as presenting 'views of the intersecting worlds that formed him as a queer, working-class, urban Chicano' (2000: 97).

[11] Sophocles' *Electra*, produced *c*.410 BCE, depicts the frustration of Electra, whose father Agamemnon was murdered by her mother Clytemnestra, who now rules with her lover Aegisthus. Although Electra's younger sister Chrysothemis has been acquiescent and urges Electra to stop her obsessive lamentation, Electra does not relent. Not even the threats of her mother can deter her. In the meantime, her brother Orestes, who has been in exile, returns in disguise with his friend Pylades. Orestes at first pretends he is a Phocian carrying an urn with his ashes, but when Electra mourns in despair, he reveals his identity as her brother. Orestes enters the palace, murders his mother, and shortly after kills Aegisthus.

[12] Produced *c*.429 BCE, Sophocles' *Oedipus Tyrannus* dramatizes the myth of Oedipus, who an oracle predicted would murder his father. To avoid this fate, the infant Oedipus with pinned feet is left to be exposed on a mountaintop, but a shepherd instead gives him to Polybus and Merope of Corinth to adopt as their son. Believing them to be his biological

Euripides' *Medea*[13] into modern-day Chicanx tragedies.[14] Identifying as both an artist and a social activist, Alfaro has been described as 'perhaps one of the most powerful voices in gay, Chicano/Latino performance'.[15] He has worked with activist organizations such as ACT-UP, an AIDS awareness organization, and addressed Chicanx queer identities in works such as his 1996 *Cuerpo Politizado*.[16] In his characteristic camp style,[17] his Greek adaptations use ancient tragedy to comment on inner-city Latinx communities that struggle with problems such as gang violence, domestic abuse, and recidivism. Thus, unlike Take Wing and Soar and the Classical Theatre of Harlem, which are both theatre companies dedicated specifically to classic and classical works, Alfaro's interest is first in the community and then in the ways that Greek drama can speak to it.

This chapter will focus on one particular aspect of Alfaro's Greek adaptations: the challenge they present to representations of 'Latinness' in the media, or what performance theorist Brian Eugenio Herrera has called 'executing the stereotype',[18] i.e. playing up a stereotype with the intention of eliminating it. Like the image of 'the black body', discussed in Chapter 1, stereotypes of Latinxs, such as the 'Latin lover', 'the gang-ster', the 'wetback', and the 'spitfire sexpot', persist in the American

---

parents, Oedipus flees his mother and father to avoid the curse. On his way to Thebes, where he solves the famous riddle of the Sphinx, he kills a man at a crossroads. Sophocles' play begins with Oedipus on the hunt to find the cause of his city's plague. Oedipus' brother-in-law Creon reports an oracle from Delphi that states the plague has resulted from the murder of the former ruler Laius. The plague will not end until the murderer is brought to justice. Oedipus vows to find the murderer. However, he refuses to believe the prophet Tiresias' claim that Oedipus himself is the murderer. Instead, he accuses Tiresias and Creon of trying to dethrone him. When a shepherd arrives to report that the man whom Oedipus believed was his biological father has died, Oedipus rejoices, thinking he has avoided the oracle's prediction, but he fears he could still have sex with his mother, as the oracle also predicted, until the shepherd, the same shepherd who had given him to Polybus and Merope, explains that Merope is not in fact his biological mother. This revelation leads to others and to Jocasta's and Oedipus' discovery that they are not only wife and husband but also mother and son. A Messenger reports that Jocasta has hanged herself. Finding her, Oedipus blinds himself with the brooches from her dress. He is exiled, and asks Creon to care for his daughters Antigone and Ismene.

[13] See Chapter 1, n. 18 for a summary of the plot of this play.

[14] For further reading on the work of Luis Alfaro, see Marrero (2000) 144, Muñoz (2000), and Román (1995) 356–69.

[15] Marrero (2000) 144.   [16] Marrero (2000) 144; Muñoz (2000).

[17] Anderlini-D'Onofrio (1998) 90 defines camp as, 'a distance, artifice, and grotesque manifestation of a self-conscious attitude toward one's sexuality'.

[18] Herrera (2015) 128–53.

cultural imaginary. I will focus on Alfaro's process of 'executing' such stereotypes in the productions of *Electricidad*,[19] *Oedipus El Rey*, and *Mojada* that I saw performed in 2005, 2014, and 2015 at the Mark Taper Forum, Los Angeles, the Dallas Theater Center, and the J. Paul Getty Museum, Los Angeles, directed by Lisa Peterson, Kevin Moriarty, and Jessica Kubzansky respectively. I will argue that in the process of remaking the Greeks, Alfaro aims to remake 'Latinness' in the tradition of playwrights such as Luis Valdez who since the 1960s 'have enacted the stereotype[20] so as to eliminate it'.[21] However, as I will discuss later in relation to the Dallas Theater Center's production of *Oedipus El Rey*, a performance can also work against the playwright's intentions and inadvertently reinforce the very stereotypes it aims to overturn.

Luis Alfaro

The world that Alfaro portrays in these plays is one that is familiar to him. A child of Mexican immigrants, he grew up in the Pico-Union neighbourhood of Central Los Angeles, where at the age of 17 he found himself arrested for heroin possession, an experience that ironically changed his life for the better. About this experience he has stated:

I was brought before a great judge who said I could choose between jail or serious community service time with a performing arts center downtown. Suddenly I was running lights, learning about stage management and all the rest. I had great mentors, which is why I try to be a mentor myself now.[22]

Alfaro's dedication to the community is clear:

For the past 10 years he has engaged in a series of residencies at regional theaters throughout the country, where, instead of hanging around the green room he has gotten out and explored the surrounding 'towns and cities in crisis'. He ventured into the impoverished areas of Hartford, Conn. that exist in the shadow of big insurance companies, interacted with teen felons in Tucson, Arizona, spent time at a clinic not far from the Oregon Shakespeare Festival that dealt with the health problems of the many migrant workers in the area.[23]

---

[19] I have quoted from the version of *Electricidad* published in *American Theatre Magazine*, since it is widely available.

[20] See Herrera (2015) 134–9 for a review of scholarship on stereotypes. See also my Introduction for further discussion.

[21] Herrera (2015) 17.

[22] Weiss (2013). On Pico-Union's gentrification, see Gross (2015).

[23] Weiss (2013).

In fact, his inspiration for *Electricidad*, his first adaptation of a Greek play, came from his experience of working at a youth authority camp. There, he met a 13-year-old Yaqui Indian girl who was serving a sentence for killing her mother. He recalls, 'She killed her mother because the mother had gotten a hit man to kill her father, a drug dealer on the south side of Tucson.'[24]

From this experience, Alfaro's relationship with the Greeks was serendipitously born. For later that day, he went into the Arizona Theatre Company's bookshop, saw Greek plays on special offer, and picked up the story of Electra.[25] Recognizing the parallels between the Yacqui girl's story and that of Electra, Alfaro thought that even now 'we're still trapped in the cycle of revenge . . . [and] . . . the poverty of ignorance'.[26]

Inspired by such real-life events, he connected the familial violence of the ancient plays to domestic violence in urban areas. He transformed the plot, the characters, and the 'corporeality'[27] of the ancient heroes into the movement, language, and Aztec mythology of his characters. Through the revisions, which have been performed on major stages and workshopped with at-risk communities, Alfaro has demonstrated the connections between ancient Greek and Chicanx culture, and the ability of the theatre to raise awareness about social justice.

'Executing Stereotypes' with Humour

One aspect of Alfaro's teaching is to 'execute' Latinx stereotypes, such as that of the Latinx gang member. In his discussion of *West Side Story*, Herrera describes the process by which this stereotype has been created. He has argued that the film-makers who adapted the famous musical gave its Latinx gang the Sharks 'a collective, articulate voice [that] elaborated [them] as characters, and in so doing, they created a template for the Latino gang member as a stock character in US popular performance—a character, in this case, named Chino'.[28] Herrera explains that:

---

[24] Harmon (2008).   [25] Johnson (2006) 64.   [26] Harmon (2008).

[27] i.e. the embodied social codes as exhibited through costume, gesture, voice, setting, etc. See Foster (1996) on corporeality and her theory of 'choreography', which she poses as an alternative to Butler's 'performativity'. Foster's choreography 'challenges the dichotomization of verbal and nonverbal cultural practices by asserting the thought-filledness of movement and the theoretical potential of bodily action' (17). Choreography addresses a *social* network of embodied knowledge as opposed to the *individual* execution of Butler's discursive 'performativity'.

[28] Herrera (2015) 121.

Chino's cinematic recharacterization, in tandem with other narratives charting the entry of Puerto Rican boys into criminal lives, emerges as perhaps the inaugural appearance of one of the most enduring stock characters in subsequent depictions of Latino masculinity in US popular performance: the Latino gang member. The film *West Side Story* thereby invests Chino's singular form with both 'juvenile delinquency' and 'the Puerto Rican problem', while also installing the 'Latin gang member' as a racialized stock character in American popular performance.[29]

Because *West Side Story*'s 'depiction of Puerto Ricans in New York was almost immediately misrecognized as a documentary account',[30] the stereotype has become indelible in the cultural imaginary.

In addition to the gang member, other images are no less pernicious. Stereotypes such as the gangster and the wetback, as well as the domestic, the sexpot, and the Latin lover are evident in popular culture, as in the media's portrayal of the former Los Angeles mayor Antonio Villaraigosa as a slick ladies' man[31] whom the popular American gossip site TMZ dubbed Mayor Suave.[32] Whatever the intentions of such words may be, they still evoke stereotypes, for, as Judith Butler has argued, racially charged words and images are contingent upon the identity of those who use them, those whose receive them, and the historical context in which they are situated.[33]

Attempting to overcome this 'indefatigable obstacle'[34] of the stereotype, Alfaro employs the performance techniques of *carpa* and *tanda*.[35] As Lisa Shaw has explained, *carpa* (literally 'tent theatre') is a popular Mexican theatrical tradition based on vaudeville improvisation that was dedicated to representing the common people and flourished in the 1920s and 1930s

---

[29] Herrera (2015) 127.   [30] Herrera (2015) 124.

[31] Gene Maddaus (2015), http://www.laweekly.com/news/villaraigosas-new-girlfriend-played-the-villain-in-terminator-3-5551743, accessed 31 October 2015.

[32] http://www.tmz.com/videos/0_zfjklw8f/, accessed 30 December 2017. See also Soto (2013). For a website that summarizes such stereotypes, see, e.g., http://brown-face.com, accessed 30 December 2017. See also *Latinos beyond Reel: Challenging a Media Stereotype.* (2012) DVD.

[33] Butler (1996) argues this point in relation to the image of the burning cross.

[34] Herrera (2015) 138.

[35] Broyles-González (1994) 7 states: 'It is impossible to define the Mexican *carpa* as one thing, for it encompassed a field of diverse cultural performance practices popular among the poorest segments of the Mexican populace.' See this work for further discussion of *carpa* and its use especially in the work of El Teatro Campesino, a Chicanx theatre troupe founded by Luis Valdez during the California farm labour movement in 1965. On *carpa*, see also Prieto (2000).

with Mexican American troupes in the US and Mexican troupes in working-class districts of Mexico City and in many provincial cities.[36] Relying on the improvisation skills of actors who brought the stock characters such as city slickers, policemen, effeminate males, harlots, and shrews to life, a *carpa* show, known as a *tanda*, was cheap to attend and characterized by audience participation in the form of applause, comments, and heckling. Highlighting the negative effects of modern life on the family, masculinity, and patriarchy, the *carpa*'s favourite theme, explains Shaw, 'was the culture clash between rural and urban society, often in the form of an encounter between a city slicker and a country bumpkin'.[37]

In his *Eletricidad*, *Oedipus El Rey*, and *Mojada*, Alfaro draws on these Mexican performance traditions that 'contested U.S. cultural representations of the Mexican'[38] in order to represent the culture clash not between the rural and the urban but between Chicanx culture and US popular culture at large. In doing so, he, like Cherríe Moraga with *The Hungry Woman*, uses skill in adapting the Greeks to address social inequalities linked to class and race. While humour may seem to be an unusual ally in the attempt to dismantle stereotypes that can lead to social inequality and even violence,[39] Alfaro sees humour as a crucial tool that is endemic to his Mexican roots. On the *Día de los Muertos*, for example, one can make fun of the dead. For Alfaro, as well, humour becomes a mask that allows the actors and audience to face the painful story and experience the gang motto of '"you laugh until you cry"—"you live it up until you get caught"'.[40]

Aiming for such laughter, he harnesses it as a tool to dismantle the cultural and racial stereotypes that deny opportunities to those struggling with living life in mainstream America. The camp portrayals of his characters are funny but also demonstrate the critical connections between the mythological ancient family dramas that high culture has revered and the real-life family dramas that many Los Angeles cholxs[41]

---

[36] See Shaw (2005) 125–6.   [37] Shaw (2005) 126.

[38] Haas (1995) 210–11. He continues: 'Immigrants drew on this transnational development of language, images, and content to define "lo mexicano" over time and to interpret the bilingual and bicultural reality in which they lived.'

[39] On the social function of laughter, see Bergson (1991).

[40] Johnson (2006) 64.

[41] Vigil defines cholxs as members of an urban subculture characterized by 'a street based amalgam of Anglo-American and Mexican features with innovative syncretisms' (1988: 41–2). His glossary definition reads: 'A Chicano street style of youth who are

and undocumented immigrants face on a daily basis. This carefully constructed mix of high and low, tragedy and comedy functions to dismantle the stereotypes such as the gang member, the wetback, and the sexpot.

This 'execution of stereotypes' works on two levels: both in the text and in the performance. On the one hand, he executes stereotypes by writing his own versions of them, e.g. the gangster (Electricidad, Orestes, Oedipus, and Creon), the wetback (Medea, Tita, and Jason), and the spitfire sexpot (La Abuela)[42] (see Figure 2.1). His poignant yet humorous construction of characters encourages the audience's identification with them, particularly through his humanistic portrayal of families in crisis. Like their ancient Greek mythological counterparts, Alfaro's characters live under extreme circumstances in an extreme world. Illustrating this connection between the elites of the heroic past and the working men and women of the underserved neighbourhoods, Alfaro encourages his audience to admire and value—and thus identify with—these people for the principles they stand for and their stoic ability to endure. In this way, his work 'executes stereotypes' by appealing to a humanistic impulse.

On the other hand, the performances 'execute stereotypes' by emphasizing difference, i.e. through hyperbolizing stereotypical corporeal features, such as tattoos, big hair, and bandanas, which, as Alfaro has stated regarding *Electricidad*, can function like a Greek mask.[43] In such cases, the direction of a performance can mark the distance between the characters and the actors playing them. The design, for example, can create a fictional world that makes clear that the actors are not attempting a realistic portrayal of cholxs. Rather, through the use of camp (an aesthetic marked by irony) the design and performance style can highlight the construction and the representation of the characters on the stage and, in the process, play up stereotypes in order to dismantle them. Thus, a production's style can encourage an audience to focus on stereotypical indicators of difference as social constructs. However, striking the right aesthetic to evoke such a response from the theatre audience is difficult, and, whatever their intentions, not all productions may do so effectively.

---

marginal to both Mexican and Anglo culture; also used historically for cultural marginals and racial hybrids in Mexico and some parts of Latin America' (177).

[42] Spanish for 'the grandmother'.

[43] Alfaro referenced the idea of the mask at a public lecture on 3 October 2015 at the J. Paul Getty Museum (Alfaro 2015).

Figure 2.1 La Ifi and La Abuela in Luis Alfaro's *Electricidad*, directed by Lisa Petersen at the Mark Taper Forum. 2005.

Mark Taper Forum Production of *Electricidad*. Photo © 2005 Craig Schwartz Photography.

The Rule of Law

A key way in which the text, plot, and dialogue of Alfaro's dramas work to challenge stereotypes is by questioning the rule of law in the US, i.e. the idea that the law functions as a common set of rules to be applied equally to all. Greek drama offers excellent source material for doing so, because, although the extant plays were performed before the Athenian democracy, they dramatize events from the heroic mythological past, a world before the invention of the law court, a point which Aeschylus exploited in his *Eumenides* when he staged the founding of the Areopagus, the real-life Athenian court in which murderers were tried.[44] Alfaro too capitalizes on the pre-law dramatic context of Greek tragedy by connecting it to the policing problems of urban areas and the formation of gangs.

For example, while Foley has explained that 'new versions of Sophocles' *Electra* [in the US] have tended to emphasize the heroine's damaged psyche over her assertive search for justice revenge',[45] Alfaro's *Electricidad* focuses on the Sophoclean murder-for-justice motif and connects it to the cholx code of gang violence.[46] The system of retribution that has affected the life of Electra also plagues her cholx teen doppelgänger Electricidad (Figure 2.2). In the myth of the House of Atreus, each transgressor's murder must be avenged in a system of retribution: Orestes must kill his mother, who killed his father, who killed his daughter, whom Artemis demanded as a sacrifice to make the winds blow the ships to Troy. No alternative to this vendetta system yet exists, for the play takes place in the mythical heroic past before the establishment of any court.[47] Moreover, as Anne Pippin Burnett has argued, Electra and Orestes' revenge can be considered moral[48] because it avenges their father's murder. They act in accordance with the Greek heroic code of 'helping friends and harming enemies',[49] even though it causes great pain.

Although *Electricidad* does not imply that the murder is moral, the play demonstrates that the crime works as a form of alternative justice, for *Electricidad* channels the Sophoclean system of retribution through

[44] Aeschylus dramatizes the foundation of this law court in the *Oresteia*, which includes his version of the Electra myth.

[45] Foley (2012a) 315.

[46] For further discussion of this play, see Powers (2011) and Moritz (2008).

[47] On justice and revenge in Greek tragedy, see Blundell (1991); Burnett (1998); and Mossman (1995).

[48] Burnett (1998) 139.

[49] On helping friends and harming enemies, see Blundell (1991).

Figure 2.2 Clemencia and Electricidad in Luis Alfaro's *Electricidad*, directed by Lisa Petersen at the Mark Taper Forum. 2005.

Mark Taper Forum Production of *Electricidad*. Photo © 2005 Craig Schwartz Photography.

its depiction of the 'old cholo order' in Boyle Heights, a gang-troubled neighbourhood, situated just east of the LA River, long known as a gateway for poor immigrant communities, who sometimes mistrust the police and the justice system in general. In this neighbourhood, 'Violence begets violence begets violence—[which] is one of the big themes of the play.'[50] Electricidad, played by Zilah Mendoza, states to her deceased father at his grave:

You are the old ways, Papa. You are the history and the reason we know how to live. I want to live the old cholo ways, Papa. Simple and to the point. You mess with me, I mess with you back. You want to party, party in your own backyard. You shoot, I shoot back. It's simple.[51]

The cycle of family violence begins in the play after Bertila Damas' Clemencia (Sophocles' Clytemnestra), snazzily coiffured, wearing all-black threads, and heavily made-up with the darkly lined lips, thin eyebrows, and the Aqua Net bouffant characteristic of cholas, kills her abusive husband Agamemnon, who 'took her virginity' (or raped her) in the back of a car when she was 13 years old (Figure 2.2). While Clemencia wants to move on and sell her Boyle Heights bungalow (set designed by Rachel Hauck) to pursue a more economically and emotionally liberated life, Electricidad, who does not wear the same make-up as her mother and sister Ifi, attempts to deny her mother's dream for a new way of life. She keeps Century 21[52] on hold by clinging to her father's stinking corpse, which she has enshrined in their front yard after stealing it from the cemetery. Despite her father's abusive behaviour, she obsessively laments his death, which also represents the death of the 'old cholo order' that has inspired her to try to persuade and eventually convince her brother Orestes, played by Justin Huen, to murder Clemencia. Through this contemporary system of vendetta justice, *Electricidad* engages with the themes of the Sophocles original, for no trustworthy police protection or justice system exists in the world of the play.

As La Cuca, one of Las Vecinas (the Neighbours), the three chatty gossips, who continue to sweep around Agamemnon's tomb performing a pun on *limpiar* ('to clean' and 'to purify'),[53] states, 'We don't dial the 911 no more,' and La Carmen, another of the Vecinas, confirms, 'No place for la policia in these barrios now.'[54] To many inner-city communities in Los Angeles, the police appear to be a worse evil than the gangs. In fact, the gangs are seen as offering protection against corrupt police and politicians: 'Thank dios for cholo protection.'[55] *Electricidad* thus

---

[50] Johnson (2006) 65. On the gentrification of Boyle Heights, see Sager (2017).
[51] Alfaro (2006) 70, col. 2.   [52] An estate agency that operates nationwide.
[53] In the manner of a Greek chorus but without any literal music and dance.
[54] Alfaro (2006) 67, col. 3.   [55] Alfaro (2006) 67, col. 2.

depicts the 'friction between barrio residents and law enforcement, much like what is found in other low-income neighborhoods',[56] a friction which has contributed in part to domestic and gang violence within these communities.

For example, scandals in the Los Angeles Police Department, such as those of the Rampart Division in the late 1990s, have done much harm to the relationship between citizens and police in certain neighbourhoods. In the Rampart scandal, several officers in the elite gang unit known as CRASH were accused of routinely planting evidence, framing, and even shooting innocent people. Since the investigation began, over 100 criminal convictions have been overturned, and several civil and criminal convictions of officers ensued.[57] Corrupt police such as these have contributed to distrust, fear, and anger with the US justice system, an anger which eventually erupted into the LA uprising of 1992, after the acquittal of several officers on trial for the brutal beating of Rodney King. The LAPD has since made many reforms, such as the practice of community policing, which have increased the public's trust in them.

However, the problem of mistrust is one that continues not only in Los Angeles but also across the nation. As mentioned in the introduction to Chapter 1 as well, a chronic mistrust of the police has been apparent in nationwide protests over the deaths of individuals such as Michael Brown, Eric Garner, and Akai Gurley, all unarmed black men who died at the hands of law enforcement in 2014. Many of these public protests reflect a collective outrage over such deaths, which gang members can use as bait to recruit youngsters, who often turn to gangs, instead of the police, for a sense of belonging and protection.

Electricidad epitomizes such feelings of mistrust and believes that she has no recourse to any legitimate judicial institution. She experiences family stress, isolation, and adolescent struggles for identity, all factors associated with gang formation and violence. As Las Vecinas explain, cholxs are not violent by nature but are 'made by man . . . the product of racism . . . and neglectful mamas'.[58] They live in America but also outside it, for as La Abuela laments, cholxs stay in the neighbourhood, because where would they go 'in a world that won't have us?'[59]

---

[56] Vigil (1988) 37.   [57] See, e.g., Sterngold (2000).
[58] Alfaro (2006) 67, col. 3.   [59] Alfaro (2006) 77, col. 2.

This problem of assimilation articulated by La Abuela is a key issue that influences the choices of all of Alfaro's characters. Cholxs feel neither completely Mexican nor completely American. They call Mexican nationals and immigrants *chúntaros*[60] and 'wetbacks', and at the same time, they deny being *engabacheado* (anglicized). While not all cholxs join gangs, many do, because conventional opportunities seem out of reach. In fact, the marginalization they experience in school and in greater society is one of the key sociocultural factors on which gangs capitalize.[61] For, by joining a gang, 'troubled youths acquire a sense of importance, self-esteem, and self-identity. In short, rather than feeling neglected and remaining socially and institutionally marginal, the gang members develop their own subcultural style to participate in public life, albeit a street one.'[62] Thus, while the humorous dialogue and garish costumes of *Electricidad* add levity to the piece, they also work like a Greek mask that cannot be in profile but must always face the inexplicable horror with wide eyes and an open mouth, a protective medium between the audience and the very real violence endured in underserved communities.[63]

Like *Electricidad*, *Oedipus El Rey* also makes visible the absence of the rule of law. Alfaro departs from the trend of US productions of *Oedipus Tyrannus* that, according to Foley, 'have until quite recently expressed open distaste for the play's apparent "fatality" [which] . . . dooms its hero before birth to be alien to a U.S. Horatio Alger mentality, which emphasizes the opportunity of even the poorest citizen to remake his or her life through hard work and discipline'.[64] Instead, the play's fatalism becomes a means to frame the sociological problems that lead to crime and the problem of recidivism.

Through the Sophoclean free will versus predetermination theme, *Oedipus El Rey* links the fate of the ancient Oedipus[65] to the fate of those individuals who sometimes seem condemned to the problems of addiction, poor health care, and abuse. These social problems breed

---

[60] According to the Urban Dictionary, a derogatory term used to describe a Mexican or someone who is a 'native Indian hailing from Michoacan', http://www.urbandictionary.com/define.php?term=chuntaro, accessed 1 October 2016.

[61] Vigil (1988) 42.   [62] Vigil (1988) 63–4.

[63] This idea of the Greek mask comes from the poet Tony Harrison. See, e.g., Jaggi (2007).

[64] Foley (2012a) 315.

[65] For an excellent study of Sophocles' *Oedipus* on the world stage, see Macintosh (2009).

crime, and for many individuals can foster recidivism, the vicious cycle of committing crime and becoming incarcerated. The production of *Oedipus El Rey* at New York's The Public Theater in 2017, for example, poignantly depicted the recently released Oedipus' search for legitimate work that ultimately ended in his looking to crime as the only way to survive. The production asks: is this way of life fated for Oedipus, or is it something he can escape?

Accordingly, the play also asks whether the law can be applied equally when social circumstances are so unequal. In this way, Alfaro uses a play that 'most typically reflects the Greeks' fatalistic or pessimistic outlook'[66] to explore 'every human being's quest for personal identity and self-knowledge in a world full of ignorance and hidden horrors—perhaps even one ruled by divine indifference or malevolent fate'.[67] Thus, as Rush Rehm has stated, 'Sophocles crafts a play that is both keenly particular (Oedipus is like no man) and broadly universal. Does any of us know who we really are, what we are doing, the full consequence of our actions?'[68]

In order to emphasize such questions about fate, while mixing ancient Greek and Aztec myth, *Oedipus El Rey* dramatizes aspects of the myth that do not appear in the Sophocles play, i.e. the plot starts at a different point in time. It begins with the prediction of El Sobrador (a healer who uses touch), who explains to Laius, the king of the neighbourhood, that Oedipus (played by Philippe Bowgen in the Dallas production) will murder him. Despite his initial scepticism, the king quickly orders Tiresias (Rodney Garza) to murder the child, but Tiresias cannot bring himself to commit the act. Disobeying his orders, Tiresias instead adopts the child as his own.

The sequence of time then jumps to many years later, and it is here that Alfaro begins to connect the Sophocles play to the problem of recidivism specifically. The audience learns that Oedipus was years ago released from a young offender institution only to rob a Costco upon his release, because, like many newly released prisoners, he finds adjusting to life outside of the institution difficult. He now finds himself released from prison for the second time, only to commit yet another crime. Trading his blue prison slippers for shiny white tennis shoes, Oedipus gets behind the wheel of an '85 Honda Civic and heads off to Calle Broadway, but along the way has a road rage incident and murders a

---

[66] Griffith and Most (2013) 12.   [67] Griffith and Most (2013) 12.
[68] Rehm (1992) 110.

man who he later learns is his biological father Laius. Instead of being caught, tried, and sentenced to prison for a third time, however, Oedipus begins a quest for personal identity and self-knowledge that frees him from the cycle of recidivism, even as it destroys him.

Unaware of the paternal blood relationship between him and the man he killed, Oedipus moves on to settle in Pico-Union, where, coincidentally, Laius used to be *el rey*. There, Oedipus stops at the Farmacia Million Dollar, which was an actual shop, on the corner of Broadway and 3rd Street in the city centre, which was not exactly a pharmacy but a *botánica*.[69] At this location, Oedipus meets and slays El Esfinge, the Sphinx-like creature, created by three chorus members, who, with hats on and hands joined, make a snake-like sound, as the actors on the top row of the theatre shake rattles. Unfazed by their warnings, Oedipus moves on to the home of the fedora-wearing, heat-packing Creon (Daniel Duque Estrada), an old friend from his young offender institution (Figure 2.3).

There, he meets Jocasta (Sabina Zuniga Varela) (see Figure 2.4) with whom he argues over faith, belief in God, and respect for religious traditions. Jocasta believes in fate, the old ways, the traditions of the barrio, the powers of healers, mystics, and shamans; but Oedipus believes in 'Me'. Although the scene begins with both actors arguing from either side of the arena, by the end, after an abrupt transition, Jocasta and Oedipus come together, kiss, and undress. While the nakedness of both actors in such an intimate setting could have shown a love and passion that was moving,[70] their love scene, in this performance at least, was instead stilted and awkward, although perhaps that was the very point.

After marrying Jocasta, Oedipus feuds with Creon over which of them will become the new king of the neighbourhood, until Oedipus discovers that he is the baby that Jocasta thought Laius had killed. The recognition and reversal of Oedipus occurs when Tiresias reveals that he did not kill baby Oedipus but brought him up as his own son. After learning the truth, Oedipus begs Jocasta to blind him, and, as she does so, he stabs her with a knife that she willingly steps into. The play closes with Oedipus and Tiresias, two blind men, exiting together, leaning on each other and their canes.

---

[69] A shop, most often associated with the syncretic religion of Santería that sells candles, herbs, charms, and other items connected to healing and spirituality.

[70] I found this to be the case in the production at New York's The Public Theater in 2017.

Figure 2.3 El Coro (seated), Oedipus El Rey (left), and Creon (right) in Luis Alfaro's *Oedipus El Rey*, directed by Kevin Moriarty at the Dallas Theater Center. 2014.

Photo © 2014 Karen Almond, Dallas Theater Center.

Through this revised plot structure, Alfaro replaces the ancient oracles that governed Oedipus' destiny with a culture of poverty that effects the same result. In an interview that was printed in the programme, Alfaro states:

... most children in South LA get their meals from fast food outlets and liquor stores. And even worse, most have no regular salads or fresh fruits in their diet. They are dependent on sugar, high sodium offerings, and processed meat. Tack on the over 50% high school drop-out rate, the single parent/working parent scenario, the access to inexpensive weapons, lack of jobs, and having witnessed a violent crime, domestic disturbance, or harm to animals before the age of 10. Do these factors help you make a very specific choice, or is this just the way of the world for some?[71]

[71] Alfaro (2014).

Figure 2.4 Jocasta in Luis Alfaro's *Oedipus El Rey*, directed by Kevin Moriarty at the Dallas Theater Center. 2014.

Photo © 2014 Karen Almond, Dallas Theater Center.

The playwright thus suggests that these social circumstances, like the ancient oracles, can effectively predetermine one's ability to succeed. In making this connection, he by extension raises a crucial question posed by the Sophocles play.

In Sophocles' *Oedipus*, the chorus anxiously wonders why they should dance if the oracles that predicted Laius' murder by his child are not true (896). For false oracles would 'undermine traditional religious observances, such as consulting the oracle and performing at festivals'.[72] However, 'when Oedipus' true parentage is known and the oracles have been truly fulfilled, the chorus has no thought of dancing but wish they had never seen him'.[73] Similarly, *Oedipus El Rey* poses not only the question of the extent to which his fate was predetermined by social circumstances, but also whether Oedipus can overcome those circumstances without rejecting or being rejected by the community that surrounds him.

Working to educate the public to sympathize with rather than reject the formerly incarcerated, the production of *Oedipus El Rey* at the Dallas Theater Center held a discussion before every show to explain the problems of crime, incarceration, and recidivism that affect the cholx community represented in the play. For those audience members unable to attend the talk, several statistics were posted on billboards in the bar area adjacent to the theatre. There, audience members could read that:

as of 2013, the United States has the highest recorded rate of incarceration in the world with 716 prisoners per 100,000 of the population. By comparison, Cuba imprisons 510 per 100,000, Russia imprisons 475 per 100,000, [and] Iran 284 per 100,000 . . . According to the U.S. Bureau of Justice, African Americans make up 39.4% of the prison population but only make up 13% of the population of the country. Hispanics make up 20.6% of the prison population and 16.3% of the population of the country . . . Most prisoners, when released, will end up incarcerated again. Nationally, 53% of arrested males are reincarcerated. In California where the play takes place, 7 out of 10 prisoners (or 70%) will return to jail within 3 years of release. California has the highest rate of recidivism in the country.

Juxtaposed with these statistics, a short summary of *Oedipus El Rey* states: '*Oedipus El Rey* can be taken as social commentary, illustrating the situation of America's growing lower class, whose members are—now more than ever—condemned at birth to fulfil an ugly, impoverished, criminalized destiny.'

Like the ancient Oedipus, whose *hamartia*[74] (mistake) of murdering his biological father and marrying his mother was no fault of his own, or

---

[72] Murnaghan (2012) 230.

[73] Murnaghan (2012) 230.

[74] Although *hamartia* is sometimes translated as 'sin' or 'tragic flaw', the concept of sin did not exist in ancient Greek thought. As Bernard Knox (1957: 29–32) has argued,

'the product of not any one quality, but the total man',[75] so El Rey is born into social circumstances that, like the ancient oracles, seem to destine him to a life of recidivism, even though he takes responsibility for the choices he made that led him to his fate. By connecting the predicament of the modern character to that of the mythological king of Thebes, the plot demonstrates that El Rey, like Oedipus, is not inherently bad, nor did he do anything to deserve his fate. Instead, factors beyond his control influenced his fate as a perpetual offender and prisoner. Thus, in this play, as with *Electricidad*, Alfaro 'executes stereotypes' by rewriting the figure of the Latin gang member as one who is a product of society (a result of social, economic, and legal injustices) rather than a terror to it.

Like *Electricidad* and *Oedipus El Rey*, *Mojada* also addresses the absence of the rule of law. Using three generations of women (Medea, Tita,[76] and Josefina:[77] Figure 2.5) as his starting point, the play demonstrates the problems encountered by immigrants, specifically undocumented women and girls, eighty per cent of whom are raped crossing the US/Mexico border.[78] While the title of the play was *Bruja* (Witch) at its premiere at the Magic Theatre in San Francisco, by the time of the initial production at the Victory Gardens Theater in Chicago, Medea was depicted as an immigrant, not a magician,[79] a choice which evokes the Medea of Moraga's *The Hungry Woman*.

The isolation and desperation of the betrayed, foreign, Euripidean Medea translates well to the situation of an undocumented worker. As discussed in Chapter 1, in the Euripidean text, Medea is a foreigner (*barbaros*). She has betrayed her family in Colchis, on the Black Sea, to help Jason steal the Golden Fleece. While a Greek woman in Medea's

---

Oedipus' *hamartia* (mistake) was no fault of his own. He was by ancient Greek standards a 'good' man and did nothing to deserve his fate. As Rush Rehm has explained, 'Oedipus errs through simple ignorance of the material facts of his own birth' (1992: 110).

[75] Knox (1957) 31.

[76] A character loosely based on Creon and Glauce. She is from the previous generation of Mexican immigrants. She married an American and became a successful businessperson.

[77] A character loosely based on Aegeus. Josefina sells doughnuts and croissants from a van to the people of the neighbourhood. Her husband is a blueberry picker. They have trouble conceiving, and Josefina asks Medea for help.

[78] Goldberg (2014).

[79] Alfaro discussed this change in his talk on 3 October 2015 at the J. Paul Getty Museum (Alfaro 2015).

Figure 2.5 Medea, Josefina, and Tita in Luis Alfaro's *Mojada*, directed by Jessica Kubzansky at the J. Paul Getty Museum. 2015.

J. Paul Getty Villa Production of *Mojada*. Photo © 2015 Craig Schwartz Photography.

situation would enjoy some protection from her father and brother(s), Medea has no family, foreign or Greek, to help her and no system of justice to which she can appeal. It is through this point of entry that Alfaro threads together the stories of these two distant Medeas.

Like the Euripidean Medea, who is a foreign woman who forsook her family to live in a land in which she has no rights, Alfaro's Medea, played by Sabina Zuniga Varela (Figures 2.5 and 2.6), follows Hason's dream, not hers, to live in the US. She has left Mexico after killing her twin brother, who physically abused her when she told him following the death of their father that she was leaving with Hason (Justin Huen) for *el Norte*. In addition to the abuse by her brother, she is brutally raped by Mexican soldiers during her border crossing, an event which is narrated by Tita (VIVIS—also known as Vivis Colombetti: Figure 2.5) and also staged in the Getty production. In my opinion, Tita's narration of this scene would have had a more profound emotional effect if there were no

Figure 2.6 Medea (background), Acan, and Armida in Luis Alfaro's *Mojada*, directed by Jessica Kubzansky at the J. Paul Getty Museum. 2015.

J. Paul Getty Villa Production of *Mojada*. Photo © 2015 Craig Schwartz Photography.

accompanying stage action to illustrate her words, but, at the same time, the staging of Medea's rape helped to reinforce through visual means a traumatic experience crucial for understanding Medea's character.

Far from the heroic, masculine Euripidean Medea,[80] she is damaged and weak, a characterization reinforced by Varela's performance.

---

[80] Foley (1989). See also Easterling (1977).

The violence she has experienced contributes to her agoraphobia and inability to adapt to her new home in Boyle Heights, where she works as an undocumented tailor earning a pittance for her exquisite, magical craftsmanship. Clinging to the traditions of the Old World, she struggles with her skateboard-wielding, Wii-playing son, Acan (Figure 2.6). Medea does not approve of his assimilation to the new American way of life that her husband Hason, in his plaid shirt and baseball cap, has also embraced. When she discovers that the aspiring Hason has betrayed her and will take Acan and marry Armida (the self-made, well-heeled, documented immigrant, played by Marlene Forte, who has been helping Hason become more successful: see Figure 2.6), Medea refuses to leave quietly.

However, Armida reminds her of her undocumented status. Medea has no family, no security, and no rights. To the gasps of the audience, Armida threatens to report the undocumented Medea to the authorities and ask a judge to grant custody of Acan to his father, who is now legally married to Armida, an American citizen.

Left with no legal recourse to fight for her son, Medea delivers to Armida a beautiful dress of hundreds of threads that come alive like snakes to suffocate her. Then, after Acan tells his mother that he wants to live with Armida, Medea does the unthinkable. She sends her son inside and follows him through the door of their Boyle Heights Victorian house,[81] machete in hand. Acan screams and pleads, but to no avail.

The play closes with Medea's exit from the bungalow to reappear *ex machina* on the balcony above the Getty Villa's portico. In this iconic image, she coos while flapping the giant leaves of a banana leaf plant, as if she were a bird with wings. Transformed into a *guaco*, the bird of her native Michoacán, she has left the world below her and returned to the self she once was when Hason first met her as a carefree little girl playing in the rain.

Whether Medea murders her child to punish Hason, to save Acan from assimilating to a new world that she distrusts, because she is mentally and emotionally broken, or at all, are questions that Alfaro leaves his audience

---

[81] Designed by Efren Delgadillo Jr, the set consisted of a scrim painted with the image of a Victorian house, a well-recognized style of architecture in Boyle Heights. The stage exit was modelled on that of Medea through the *skēnē* door in the Euripides.

to ponder.[82] However, while Medea's psychological break in this performance, to me, felt sudden and the murder abrupt, it is clear that her decision resulted from her desperation. Unlike the fierce Euripidean warrior whose desire for masculine, heroic glory (*kleos*) overcomes her maternal love for her children,[83] this Medea is calm and gentle, if frustrated and tired. The first glimpse the audience sees of her potential for violence appears late in the play, when she explains why she murdered her brother. Her anger, however, comes not only from any damaged pride but also from helplessness. She lacks power and protection, and has no recourse to justice. She cannot part with her son, nor can she keep him in a world where she can lose him to the new way of life in the US.

Framing this predicament through the structure of an ancient tragedy, Alfaro makes sympathetic the common plight of the millions of undocumented workers living in the US. He thus 'executes the stereotype' of the wetback by illustrating the struggles of women like Medea and allowing audience members such as me not only to intellectualize these problems but also to experience them emotionally and connect them to a historical antecedent. While none of these plays asks easy questions or offers easy answers, all of them present a plot structure that encourages audiences to recognize the social ills caused by poverty, their impact on the rule of law, and their consequences on the justice system. In the process, through appealing to the head, the heart, and one's sense of humour, the productions work to 'execute stereotypes' by evoking empathy for those who turn to crime because they think they have no other choice.

Family

In addition to questioning the rule of law in the US, Alfaro's work also revises stereotypical images of the Latinx family. For what connects the ancient material so well to life in Boyle Heights and Pico-Union is not only the absence of a structured justice system but also, as Mary Louise Hart has stated, the importance of family.[84] Electra, Oedipus, and Medea,

---

[82] Alfaro raised this point in his talk on 3 October 2015 at the J. Paul Getty Museum (Alfaro 2015).

[83] On Medea's desire for *kleos* (masculine, heroic glory), see Foley (1989).

[84] In a public talk with Luis Alfaro at the J. Paul Getty Museum on 3 October 2015, Mary Louise Hart pointed out that Alfaro's adaptations connect with the ancient dramas in part through the idea of family.

in both the ancient versions and Alfaro's, live in a world where the best source of protection is family but where that very family can also be what one most needs protection from. In these worlds, children murder parents, parents murder children, husbands murder wives, and vice versa. Such violence can occur in any culture or economic demographic, but what particularly unites these two distinct worlds is the use of such violence because of the perception that there is no recourse to a legitimate, institutionalized means of justice.

The ancient tragedies have thus become a way for Alfaro to explore the dysfunction of the 'organizing principle of traditional Latino life, the family'.[85] For, prior to his work on the Greeks, Alfaro's work has seemed to reinforce the 'conservative notion of the centrality of the family' in Latinx culture.[86] '"Blood is thicker than water"' says Alfaro in his solo, autobiographical performance *Downtown*, '"Family is greater than friends, and the Virgin Mary watches over all of us."'[87] According to David Román, in *Downtown*:

Alfaro links the bonds of family to the bonds of Catholicism for the immigrant imaginary when he recalls how the haunting words of his family elders have now become his own despite his own reluctance to adopt them. Alfaro presents this invocation of the family bond's hegemony as nearly inevitable. The family remains so deep rooted in the Latino psyche that its force cannot be constrained, regardless of one's own position within it. Alfaro gives voice to this prevalent theme in the literature by and about Latinos.[88]

This interest in the power of family may be what has continued to attract Alfaro to Greek tragedy. Through working with the genre, he has expanded his exploration of the subject from a conservative notion, which Román has discussed, to a cross-cultural, ancient/modern model that has allowed him to explore the dysfunction of the patriarchal family structure and positive alternatives for its replacement.

As the Chicanx theatre scholar Jorge Huerta has argued, the frequent depiction of family relationships in immigrant dramas often shows the dysfunctional family as the rule rather than the exception, but Román has contrasted this usual scenario in Latinx works with that presented by John Leguizamo in his Broadway performance of *Freak*.[89] According to

---

[85] Román (2005) 117.   [86] Román (2005) 118.
[87] Alfaro (1998) 323, quoted in Román (2005) 118.
[88] Román (2005) 118.   [89] See Leguizamo and Katz (1997).

Román, Leguizamo explores the issue further by presenting familial dysfunction:

as that which enables the rejection of the family unit. *Freak* not only models how one might reject the family; it goes so far as to represent that rejection as a mark of power . . . In Leguizamo's world, the broken nuclear family does not represent a negative value; women and children benefit from its demise.[90]

Yet *Freak*, Román continues, 'is not about the disavowal of the family. It is about generating alternative and more expansive models of Latino relations.'[91]

Using the Greeks as a starting point, Alfaro too explores familial dysfunction to generate alternative models of positive familial relations. His adaptations challenge the patriarchal model of the family by challenging the 'normative impulses embedded in Latino/a culture, impulses that presume the centrality of the biological family model for the Latino imaginary'.[92] He does so by presenting, for example, women characters who are searching for a way out of their abusive environments. Clemencia, Jocasta, and Medea all attempt to escape an environment in which women have limited opportunities. However, their means of escape is not something positive, such as education. Rather, they become perpetrators of violence. Although Clemencia, Jocasta, and Medea do not exactly enact positive alternative choices themselves, their violent actions reject the traditional patriarchy and allow for the creation of new, alternative family structures.

In *Electricidad*, for example, Clemencia's violence allows for the forgiveness of La Ifi (Figure 2.1), who creates for herself a new family at the convent. Using themes from the Euripidean plays *Iphigenia in Aulis* (in which Iphigenia is replaced on the altar by a deer, when her father attempts to sacrifice her to make the winds blow the Greek ships to Troy[93]) and *Iphigenia in Tauris* (in which she is in Tauris as a priestess of Artemis), Alfaro introduces Electricidad's 'born-again' sister in place of Electra's Sophoclean sister Chrysothemis. In so doing, he seriously undermines Clytemnestra's claim in all the Greek versions that Agamemnon's murder is merely in retaliation for the king's sacrifice of their

---

[90] Román (2005) 120–1.   [91] Román (2005) 133.   [92] Román (2005) 135–6.
[93] This ending in the manuscript may not be authentic to the Euripidean version. See Rutherford (2005).

daughter Iphigenia, and instead makes Clemencia's act of revenge a product of her husband's abusive behaviour.

With a wonderful physical characterization by Elisa Bocanegra, La Ifi is clad as a dowdy nun wearing a puffy, black goose-down jacket. Tattooed in skull and crossbones, she has a very butch appearance in spite of her nun duds and humorously swings between her past aggressive behaviour and newly found pious demeanour. Born-again, she has rejected the cholx code in favour of her new religion and attempts to instruct her family in the practice of forgiveness:

IFIGENIA: 'Forgiveness is a virtue.'

ELECTRICIDAD: What are you talking about, macha?

IFIGENIA: I just learned that one. I don't know what the hell it means.[94]

Despite the lightness of the comic relief, La Ifi's quips convey a more serious point. She explains that the way out of the area and its violence is through unconditional love, or as she calls it, 'love, like...beyond the barrio'.[95] Thus, although the Sophoclean version depicts Electra's revenge as justified or even righteous,[96] *Electricidad* condemns such violence by presenting Christian forgiveness as a peaceful alternative.

In fact, La Ifi's Christianity is a necessary and intrinsic part of the cholx terms and culture into which Alfaro translates, for 'being born-again has become a big thing in gang culture, a way of avoiding violence'.[97] La Ifi demonstrates that not everyone in the area is a criminal, and those who are do not have to be. She shows that forgiveness is the only antidote to family violence. In fact, Alfaro has constructed the character of La Ifi in part because he 'thought it was important for everyone to see the choice Electricidad is making. She sees other options, Ifigenia presents one, and yet she *chooses* to do what she does.'[98] For the young students who have participated in Alfaro's workshops, La Ifi's perspective illustrates an alternative way of life. She tries to convince her mother that 'a stick is not the answer. Love is.'[99] Although her message is

---

[94] Alfaro (2006) 73, col. 1.   [95] Alfaro (2006) 78, col. 3.

[96] For a commentary on *Electra* that avoids a Christianizing view of the revenge, see March (2001).

[97] Johnson (2006) 65.   [98] Johnson (2006) 65.   [99] Alfaro (2006) 79, col. 1.

never received, the born-again La Ifi illustrates that family does not have to be inherited. It can also be created.

Oedipus too must reject his old family and begin to create a new one. He screams at Tiresias and blames him for saving him. He wanted to control his own destiny, but he wonders if he ever had the chance. Was everything already decided? 'Am I the lesson?' he asks. To which, Tiresias replies that he did the best he could. He is just a man who looks for answers not out in the world, but inside.

Ironically, in the violent act of killing his mother, Oedipus escapes the social and familial ties that bind him. Through the death of his old life, as represented by Jocasta's death in which she participates, he can seek redemption. For it is only by recognizing that he has fulfilled the prophecy—that he is bound by the chains of fate and that his story 'has been written'—that Oedipus is finally able to be free. His recognition of the prophecy thus functions as a metaphor for a recognition of the social and familial circumstances that may contribute to one's demise. Only by recognizing these oppressive circumstances and their effects can Oedipus break free of them.

Like *Electricidad* and *Oedipus El Rey*, *Mojada* too explores the dysfunction of the family and the need to create new models. Through the dramatization, Alfaro shows that some women, like Armida and Josefina, are able to create new lives and structures, and others, like Medea, cling to the old ways. Traumatized by her rape, she thinks she has no way of moving forward. While Medea fears the Americanization of her family, Armida and Josefina embrace their new life and the economic opportunities that it presents.

Through illustrating the choices and perspectives of these three women characters, Alfaro demonstrates that assimilating to life in the US can affect the family. On the one hand, Medea's resistance to conformity destroys her son, literally; on the other hand, Armida's crass exploitation of Medea's undocumented status pushes Medea to a psychological break. Midway between these two perspectives is Josefina, who, despite her lack of children, the long hours selling doughnuts and croissants from her van, and her husband's long hours as a blueberry picker, remains loyal, optimistic, and cheerful. Like Medea, Josefina misses home. She came to the US to survive, but she is willing to adjust to her new life. Like Armida, she works at her business, but unlike Armida, she has integrity and remains loyal to her friends. These three women and their three perspectives represent the choices, possibilities, and challenges that face some US immigrants. Some, like Medea, cannot acclimatize; others, like Armida and Josefina, do, but in the process encounter challenges in their search for new families and ways of living. By questioning the traditional family structure and presenting alternative models through these various characters, Alfaro thus questions stereotypes about the traditional Latinx patriarchal family structure.

Corporeality and Humour

Also at work in 'executing stereotypes' is the play's corporeality, i.e. the embodied elements of the performances, such as gestures, performance style, costume, and set.[100] In all three of the productions which I have discussed here the corporeality of the performances merges the historical environment of their precursors with the sociocultural environment of Boyle Heights and Pico-Union. From Electricidad's plaid shirt and baggy trousers to the tattooed crown of El Rey to Medea's long white dress and turquoise tasselled shawl, the costumes and comportment of the actors reflect the dress and style of Mexican-American and, in the case of Medea, Mexican culture. In fact, as sociologist James Diego Vigil has discussed, the cholx style, such as that donned by Electricidad and Oedipus in particular, is a key part of cholx identity, and, together with these clothing choices, 'other gestural and demeanour patterns also reflect the cholo style' and demonstrate 'one's closer associations to the barrio gang'.[101] Thus, the medium of performance creates an environment in which these characters not only retell the ancient myth but also embody it through a syncretic fusion of ancient Greek and modern cholx style.

In Alfaro's work, tattoos, graffiti, low-riders,[102] dancing style, and a leisurely gait function as identity markers, but the performance presents

---

[100] Although *Electricidad* follows the plot of the Sophoclean tragedy fairly closely, the play's marked use of tragicomedy and innovative dramaturgy resembles the style of Euripides. Euripides' late tragedies, especially, take on comic elements that scholars such as Oliver Taplin have attributed to the turbulent, war-torn environment of late fifth-century BCE Athens. Taplin (1986, 165–6) has argued that Euripides takes his use of comic touches, which characterize his later plays, to a new degree especially in *Bacchae*.

[101] Vigil (1988) 112. See also Berrios (2006).

[102] A car that has had its ground clearance modified so that it no longer fits the manufacturer's design specifications. Low-riders are popular in Chicanx culture and are often painted to reflect their Chicanx associations.

them with a humour that humanizes the characters. When Hason spits a gob of phlegm, or when Electricidad's *abuela* pulls a joint out of her cleavage, or when the infamous Sophoclean Sphinx appears as Esfinge, a vendor at the Farmacia Million Dollar,[103] the corporeality of such scenes captures Pico-Union culture, with a wink. However, the costumes, gestures, and actions are also funny, because of the mixture of the 'highbrow' classical play and 'lowbrow' modern setting.

Such camp portrayals, which are characteristic of Alfaro's work, endear the characters to the audience, as the dialogue simultaneously functions to explain the root causes of the problems they encounter within their environment. As Jessica Kubzansky, the director of the Getty's *Mojada*, has stated:

The adaptation of these given circumstances (Medea is an immigrant, but in this adaptation she and her family flee Michoacán, endure a rough border crossing, and end up in Boyle Heights undocumented) helps me to understand the humanity of *all* these characters in a whole new way. Because now they're in my world. Instead of just watching from afar and wondering at their reactions, I empathize with each of their plights and as the drama unfolds with terror and inevitability, I breathe and suffer with them every step of the way. This is the particular and prodigious gift of Luis Alfaro, who takes a Greek play, sets it somewhere modern and very specific, and from that specificity finds a way to universally show us ourselves.[104]

Alfaro's characters, like their real-life Boyle Heights and Pico-Union counterparts, are not people to fear and loathe. Instead, like their mythological templates, they are humans struggling against the vicissitudes of life, both those divinely inherited and those socially constructed. In this way, the corporeality of performance brings to life a humour that appeals to the head and addresses the heart. Such humour fosters a sympathy

---

[103] The character of Esfinge is like a *curandera* (healer). Items such as candles, herbs, and other types of alternative healing mechanisms sold in *botánicas* like the Farmacia Million Dollar are often used in spiritual practices of *curanderismo*, a healing art of Mexico, *espiritismo*, a Latin-American and Caribbean tradition of spiritualism, and Santería, an African Caribbean syncretic religion that fuses elements of Roman Catholicism with West African or Amerindian traditions. To serve their communities, which often have limited access to modern Western health care, these religions encourage the use of items from the *botánicas* for healing practices and magic to help with problems ranging from illness to heartbreak.

[104] Program Notes, *Mojada*, J. Paul Getty Museum at the Getty Villa (Kubzansky 2015a), with some minor amendments sent by email 6 January 2018.

and identification with the characters that work to foster the empathy necessary to understand and appreciate difference.

For example, in all three plays, pop references cast generic American cultural references into the framework of the immigrant experience. In *Electricidad*, Las Vecinas describe Electricidad's mother Clemencia as a power-hungry villain who wants 'Power... Her own business... Her own territory... Wants to own the block... the casa... the carro... Be a queen... an entrepreneur... Como la Oprah.'[105] If laughter has a 'social signification', as Henri Bergson suggests,[106] such punchlines play on the cultural anxiety about the integration of immigrant minorities into mainstream, white, middle-class American culture. In the case of this particular joke, the anxiety surrounds not just the issue of assimilation but also that of women of colour in positions of power. At first characterizing Clemencia as a power-hungry, materialistic cholx not to be messed with, Las Vecinas then undo their villain-like description of her by comparing her drive and ambition to the well-loved, former, TV chat show host Oprah Winfrey. Clemencia's entrepreneurial ambitions are as American as 'Oprah-pie'. The humour in the punchline 'Como la Oprah' arises in the juxtaposition of an image of a power-hungry villain with that of one of the most successful, cheerful, and well-loved yet fiercely powerful women in the American entertainment industry.

At the same time as the humour in this dialogue highlights a cultural fear of women of colour in power, the joke also points to an anxiety concerning the mingling of class and cultures. For Alfaro often casts 'apple-pie American' household references such as Oprah and 'The Price Is Right' into Spanglish phrases, and he references many consumer chains, such as Krispy Kreme,[107] El Pollo Loco,[108] Target,[109] and Food 4 Less,[110] and household goods, such as wine coolers, malt 40s,[111] tamales, and pointy bras from Woolworths, that all have clear class

---

[105] Alfaro (2006) 68, col. 1. 'Como la Oprah' is just one of a number of other pop-culture references mixed into the play's framework.

[106] Bergson (1991) 65. See also Freud (1989).

[107] A popular US doughnut chain.

[108] El Pollo Loco (The Crazy Chicken) is a popular US fast-food chain primarily located in the Southwest and Western areas of the country.

[109] A popular US retail chain known for its affordable, everyday goods.

[110] A chain of affordable supermarkets primarily located in Southern California.

[111] Low-price 40-ounce (1.183 litre) bottles of beer with an alcohol content of more than 6 per cent.

connotations. One such joke that hinges on class occurs when Orestes looks at the tattoo of Electricidad that he has just imprinted on his chest, and Nino (the pedagogue who trains Orestes to be a warrior while they are in Las Vegas) declares, 'Better than the Sears[112] family portraits!'[113] As Nino speaks of kitsch consumer goods as if they were luxury items, he evokes a laughter produced from a social anxiety surrounding class and racial stereotypes and the social and economic obstacles faced by many under-represented communities.

The anxiety over hybridity[114] and assimilation which fuels such jokes resonates in both Anglo-American and Chicanx culture, because, as Alfaro has stated, Chicanxs:

are dealing with our Americanism—we've got one foot on each side of the border—not necessarily the way you think about Mexico/U.S., but about assimilation and tradition. We truly possess an American psyche, and we're dealing with what it is to be American. It's natural to use what's in the culture at the moment.[115]

Pop culture thus functions as a syncretic site that Alfaro expertly exploits to defuse the tension that arises in the struggle between holding onto a traditional identity and assimilating into a new culture.

Therefore, while the humour in these plays could easily detract from their serious points, it instead allows the audience to laugh at what they might otherwise find themselves fearing, just as on the *Día de los Muertos*, one can laugh at Death itself. The syncretization of popular American and Boyle Heights/Pico-Union cultures becomes the power source for much of this humour, which humanizes Alfaro's characters, as the dialogue demonstrates the social circumstances that contribute to their problems. In this way, the characteristic humour and the syncretic corporeality and language (Spanglish) of his plays operate as poetic tools to dismantle stereotypes and in their place construct a bridge between classes and cultures.

Reinforcing Stereotypes

Nevertheless, as Alfaro has clearly aimed to 'execute stereotypes', his work could also inadvertently propagate the very stereotypes he wishes

---

[112] A US chain of department stores selling affordable clothing.
[113] Alfaro (2006) 80, col. 1.   [114] On hybridity, see Chapter 1.
[115] Johnson (2006) 64.

to destroy. In my classes, I ask my students how these characters might read differently to distinct audiences. How might the jokes reach some members of the audience who understand the cultural references, but not others? How might a middle-class, theatre-subscriber audience conflate Alfaro's characters with Latinxs at large? How might the audience exoticize rather than identify with the characters, and thereby reinforce stereotypes about Latinxs as gangsters and wetbacks?[116]

On the one hand, Alfaro's works inform mainstream, middle-class theatre-going audiences and empower the Latinx performers and also LA communities. On the other hand, this same attempt at education inevitably has risks. As a self-described people person who likes to go to Krispy Kreme openings[117], Alfaro seems to look for the best in people. He trusts his audience, but an audience's responses are clearly unpredictable. From the cosy cushions of their fifty-dollar seats, theatregoers such as myself cannot help but voyeuristically witness the characters' dramatized troubles from a comfortable distance.

Unlike the ancient Greek audience who witnessed the dramas of mythical kings and queens from the heroic past, Alfaro's audiences witness the real-time, present-day trials of working-class and undocumented families. This unequal power dynamic between the characters and the audience could easily result in the exoticization of the Boyle Heights and Pico-Union communities, because, despite the intentions of the performance, distinct audiences will inevitably receive these performances in various ways, and the demographic of the audience affects the performance itself.[118]

This unavoidable risk is a challenge that Alfaro faces in his writing, but is especially a challenge for the directors of the performances. For the performance walks the fine line between reinforcing a stereotype and challenging it.[119] This risk was especially apparent in the matinee

---

[116] While such commentary shows an attention to issues of class and culture, it also perhaps indicates a resistance to pan-Latinx cultural politics in favour of nationalism. See Román (2005) 134–6 on this issue.

[117] Alfaro (2015).

[118] On the 'theatrical event', see the Introduction. For studies of the theatre audience, see Carlson (1989); Bennett (1997); Blau (1990); Davis and Emeljanow (2001); Dolan (1988); Lee-Brown (2002); McConachie (2008); Tulloch (2005); and Sauter (2000).

[119] Herrera (2015) 28–33 explains this fine line in his discussion of the performances of Rita Moreno, whose performances, he argues, worked to challenge stereotypes versus Googie Gomez, who he suggests reinforced them.

performance of *Oedipus El Rey* at the Dallas Theater Center that I attended in January 2014, where the costume design of the performance reinforced the gangster stereotype. The production's male characters have slicked-back braided ponytails, goatees, blue bandanas, boleros, dark sunglasses, hairnets, stocking caps, fedoras, tattoos of spiderwebs (on their necks), and a variety of Christian iconography, such as Jesus with a crown of thorns and the Virgin of Guadeloupe—all stereotypical markers of the Latin gang member (see Figure 2.3). The costumes in the Taper's *Electricidad* have also used such stereotypical markers. However, the consistent application of a hyperbolized, camp aesthetic to all of the characters' costuming, from La Ifi's exaggerated eye make-up (see Figure 2.1) to Clemencia's snazzy coiffure (see Figure 2.2), has functioned, in Alfaro's words, 'like a Greek mask', i.e. in a manner which aestheticizes the features and avoids any claim to a realistic presentation of them. In contrast, the Dallas production failed to create such an aesthetic, in part because the stereotypical features of the male characters' costumes (see Figure 2.3) contrasted with the absence of such features in Jocasta's costume (see Figure 2.4).

In other words, the lack of consistency in the production design was confusing, for, while the male characters' attire played into the stereotype, Jocasta's did not (see Figure 2.4). Unlike the Jocasta in The Public Theater's 2017 production, whose wrap dresses and lace wedding gown referenced the attire of the *pachucas* (the women counterparts to the zoot-suiters of the 1940s who inspired chola style),[120] the Dallas Jocasta had an ethereal demeanour that contrasted with the apparent cultural specificity of her male counterparts. With long, flowing hair, often tied up in a bun to emphasize her large, gold hoop earrings, her nondescript ankle-length, white, jersey, spaghetti-strap, slip dress, with slits up the sides and a low-cut back, reveals a large tattoo of angel wings on her shoulder blades, as well as two other tattoos on her breast and just above her sacrum. However, such make-up and costume would easily suit a hipster on Venice Boulevard and are in no way specific to the Pico-Union subculture as it is represented in the play, nor are they a match for the hyperbolized depiction of the culture represented in the men's costumes.

---

[120] www.http://www.museumofthecity.org/project/la-pachuca-mexican-subculture-in-1940s-los-angeles/, accessed 31 December 2017.

Striking the right aesthetic is particularly important for this production, because, unlike the Los Angeles productions of *Electricidad* and *Mojada* that I attended, the Dallas production's audience was composed primarily of middle-aged Euro-Americans, and thus the risk of exoticization was greater. If any community outreach was done (as with the Boston Court/Getty production,[121] which provided subsidized tickets and bussed people in) to advertise the production in working-class Latinx communities, it was not apparent at this performance.[122]

The result of this demographic, for me personally, was to feel more like a voyeur of the culture than a participant in its experience. This was quite distinct from my experience at the Getty. There, I was surrounded by a mix of cultures, ages, and classes, from a Latinx family who brought their small toddler to the show to some young twenty-somethings, who on their way out agreed, 'It was, like, worth the forty dollars.' Another key distinction was that in Dallas the audience rarely laughed, whereas the Getty's audience not only laughed heartily at jokes with Spanish punchlines, but also gasped and even yelled at moments such as when Armida declared she would report Medea to the authorities.

Perhaps in an effort to address the cultural disparity between the demographic of the audience and that depicted by the actors, the performance in Dallas, unlike those at the Taper or the Getty, began with a pre-performance lecture and ended with a post-performance discussion.[123] As previously mentioned, about forty-five minutes before the performance, an actor from the show gave a presentation. Before the performance I attended, approximately fifteen of the nearly one hundred audience members who attended the show attended the lecture. Daniel

---

[121] In an interview with me, director Jessica Kubzansky (2015b) explained that Alfaro insisted that the portrayal of the characters should be as 'authentic' as possible, and one way they worked to do this was to workshop the play with the community in advance of the show's opening. The production even employed a community organizer, because they wanted people in East Los Angeles, in neighbourhoods like Boyle Heights, to know about the production, and a bus was hired to bring people from the neighbourhood to both a staged reading and then the full production at the Getty as well. I am most grateful to Ms Kubzansky for her thoughtful comments and stimulating discussion about the production.

[122] I was unable to contact director Kevin Moriarty for an interview.

[123] The Mark Taper Forum and the J. Paul Getty Center at the Getty Villa have hosted talks with Alfaro (and in the case of Taper, with the cast as well), but these were one-time events and not part of every performance.

Duque-Estrada, who played the role of Creon, began the talk by summarizing the Sophoclean version of the story and giving a brief explanation of the director Kevin Moriarty's interest in the political aspects of *Oedipus Tyrannus*. While the director wanted to focus on the human story in the play, the pre-performance lecture closed with an explanation of Alfaro's political interests in writing *Oedipus El Rey*. For the majority of the audience members who did not attend the pre-performance talk, several statistics, such as those cited previously, were posted on billboards in the bar area adjacent to the theatre. However, from my observation, few people actually read the billboards, but interviews with Alfaro and Moriarty about the prison industry were printed in the programme.

The post-performance discussion had twenty-nine patrons in attendance and lasted approximately fifteen minutes. In response to a question from an African American woman who mentioned she was interested in the depiction of Latinx culture, one actor explained the distinction between his own Latinx identity and that of the characters in the play, whose vocabulary and cultural landscape were foreign to him. However, instead of delving further into the problem of the possible conflation of the Pico-Union cholxs with all US Latinxs or into questions about stereotypes or recidivism, the discussion quickly moved on to a conversation about Sophocles' Oedipus, his struggle, and his fate, despite my attempt to redirect the focus by asking a question about stereotypes. Thus, even though educational material about the prison industry surrounded this audience, the post-performance discussion that I attended primarily focused on such apolitical, study-guide-type topics. No mention was made of the problem of recidivism, of Oedipus El Rey's being a repeat offender, or any of the other sociological problems that the play addressed, such as the poverty, violence, and isolation faced by the characters.

Conclusion

The problem of stereotypes is indeed quite complex, for, in the process of attempting to challenge them, one can easily effect the opposite result. Alfaro himself has grappled with this problem not only in his writing but on a personal level as well. In response to a question from an audience member during his talk at the Getty, he shared that he lost friends over his choice of *Mojada*[124] as the title of his play. The decision was even vehemently protested on his Facebook page. People could not understand his decision to reinforce (in their opinion) the use of this pejorative word, despite the ways in which it is used so specifically in the play by Medea to convey her desperation. After sharing this anecdote, Alfaro explained that he believed in the ability to 'reclaim' such pejorative terms, as the LGBTQ community has done with the word 'queer'.[125] Members of these communities clearly remain in disagreement about the use and function of such terms and who has ownership over them.[126] While some, like Alfaro, believe in the power of reclaiming words, others insist that doing so only reinforces the hateful stereotypes. This perennial debate illustrates the inherent difficulty in any attempt to 'execute the stereotype', namely the problem that 'those who loudly oppose stereotypes may [ironically] be their best allies'.[127]

The three productions discussed here have nevertheless aimed to challenge stereotypes while pursuing a more diversified trajectory of the performance of classical theatre. They have called on Americans to acknowledge the social circumstances that influence individuals to make the wrong choices, and to question a judicial system that aims to apply the law equally but instead appears to be rigged against people of colour and the poor. In the process, these works, through the fusion of cultures, have presented a new American classicism, a term which Mabou Mines founder Lee Breuer has coined to refer to productions of the classics with hybridized characteristics of American language, culture, and identity, as opposed to Anglo-European characteristics.[128]

---

[124] Alfaro (2015).   [125] Alfaro (2015).

[126] Judith Butler (1993) has analysed the critical uses of 'queer', stating that while:

> it is necessary to assert political demands through recourse to identity categories, and to lay claim to the power to name oneself and determine the conditions under which that name is used, it is also impossible to sustain that kind of mastery over the trajectory of those categories within discourse ... If the term 'queer' is to be a site of collective contestation, the point of departure for a set of historical reflections and futural imaginings, it will have to remain that which is, in the present, never fully owned, but always and only redeployed, twisted, queered from a prior usage and in the direction of urgent and expanding political purposes.
>
> Butler (1993) 227–8.

[127] Rosello (1997) 33, quoted in Herrera (2015) 139.

[128] Lee Breuer has used the phrase 'American classicism' to describe his *Gospel at Colonus* (a version of *Oedipus at Colonus* set in an African American Pentecostal church).

Therefore, as these performances work to challenge monolithic views of Greek drama, they also challenge normative views of American identity. Like *The Gospel at Colonus* (1988), whose performance on Broadway coincided with the election of more black mayors than ever before in US history, Alfaro's plays have accompanied the advancement of representational power of Latinxs in the US. From the election of Mayor Antonio Villaraigosa on 17 May 2005, just a month after *Electricidad*'s opening at the Mark Taper Forum, Los Angeles, to the recent service of six Latinx members of Congress,[129] to the appointment of Sonia Sotomayor as Supreme Court Justice, Latinxs have been increasingly transporting their political power from the page to the stage and into the political arena; Alfaro's adaptations of *Electra*, *Oedipus*, and *Medea* have contributed to these successes in part by showing how much more work still needs to be done.

Breuer recognizes that 'a different tradition is at work here [i.e. in the US] and a different classicism has to be developed' (Rabkin 1984: 51, citing Breuer).

[129] From 2003 to 2015, John Sununu (New Hampshire, Republican), Mel Martínez (Florida, Republican), Ken Salazar (Colorado, Democrat), Robert Menendez (New Jersey, Democrat), Marco Rubio (Florida, Republican), Ted Cruz (Texas, Republican). With the exception of Salazar, who is of Mexican descent, and Sununu, who is of Salvadorian and Cuban descent, all of these representatives are of Cuban descent.

3

Representing 'Woman' in Split Britches' *Honey I'm Home*, the F-RTC's *Oedipus Rex XX/XY*, and Douglas Carter Beane and Lewis Flynn's *Lysistrata Jones*

In 1985, Sue-Ellen Case laid down the gauntlet. In her pioneering article 'Classic Drag',[1] Case, who has since become one of the most influential theorists in feminist and queer theatre, boldly declared: 'Feminist scholars and practitioners may decide that such [Greek] plays do not belong in the canon.'[2] Inflamed in part by this statement, many classicists

---

[1] See also Case's seminal *Feminism and Theatre* (1988) for her views on Greek theatre.

[2] Case (1985) 327. Using the word 'may', which implies option, as opposed to 'should', which implies recommendation, Case challenged feminists to consider and explain their reasons for and approaches to representing women characters who were constructed by and for ancient men:

> The feminist theatre practitioner may come to a new understanding of how to reproduce the classic Greek plays. For example, rather than considering a text such as *Lysistrata* a good play for women, she might view it as a male drag show with burlesque jokes about breasts and phalluses playing well within the drag tradition. The feminist director may cast a man in the role of Medea, underscoring the patriarchal prejudices of ownership/jealousy and children as male-identified concerns. The feminist actor may no longer regard these roles as desirable for her career. Overall, the feminist practitioners and scholars *may* [my italics] decide that such plays do not belong in the canon—that they are not central to the study and practice of theatre.
>
> Case (1985) 327.

and some theatre historians continue to challenge the work.[3] However, through its pervasive dissemination in W. B. Worthen's *Wadsworth Anthology of Drama* (2010), the article continues to be a key resource on a topic that nearly thirty years later continues to inspire debates, including one between Case and Steve Wilmer, who revisited the work to assess the feminist reception of Greek drama.[4] For, despite her admonition, or perhaps because of it, women, without question, have been embracing Greek drama while employing feminist strategies for its reperformance. New York productions such as Deborah Warner's *Medea* (2002), Ann Bogart's *Trojan Women* (2012), Mariah MacCarthy's *Lysistrata Rape Play* (2013), and Seonjae Kim's *Riot Antigone* (2017) represent just a few productions in recent years that have engaged in feminist revisions of ancient works.[5]

The appeal of Greek drama to American women has had a long history. Kathryn Tingley (1847–1929), Eva Sikelianos (1874–1952), Margaret Anglin (1876–1958), Isadora Duncan (1877–1927), and Ellen Van Volkenburg (1882–1978) are just some of the women who famously pioneered the reception of Greek tragedy on the early-twentieth-century American stage.[6] According to Helene P. Foley:

> Despite other significant early performances, the inspiration and passionate dedication of one specific actress, Margaret Anglin, ignited the greatest interest in Greek tragedy on the American stage during the first quarter of the twentieth century and defined standards of performance for the production of the original plays in her era.[7]

Edith Hall has also studied the use of Greek tragedy by American modernist feminists, including Duncan, Hilda Doolittle (1866–1961), Willa Cather (1873–1947), and Susan Glaspell (1876–1948). These women used tragedy in the reconfiguration of American identity[8] by crafting innovations in aesthetic form,[9] and, in the case of Cather and Glaspell, by using the Greeks 'to face the challenge that disparities in income and class status posed to "official" American ideals of equality

---

[3] See Wilmer (2007).   [4] Case (2007). Cf. Wilmer (2007).

[5] For further reading on this topic, see Gamel (1999).

[6] For further reading on these women's contribution to the staging of Greek tragedy on the American stage, see Foley (2012b) 27–75.

[7] Foley (2012b) 47.   [8] Hall (2015) 150.   [9] Hall (2015) 163.

and freedom'.[10] Hall positions these advances within their historical moment, arguing that:

> as women gradually began to assert independence in the first two decades of the twentieth century, they sustained a consistent dialogue with Greek drama, demonstrating the seismic transformation of social and cultural life that had been ushered in by late nineteenth-century feminism. This had been presaged by the election of Susanna Salter as the first female mayor in the United States in Argonia, Kansas in 1887, and by the award of the right to vote to the women of Colorado in 1893, even though women in most states could neither vote nor sit on juries for years to come.[11]

Thus, American women have had a long, historical relationship with Greek drama that has participated in their political advancement and furthered their role in the development of American theatre and literature.

Nevertheless, the question raised by Case about how contemporary directors represent 'Woman',[12] i.e. the male 'invention of a representation of the gender "Woman"' on the ancient cross-dressed stage, continues to challenge scholars and practitioners alike.[13] In this chapter, I explore this crucial question of the contemporary representation of 'Women', who scholars such as Nicole Loraux have argued operate in Greek dramas not

---

[10] Hall (2015) 163.   [11] Hall (2015) 163.

[12] Case explains the concept of 'Woman' in her 'Classic Drag: The Greek Creation of Female Parts' (1985) 318:

> The result of the suppression of actual women in the classical world created the invention of a representation of the gender 'Woman' within the culture. This 'Woman' appeared on the stage in the myths, and in the plastic arts, representing the patriarchal values attached to the gender of 'Woman' while suppressing the experiences, stories, feelings, and fantasies of actual women. The new feminist approach to these cultural fictions divides this 'Woman' as a male-produced fiction from historical women, insisting that there is little connection between the two categories. Within theatre practice, the clearest illustration of this division is in the tradition of the all-male stage. 'Woman' was played by male actors in drag, while actual women were banned from the stage.

For further reading on 'Woman', see de Lauretis (1984).

[13] Little evidence can confirm that all women were entirely excluded from the stage or the audience. For example, some scholars have suggested that *hetairai* (sex workers for elite men at symposiums, for example) played the roles of naked women in comedy, such as Peace/Reconciliation in *Lysistrata*. However, most scholars agree that ancient male actors relied on their costumes, masks, properties, and performances to indicate their characters' gender. See Powers (2014) on the debates surrounding the issue of women in the audience.

as subjects but as objects circulated within masculine sign systems.[14] I do so by focusing on the representation of various characters in three distinct contemporary productions of Greek drama on the US stage: Split Britches' *Honey I'm Home: The Alcestis Story* (1989),[15] the Faux-Real Theatre Company's *Oedipus Rex XX/XY* (2013), and Douglas Carter Beane and Lewis Flynn's *Lysistrata Jones* (2011),[16] versions of Euripides' *Alcestis*,[17] Sophocles' *Oedipus Tyrannus*,[18] and Aristophanes' *Lysistrata*.[19]

---

[14] Loraux (1987). On women in ancient Greece, see also Foley (2001) and (1981).

[15] I recognize that some scholars question *Alcestis*' classification as a tragedy. On the subject of the genre of *Alcestis*, see Marshall (2000), who has argued controversially that Euripides removed satyrs from this fourth play in protest against a restriction on the use of comedy during the archonship of Morychides (440/439 BCE).

[16] Lewis Flynn is Douglas Carter Beane's partner in a relationship which, according to Michael Giltz (2012), made for 'one of the first, if not the first time, an openly gay couple has created a Broadway musical'. Former partners Scott Wittman and Marc Shaiman are another famous Broadway musical couple.

[17] Produced in 438 BCE, *Alcestis* is the oldest extant work by Euripides and was entered in the drama contest as the fourth play in the tetralogy (three tragedies and a satyr play) in place of a satyr play. It dramatizes the myth of Alcestis, whom ancient authors, such as Plato, praise as the quintessential good Greek wife. The tragedy begins with the god Apollo's explanation that he has awarded Admetus, the ruler of a city in Thessaly, the ability to have someone die in his place in return for the great hospitality that Admetus once showed the god. Admetus' elderly parents refuse to oblige, and his father berates Admetus for his request. Alcestis, however, agrees to die in his place, so as not to leave her children fatherless or endure the pain of losing him. However, she makes Admetus promise not to take a new wife, because she fears, in part, that a second wife could become a cruel stepmother to Alcestis' children. Admetus agrees not to remarry. Death comes for Alcestis, and Admetus laments. Yet soon, without notice, the hero Heracles arrives as a guest. Known for his hospitality, Admetus does not want to turn away his friend or sadden him, so he decides not to tell Heracles of the household's loss. As Heracles gets drunker and drunker, one of the servants finally informs him of Alcestis' death. Embarrassed by his behaviour and wanting to help Admetus, Heracles, who in myth is known to have travelled to the underworld, goes to battle with Death to wrestle Alcestis away from him. Winning back Alcestis, Heracles decides to surprise Admetus by presenting him with a veiled woman, who he insists Admetus accept as his new wife. Despite his promise to Alcestis that he would not take a new bride, Admetus finally agrees. He then learns it is Alcestis herself.

[18] See Chapter 2, n. 12 for a plot summary of this tragedy.

[19] Aristophanes' *Lysistrata*, produced in 411 BCE, is a comedy in which the title character persuades the women of Sparta and Athens to hold a sex strike until the men sign a peace treaty and put an end to the Peloponnesian War. As the younger women withhold sex, the chorus of older women seizes the Acropolis at Athens where the treasury is located. They fend off the chorus of old men, who seek to smoke them out of the temple, and are ultimately victorious. After hilarious scenes (that surely took full advantage of the comic costuming of the phallus), such as when Myrrhine teases her husband Kinesias and leaves him in pain, and the Spartan herald in desperation pleads for a treaty, the men finally begin to consider peace. Lysistrata arrives with the naked Peace at her side, and the men proceed to grope Peace, carving out their territory on her body. After both sides agree to the treaty, a celebration follows with song and dance.

Each of these productions employs women actors, as opposed to cross-dressed men, in distinct ways. For example, Peggy Shaw's perform-ance of Admetus in Split Britches' *Honey I'm Home* challenges gender norms with a 'butch-femme aesthetic', i.e. what Case has theorized as the gender masquerade of the 'coupled' lesbian subject.[20] Stephanie Regina's cross-dressed performance of Oedipus, in the otherwise all-male cast of Faux-Real's *Oedipus Rex XX/XY*, draws on queer performance tech-niques to demonstrate the performative nature of gender. In contrast to these productions that highlight the construction of gender in the ancient dramas through cross-gendered casting, *Lysistrata Jones* casts women actors in the Aristophanic cross-dressed roles.

Analysing these three examples, I will argue that the employment of women actors in a play written by and for ancient men does not preclude a feminist critique. For Split Britches' and Faux-Real's performances used feminist performance techniques to challenge normative views of gender. However, in some cases, such as *Lysistrata Jones*, reperforming Greek drama may inadvertently result in the reinforcement of negative depictions of women and essentialist ideas that attach sex (the physical body) to gender (the cultural performance of that body).

Split Britches, Faux-Real, and Beane and Flynn

Each production's creators have a distinct history that influenced their reception of the Greeks. Peggy Shaw, Lois Weaver, and Deb Margolin founded Split Britches in 1980, and 'Split Britches continues with the duo and solo work of Lois Weaver and Peggy Shaw which spans satirical, gender-bending performance, methods for public engagement, videog-raphy, digital and print media, explorations of ageing and wellbeing, and iconic lesbian-feminist theatre.'[21] Shaw is currently a:

writer, producer and teacher of writing and performance . . . Her book, *A Meno-pausal Gentleman*, edited by Jill Dolan and published by Michigan Press, won the 2012 Lambda Literary Award for LGBT Drama. Peggy was the 2011 recipient of the Ethyl Eichelberger Award for the creation of *RUFF*, a musical collaboration that explores her experiences of having a stroke. She was named a Senior Fellow by the Hemispheric Institute of Performance and Politics in 2014 and is the 2014 recipient of the Doris Duke Artist Award, and 2016 USA Artist Award.[22]

---

[20] Case (1996) 28.
[21] http://www.split-britches.com/home, accessed 4 January 2018.
[22] Programme notes to *Unexploded Ordnances (UXO)*, 7 January 2018.

Lois Weaver:

is an artist, activist and professor of Contemporary Performance at Queen Mary, University of London . . . Lois was [also] named a Senior Fellow by the Hemispheric Institute of Performance and Politics in 2014. She is a 2014 Guggenheim Fellow and a Wellcome Trust Engaging Science Fellow for 2016–18. In 2017, Split Britches were awarded the Artistic Achievement Award at the thirteenth annual New York Innovative Theatre Awards.[23]

Their pioneering work in the development of lesbian-feminist performance techniques has inspired the writing of leading performance theorists such as Sue-Ellen Case, Jill Dolan, and Katy Davy.[24] Most recently, Shaw and Weaver toured *Unexploded Ordnances (UXO)*, 'a new exploration of ageing, anxiety and "doomsday" created through conversation and collaboration with an array of elders and artists'.[25]

In 1989, the company, together with their production manager Heidi Blackwell, did a residency at Hampshire College for a Feminism and Theatre course. As part of the grant, they produced Euripides' *Alcestis*, a play, which, John Given has explained, 'is quite accessible to a non-specialist audience, whether on page or on stage, with its central love story, heart-rending death scene and boisterous drunken revel'.[26] It raises questions about themes such as husband and wife, life and death, *xenia* (hospitality), and *charis* (favour and return-favour). Nevertheless, according to Sabrina Hamilton, who designed the lighting for the show, the choice of material did not at first agree with Shaw because of the play's 'inherently heterosexual plot line',[27] in which Alcestis volunteers to die in place of her husband Admetus, who has been given the opportunity to have someone die for him because of the hospitality he once showed to the god Apollo.[28] Despite these concerns, they eventually made it work.

Because of the significance of Split Britches' work and their representation of a lesbian voice, I have included here a discussion of *Honey I'm*

---

[23] Programme notes to *Unexploded Ordnances (UXO)*, 7 January 2018.

[24] For further reading on Split Britches, see Case (1996).

[25] http://www.split-britches.com/uxo, accessed 4 January 2018.

[26] Given (2015). For an excellent study of this play, see Slater (2013).

[27] Hamilton (1993) 134.

[28] According to L. P. E. Edwards (2003), the Euripidean *Alcestis* has its origins in folk tale. She traces a variety of treatments of the story over the centuries to reveal a diversity of approaches to the tale. On the reception of the play, see also N. W. Slater (2013) 67–94.

Home, even though this work is the one production that I have not seen live and that falls outside of the approximate ten-year range of dates of the other productions discussed in this book. Moreover, the perform-ance, produced in the late 1980s, offers a valuable historical perspective on the reception of Greek drama by feminists, who at that time, shortly following the publication of Case's 'Classic Drag' (1985) and her renowned *Feminism and Theatre* (1988), were questioning the benefits of producing Greek drama perhaps more than at any other time in American history.

That historical moment is quite distinct from the one in which Faux-Real worked when Mark Greenfield directed *Oedipus Rex XX/XY* at La MaMa E.T.C. in 2013. This was nearly twenty-five years later, after famous Greek works had been 'staged by female (and feminist) directors such as, Ariane Mnouchkine, Deborah Warner, Katie Mitchell, and Rhodessa Jones and reinterpreted by women writers such as the play-wrights Hélène Cixous, Suzanne Osten, Cherríe Moraga and Marina Carr, as well as the novelist Christa Wolf'.[29] Feminist productions of the Greeks have now become common, and production companies such as Faux-Real have embraced this moment. Their stylized aesthetic, as their name suggests, 'synthesizes contrasting elements making ancient texts and challenging contemporary works exciting to a populace audience'.[30] Their various productions such as Euripides' *Bacchae*, Aristophanes' *Lysistrata*, *Queer USA*, *FunBox*, and *The Naked Show* demonstrate a keen interest in challenging normative constructions of gender.

The small-venue, avant-garde, anti-commercial approach of these two companies stands in stark contrast to Douglas Carter Beane and Lewis Flynn's *Lysistrata Jones*, which was directed and choreographed by Dan Knechtges on Broadway just a year before Faux-Real's *Oedipus Rex XX/XY*. Unlike the members of Split Britches and Faux-Real, the musical's

[29] See Wilmer (2007) 106.
[30] http://www.fauxreal.org/mission/, accessed 15 March 2016. According to their web-site, Faux-Real:

> creates original theatrical works; invigorates classic texts; mounts site-specific indoor and outdoor productions and makes high quality theatre accessible to a broad spectrum of New Yorkers. Productions often cross the boundary between spectator and actor, inviting audiences to engage directly with characters . . . . Faux-Real combines the entertainment value of physical theatre with the revelatory power of naturalism in productions that make erudite texts and challenging ideas accessible and exciting.

librettist Douglas Carter Beane has achieved major commercial success. His Broadway credits include such popular hits as *The Nance*, *Cinderella*, *Xanadu*, *Sister Act*, and *The Little Dog Laughed*; and he is a three-time Tony award nominee, including one nomination for *Lysistrata Jones'* book. Therefore, although *Lysistrata Jones* started in the smaller venues of the Dallas Theater Center in 2010, under the title *Give it Up!*, and The Gym at Judson for its off-Broadway run in 2011, the musical's short 2012 Broadway run, like many of Beane's works, aimed for commercial appeal. Despite its short run, the show has enjoyed an afterlife, playing in various small theatre venues as of 2016, such as the Chase Theater in Anaheim Hills, CA, and various universities, such as the University of Liverpool and the University of Cincinnati.[31] The production's website has even announced that a major motion picture is in development under the direction of Andy Fickman.

Cross-Dressing in Context

In contrast to the women performers in *Lysistrata Jones*, Peggy Shaw in *Honey I'm Home* and Stephanie Regina in *Oedipus Rex XX/XY* recreate not the female characters of the past but rather the iconic, male characters of Admetus and Oedipus respectively. Both companies have followed the plots of the ancient works fairly closely, but they offer feminist commentary on the dramatic events by using feminist performance techniques, such as interrupting the plot line, making use of cross-dressing, deflecting emotion at critical climaxes, and relying on the visual or physical as opposed to the verbal.[32] While Faux-Real set their *Oedipus* in a time-out-of-time framework, embellishing ancient styles of dress with modern accents, Split Britches set *Alcestis* in 1950s America and conceive of Alcestis, the quintessential Greek wife, as a proper housewife and Admetus, the quintessential host, as a doctor or, to be more specific, a 'jerky doctor'. Rather than give a broad description of these productions as others have done,[33] I will narrow my discussion here to Shaw's

---

[31] http://lysistratajones.com/database/, accessed 12 June 2017.

[32] For further discussion of the use of such techniques, see Diamond (1997).

[33] On *Honey I'm Home*, see Hamilton (1993); Blair (1993); and Case (1996). An unpublished paper with excellent detailed descriptions of *Oedipus Rex XX/XY* has been written by Manuel Simons (2013). The paper has been revised for publication in *Didaskalia* (2018).

and Regina's performances of these cross-dressed parts and their decon-struction of the masculinity inscribed in the ancient male characters.

It is first important to note, however, that these women's cross-gendered performances do not function in the same way as the Athenian men's performances of women, for distinct types of dressing-up such as theatrical cross-dressing, drag, and butch-femme role play must be contextualized on a case-by-case basis within a cultural and historical moment with specific views on gender. For example, drag is like theat-rical cross-dressing, for both are male appropriations of feminine attri-butes. However, because drag is parodic and reflects the socio-sexual mores of the modern age, the practice of theatrical cross-dressing in ancient Athens was not at all the same.[34]

As Stephen Orgel has explained, contemporary theatre is 'a theatre of named, known, and ... gendered actors ... We want to believe that the question of gender is settled, biological, controlled by issues of sexuality, and we claim to be quite clear about which sex is which—our genital organs, those inescapable facts, preclude any ultimate ambiguity.'[35] In Athens, however, 'Graeco-Roman medical writing and popular texts alike embed both sex, understood primarily in terms of genitalia and reproduct-ive capacity, and gender in the physical body while recognizing how that body can change under certain conditions and in response to certain practices.'[36] Brooke Holmes has explained that the Athenians had a distinct view of sex and gender that challenges not only contemporary views of the subject but also the whole notion of using sex and gender as an organizing principle for examining the ancient evidence.[37] Holmes states that:

what we define as same-sex erotic behaviour was parsed according to the categories of active and passive, masculine and feminine, free and slave. The definition of masculinity that has dominated research on the sexed brain—namely, that to be masculine is to desire women—simply doesn't make sense

---

[34] See Drouin (2008) for further discussion of such distinctions.

[35] Orgel (1996) 19. Orgel's *Impersonations* studies the ways in which modern discourses have obscured an understanding of the historical practice of boys playing the roles of women in Shakespeare's England. Orgel has used the example of the Irish film *The Crying Game* (1992) to explain the ways in which contemporary notions of gender influence views of historical practices of cross-dressing. For further reading on cross-dressing, see Senelick (2000).

[36] Holmes (2012) 182. For further reading on sexuality and gender in the classical world, see McClure (2002).

[37] Holmes (2012) 11.

in antiquity. And yet, in our ancient sources gender is inextricable from sexuality, and sexuality from power, challenging us to reflect on how these associations persist in our own thinking about sex, power, social norms and domination. Or consider, finally, the ways in which gender participates in more specific identities in antiquity, identities complicated by status (including the status of being human), age, kinship and lineage, as well as the ways in which it refracts light differently according to the circumstances under which it becomes salient.[38]

In sum, gender, sex, and sexuality are not timeless and universal but historically constructed categories that influence both the practice and reception of dressing up.

Mindful of the distinct views on sex and gender in the ancient and contemporary worlds, Kirk Ormand in his study of cross-dressed roles in Greek tragedy has explained that 'the ancients did not think of men and women as hetero- or homosexuals. In so far as they developed categories of sexual actors, they thought of players as either active or passive, or more precisely, penetrating and penetrated.'[39] If, as Ormand states, Greek gender is expressed in non-sexual terms,[40] then cross-dressing does not 'challenge the binarism of Greek gender',[41] for episodes of cross-dressing in fifth-century drama do not 'interact with notions of sexuality in the same way as they do for us'.[42]

Moreover, the expectations of dress and comportment in everyday life are not those of the stage. Unlike cross-dressing on the streets, cross-dressing on the stage may not have provoked any more thought about gender for ancient audiences than watching a realistic style of acting does for modern audiences. It is simply a function of the performance.[43]

For example, in theatrical traditions such as Kabuki and Noh, or Shakespearean performance in Renaissance England, cross-dressing is the expectation, just as it was for Stephen Orgel when he performed in cross-dressed roles at the Horace Mann School for Boys in New York in the late 1940s. Regarding his experience, Orgel states: 'Transvestite theatre was an unproblematic reality...I regularly played both male

---

[38] Holmes (2012) 182–3.   [39] Ormand (2003) 6.

[40] See Chapter 4 for further discussion of gender in ancient Greece.

[41] Ormand (2003) 10.   [42] Ormand (2003) 6.

[43] On cross-dressing on the ancient stage, see Llewellyn-Jones (2005) and Powers (2014) 105–7.

and female roles, with no sense that any stigma was attached to performing as a woman. This is how the Drama Club had always operated.'[44] Likewise, in ancient Athens, Aristophanes' character Agathon in *Women at the Thesmophoria Festival* could be ridiculed for his apparent effeminate style of dress, even though the cross-dressed actor playing Agathon would probably not have been ridiculed.[45]

For this reason, Karen Bassi has argued that ancient cross-dressing is not an attempt at challenging hegemonic notions of gender identity. Instead, she sees it as an example of what Stephen Greenblatt has called 'appropriative mimesis, imitation in the interest of acquisition',[46] i.e. Athenian cross-dressing aims to 'master the other'.[47] When 'Greek males wear women's clothes in front of an audience, they at once display the duplicity they ascribe to women and wear, as it were, the trappings of their own power over women'.[48]

Unlike this appropriative form of cross-dressing, Shaw's and Regina's performances highlight the social construction of the categories 'male' and 'female' by presenting the gender of the characters as a symbolic system of meaning in the portrayal of power relations. Their performance styles thus reflect and comment on the contemporary system of gender in which 'to be seriously deceived by cross-gendered disguising is for us deeply disturbing, the stuff of classic horror movies like *Psycho*'.[49] Revising the ancient tradition of cross-dressing, which scholars such as Bassi see as a

---

[44] Orgel (1996) xiii.

[45] See Zeitlin (1980) for further discussion of metatheatre in this play.

[46] Greenblatt (1991) 89.   [47] Zeitlin (1980) 80.

[48] Bassi (1998) 141. There are various perspectives on the issue in addition to Bassi's. Case has argued that the Athenian all-male stage, 'reveals the construction of the fictional gender created by the patriarchy' (Case 1985: 318). Edith Hall has stated, 'Athenian tragedy's claim to having been a truly democratic art form is . . . paradoxically, far greater than the claim to democracy of the Athenian state itself' (Hall 1997: 126). And Alisa Solomon (1997) has argued in her ground-breaking work *Re-Dressing the Canon: Essays on Theater and Gender* that: 'theater has always, by its very artifice, managed to interrogate its own representational strategies and in so doing to qualify, even to subvert, the "natural order" of those power structures that critics of transvestism fear are threatened by it' (Solomon, quoted in Bulam 2008: 11). Nancy Rabinowitz has argued for a middle ground. She has posited that the audience of Greek tragedy can respond on two levels: the 'narrative level', that is, taking what it saw presented as real and happening for the first time, and the 'authorial level', that is, aware that they were watching a representation constructed by an author. For this reason, cross-dressing need not only be a way for the patriarchy to control the representation of women on the stage. It can also be a site of resistance to it (Rabinowitz 1995. See also Rabinowitz 1998).

[49] Orgel (1996) 19.

marker of that society's oppression of women, both actors challenge their society's idea of the relationship between sex and gender identity.

Reclaiming Cross-Dressed Parts

Shaw and Regina pose this challenge in part by distinguishing their performance of gender from their bodies otherwise marked as female. For example, while their performance styles are quite distinct, both women embody the ancient, male characters without attempting to disguise their anatomy. In other words, the audience sees their waist, breasts, hips, etc. and must negotiate these feminine forms with an otherwise masculine comportment. Neither actor is trying to 'pass' as male. Instead, in their distinct ways, they put on male attitudes to demonstrate the performance and construction of masculinity.

For example, Shaw saunters on stage in a parody of 'man'. She wears loafers, light grey, wide-legged trousers, and a dark grey, long cardigan over a checked, buttoned-up polo shirt and tie. She sports close-cropped hair, slicked down on the sides with an Elvis-esque bouffant. The hairdo nicely complements her performance, when in a nasal register she lapses into an exaggerated performance of the Shirelles' 'A Thing of the Past', a duet she sings with Lois Weaver, who plays the Marilyn Monroe-esque Alcestis character (Figure 3.1).

Apart from the tie, in which Shaw often performs, the costume itself could easily be unisex by today's standards, but the costume clearly reads as masculine in this context, not only because of Shaw's hairstyle and comportment but also because of its contrast with the 1950s-style clothing of the chorus (Figure 3.2). In some scenes, this includes debutante dresses, complete with crinoline petticoats and white gloves, worn by Weaver and the chorus. Nevertheless, despite Shaw's comportment (e.g. her slightly hunched, rounded shoulders, forward-leaning, slouching torso, and pro-truding neck, as opposed to the proper, straight-backed posture of the ladies), the fit of the cardigan does not conceal her breasts or feminine hips; and Shaw makes no attempt to alter the register of her voice.

Shaw's 'butch' ('a female desirer . . . fixed in a mannish posture that copies heterosexuality'[50]) works together with Weaver's belted waist, red

---

[50] Anderlini-D'Onofrio (1998) 90.

Figure 3.1 Alcestis and Admetus in Split Britches' *Honey I'm Home: The Alcestis Story*. 1989.
Photo © 1989 Split Britches.

lipstick, blonde 'femme' ('a lesbian and woman-wife' who is an 'enlargement of woman as "Other"'[51]) (Figure 3.3) to create what Case has theorized as the 'coupled subject' of a butch-femme aesthetic. With its

---

[51] Anderlini-D'Onofrio (1998) 90.

Figure 3.2 The chorus in Split Britches' *Honey I'm Home: The Alcestis Story*. 1989.
Photo © 1989 Split Britches.

duplicitous husband[52] and noble wife love story (an unusual scenario for Greek tragedy, which is known for its 'bad women'[53]), *Alcestis* offers classical material ripe for Split Britches' butch-femme role playing,[54] 'a practice adapted from drag queens [that] wittily inverts the direction of gender masquerade within the tradition, and complicates its signifying practices'.[55] As in other performances, such as *Belle Reprieve*, Shaw performs this 'gender masquerade' as both butch and 'man'.[56]

---

[52] As D. J. Conacher (1988) has explained, 'interpretive arguments concerning the *Alcestis* have revolved around the "justification", or otherwise, of Admetus' (46). Conacher reads the play as having 'a series of ironic variations on the themes of *xenia* (guest-friendship) and *charis* (favour for favour), and on certain ambiguities which seem, in the circumstances, to surround them' (45), as Admetus negotiates his obligation to the important Greek custom of *xenia*, which requires him to be hospitable to his surprise guest Heracles, and his obligation to mourn his wife and keep the promise he made to her not to accept another bride.

[53] See Foley (2004) on the 'bad women' of Greek drama.

[54] Although their role play typically targets the heterosexist ideology inscribed in realism (Case 1999: 197), the butch-femme dyad in this case operates against the formalist aesthetic of Greek drama.

[55] Case (1996) 17.

[56] Case (1996) 28 identifies Shaw's performance in *Belle Reprieve* in these terms.

Figure 3.3 Alcestis and Admetus with Death (background) in Split Britches'
Honey I'm Home: The Alcestis Story. 1989.
Photo © 1989 Split Britches.

For example, in a hilarious scene, about an hour into the show, Shaw,
with three male back-up singer-dancers, performs 'I'm a Man', a song set to
the tune of George Thorogood's 'Bad to the Bone' but with lyrics such as:

When I was a little boy, at the age of five, I had something in my pockets kept a lot
of folks alive, now I'm a man, I'm age 21, you know baby, we can have a lot of fun,

cuz I'm a man, spelled M-A-N, MAN, Ohhh, Ohhh, Oww, All you pretty women, standing in line, I can make love to you, baby, in an hour's time, cuz I'm a man, spelled M-A-N, MAN.

[The back-up singers drop to do press-ups.][57]

Despite the title of the song, however, Shaw does not attempt to impersonate a male, but rather, with her characteristic irony, she and Weaver use a butch-femme aesthetic and an ironic, melodramatic tone throughout the performance to mock the idea of the 1950s patriarch.

Writing in 1988, near the time of this performance, feminist theatre critic Jill Dolan saw such butch-femme role-playing in utopian terms, commenting that, 'In the lesbian performance context, playing with fantasies of sexual and gender roles offers the potential for changing gender-coded structures of power.'[58] Dolan's view, which aligns 'lesbian' with gender, contrasts with Case's in 'Towards a Butch-Femme Aesthetic', in which Case uses Split Britches' work to consider 'lesbian' 'in the play of seduction, as artifice through butch-femme role playing'.[59] However, despite this distinction, both theorists see the political imperative in butch-femme role play. For as Case concludes:

In recuperating the space of seduction, the butch-femme couple can, through their own agency, move through a field of symbols, like tip-toeing through the two lips (as Irigaray would have us believe), playfully inhabiting the camp space of irony and wit, free from biological determinism, elitist essentialism, and the heterosexist cleavage of sexual difference. Surely, here is a couple the feminist subject might perceive as useful to join.[60]

Targeting the iconic roles of Admetus and Alcestis, and interpreting them in terms of the patriarchal values of the 1950s nuclear-family home, Shaw and Weaver use butch-femme role play to revise and challenge the power structures inscribed in the traditional 1950s middle-class husband-wife relationship by reimagining the ancient tradition of cross-dressing in butch-femme terms. In the process, they work to unmask the patriarchal structures that created 'Woman' as a means to marginalize women.

---

[57] Quoted from a video of the production kindly provided to me by Lois Weaver. My grateful thanks to Lois and Peggy for all of their generous help and support. As Shane Breaux has noted, this performance is also likely a parody of Peggy Lee's "I'm a Woman," which is rife with gendered stereotypes.

[58] Dolan (1988) 68. See Case (1996) for further discussion of the contrast between her work and Dolan's. For another critique of Case's discussion of camp, see Davy (1994).

[59] Case (1996) 13.   [60] Case (1999) 197–8.

Figure 3.4 Jocasta and Oedipus with their arms around each other in the Faux-Real Theatre Company's *Oedipus Rex XX/XY*, directed by Mark Greenfield. 2013. Photo © 2013 Peter James Zielinski.

Like Shaw in *Honey I'm Home*, Stephanie Regina as Oedipus in *Oedipus Rex XX/XY* signals the performative codes of both genders but plays with and against Tony Naumovski's cross-dressed Jocasta (Figure 3.4). Manuel Simons vividly describes Regina's performances thus:

Oedipus strides confidently on stage in green leather work boots, hip and waist defining brown leather pants with thick black belt, and a form-fitting top made of silver-threaded mesh through which protrudes a [white] sports bra, its spandex shaped by the roundness of breasts. Consistent with Sophocles' text, Oedipus is always referred to with the masculine pronoun *he*. This Oedipus evokes 1980s, phallic-woman, rock-and-roll images a la Joan Jett, Pat Benatar, or Patti Smith. Yet, the costume's brown leather and silver mesh also suggest animal skins and chainmail characteristic of ancient and medieval images of warrior masculinity. Regina's long, dark hair is pulled back into a tight ponytail and she wears no make-up . . . [Her] performance evinces powerful masculinity, not only through the 'butch' styling of her costume that conjures associations with animal skin and chainmail, but most strikingly through movement and gesture. Her Oedipus walks with a wide-stepped, heavy-footed gait and gesticulates fiercely—pointing to his subjects, commanding his servants, and raising fists to his enemies—with the muscularity and resistance of arms that move as though strengthened by years of wielding swords and shields in combat. Regina's deep, grounded breathing supports a rich, alto-pitched voice that vibrates from her chest resonator; the boom of her voice fills La MaMa's ground-floor theatre. Her curt, 'square' line-phrasings hit hard upon consonants and de-emphasize vowels to maximize the forceful angularity and percussive rhythm in the language and minimize its lyricism. While her powerful, alto pitch evokes fierce strength and confidence, she neither attempts nor intends to produce masculine baritone pitches; this is a woman's voice.[61]

Like Shaw, Regina aims to perform 'man', but she does so while maintaining a tragic, as opposed to Shaw's comic, register.[62] While the chorus in this production at times uses the performance style of camp,[63] such as a sassy finger snap,[64] Regina's performance avoids the style.

Offsetting Oedipus' performance of masculinity is the femininity of Tony Naumovski's Jocasta, whom Simons has described as having:

long, wavy, platinum-blonde locks [that] caress silken, chartreuse robes, which flutter in the breeze like the billowing chiffon curtains of some Venetian piazza in a 1980s music video.[65] Jocasta's white gown with halter top fashions a deeply plunging neckline, which exposes the body: Naumovski's bare and broad shoulders, chest, and arms are muscularly developed. There is no attempt to mimic female anatomy; there are no breasts in the halter, which lays [sic] flat against the actor's chest. He wears full make-up, but his acutely square jaw-line, prominent nose, and thick eyebrows harden and contrast the soft flush of the make-up ... Jocasta's arms move fluidly and delicately; her walk is measured in small, refined steps. She moves with utter grace as though carefully schooled

[61] I am most grateful to Manuel Simons for granting me permission to quote these detailed descriptions from his excellent paper, which he submitted for my graduate seminar 'The Body in Performance' at the CUNY Graduate Center in 2013. Simons' perspective is particularly insightful because he performed as a member of the all-male chorus and has been a long-standing member of the company. A revised version of this paper has been accepted for publication by *Didaskalia* and has an expected publication date of July 2018.

[62] The contrast in the tone of Shaw's and Regina's performance is also perhaps in keeping with the distinctions between the genres of the ancient plays, for some scholars have argued that *Alcestis* could in fact have been performed as a satyr play rather than a tragedy. See Marshall (2000).

[63] Anderlini-D'Onofrio (1998) 90 defines camp as, 'a distance, artifice, and grotesque manifestation of a self-conscious attitude toward one's sexuality. From this distance the butch-femme couple critiques the cultural construction of heterosexuality.'

[64] Simons (2013).

[65] Simons (2013) references Madonna's *Like a Virgin* music video. Madonna, 'Madonna Videos', *Like a Virgin* video, 3:46, directed by Mary Lambert, 1984, http://madonna.com/media/video/19, accessed 27 May, 2013.

in the etiquettes of 'feminine' virtue and beauty. Her voice is low-pitched, but her speech is highly melodic and her phrasings have a marked sense of rhythm and musicality. Furthermore, Jocasta, uniquely among all of the characters in this production, sings some of her dialogue—alternating dramatically between song and speech at key moments in the play. Song is used here to signify the feminine.[66]

Like Regina, Naumovski does not aim to impersonate a woman but rather to reference the gender characteristics associated with it through his body.

Like Shaw and Weaver, Regina and Naumovski create a gender masquerade in part by playing on and against each other. However, their relationship does not create a butch-femme aesthetic but rather a cross-gendered performance that aims for 'real disguise'[67] (i.e. for a performance that will allow the audience to identify with each character, as if he or she were a man and woman) while simultaneously showing the artifice of that disguise by referencing performance styles, such as drag, camp, and butch-femme role play. In other words, their costumes and gestures reference queer performance techniques, but they play it straight, so to speak, without committing to a consistent use of camp and its accompanying irony. The result is two cross-dressed actors performing Robert Fagles' translation of the play without relying on their biology to signify Oedipus' and Jocasta's gender identity.

By highlighting not only the construction of the feminine but also that of the masculine, Oedipus Rex XX/XY's cross-dressed woman/cross-dressed man relationship allows the play's iconic son/mother relationship to be understood in terms of gender rather than sex, in terms of a dynamic that is fluid, not one that is fixed, thereby alluding to the limitations of understanding gender and sexuality through Freud's theory of the Oedipus complex.[68] The unmasking of this gendered power relationship reaches its zenith in the critical moment when Jocasta pleads with Oedipus to abandon the search for his identity. In a fit of rage, Oedipus 'seizes her [hair] in his hand and shoves her to the ground. Her blonde wig flies from her head and lands at the feet of the first row of audience members. In stunned silence, the audience and everyone on

---

[66] Simons (2013).   [67] Baker (1994) 14.
[68] For a feminist study that reassesses the Oedipal and pre-Oedipal in relation to gender polarity and the fluidity of gender categories, see Benjamin (1998).

stage see that Jocasta (or Naumovski?) is bald.'[69] Ironically, it is through un-wigging Jocasta and revealing the mark of masculine baldness that she appears most deprived of power.

Yet while Shaw and Regina deftly deconstruct masculinity, neither actor plays up her male character's feminine traits, which would have been apparent in the ancient context. In her seminal article 'Playing the Other', classicist Froma Zeitlin discusses the ways in which the male actors and spectators honour the god of masks, Dionysus, through exploring the feminine 'other' that is inscribed in the theatre's presentation of the body, architectural space, use of plot, and mimetic representation.[70] Classic examples of so-called feminine behaviour, of the sort that Plato condemned in *Republic* Book X, are laments, wounded bodies, expressions of pain, and deceptive behaviour. Admetus' lament with the chorus after Alcestis' death and Oedipus' blinding are two such examples; yet neither Shaw nor Regina seizes the opportunity to play the man 'playing the other'. Instead, they remain fixed in their characterization and critique of masculinity.

For example, in *Alcestis' kommos*, a lyrical exchange between a principal character and the chorus at times of heightened emotion, Admetus grieves for his recently deceased wife, at first wishing he were dead and then that he were unmarried and childless so that he would not have to endure such grief. In place of this emotional moment, Shaw begins to give a melodramatic speech over Weaver's body. However, she then forgets her lines, or pretends to, only to be prompted by Weaver's dead Alcestis—a moment that, like Jocasta's un-wigging, leads the audience to wonder whether this mistake is accidental or a part of the performance, as the actors digress into a debate over whether or not they should be performing this play at all:

ADMETUS/SHAW: I told you from the beginning I don't want a lot of lines . . . and I don't want to play a man.

ALCESTIS/WEAVER: But these are lovely lines . . .

ADMETUS/SHAW: But look who's saying them, a jerky junior executive.

---

[69] Simons (2013). For me, the emotional experience of this moment was incredibly powerful and moving.

[70] Zeitlin (1996) 68–9.

ALCESTIS/WEAVER: He's a doctor.

ADMETUS/SHAW: I don't care what he is.

ALCESTIS/WEAVER: But look who's expressing them.

ADMETUS/SHAW: This guy is expressing them.

ALCESTIS/WEAVER: You're expressing them.

ADMETUS/SHAW: A woman playing a man is expressing them . . . I'm a woman playing a doctor who's a man whose wife is dying for him who is expressing them . . . What does that mean?

ALCESTIS/WEAVER: What does any of this mean?

ADMETUS/SHAW: I don't think what we're doing is responsible. No matter what we're doing we're portraying a lesbian relationship in a bad light. There are students here!

ALCESTIS/WEAVER: Well, look at me. I have to die, just so I get to play the tragic heroine—all the leading roles for women still have to die in the end . . .

ADMETUS/SHAW: What's the audience supposed to think when one of them is dying for her husband, one of them is a jerky doctor, and one of them is strutting around in this outfit [*as she points to Death*] killing women while some guy plays the violin.

WOMAN PLAYING DEATH: But this is what I choose to wear.

ADMETUS/SHAW: What does that mean?

WOMAN PLAYING DEATH: I don't know.

ALCESTIS/WEAVER: Maybe we should just get on with it.[71]

The hilarious scene, which pokes fun at the ancient Admetus as well as the feminist critique of him, continues as Alcestis exits the stage with Death. For, instead of breaking into a 'feminine' lament at this moment, as the Euripidean Admetus does to 'play the other', Shaw sings, to the laughter of the audience, 'Dum, dum, dum, dee, dum, dooo, doobie', while making melodramatic gestures of despair.

Likewise, despite the director Mark Greenfield's attempt to feminize the blinded Oedipus through costume and design choices, Regina, like Shaw, shies away from performing any of the 'feminine' traits inscribed in the wounded ancient character, who, as Ormand has argued, 'is emasculated when exposed to great pain and great self-abasement . . . [stripping him] of both masculinity and the authority that has been his as a man

---

[71] Quoted from a video of the production kindly provided to me by Lois Weaver.

Figure 3.5 The blinded Oedipus and the chorus in the Faux-Real Theatre Company's *Oedipus Rex XX/XY*, directed by Mark Greenfield. 2013.
Photo © 2013 Peter James Zielinski.

and king'.[72] According to Zeitlin, 'it is at those moments when the male finds himself in a condition of weakness that he too becomes acutely aware that he has a body—and then perceives himself, at the limits of pain, to be most like a woman'.[73]

Nevertheless, Regina resists this feminization, even though, as Simons has described, the production design suggests it by accentuating the actor's feminine features through a costume change. Blinded and in pain, she now appears with long hair and bare feet in a sleeveless top, burlap skirt, and bloody mask, with two large, bloodshot eyeballs protruding nearly six inches from their sockets (Figure 3.5).[74] Thus, despite her feminized appearance, Regina softens neither the tone of her speech nor her gestures and comportment. Her performance does not match either the text's or costume design's attempt to feminize the king.

---

[72] Ormand (2003) 28.   [73] Zeitlin (1996) 69.

[74] According to Simons (2013), 'In this highly gendered production, it is impossible to avoid "seeing" these as disembodied testicles, his feminized body penetrated and castrated by "the long-gold pins" of Jocasta's brooches.'

Just as Shaw refuses to play the sensitive man in grief, so Regina refuses to play the wounded, vulnerable king. Both women successfully play male roles, but both also resist playing up the so-called 'feminine' qualities of these characters when they are wounded, emotionally and physically. Whether this resistance is a conscious choice or a failure of their performances is irrelevant. The result is what is significant. Shaw and Regina have denied projecting an image of a feminized male or a man resisting the failure of his own masculinity. They thus 'reclaim' the ancient construct of 'Woman' not only by deconstructing the masculinity inscribed in the ancient characters, but also by refusing to portray ancient tragedy's feminization of those characters in a way that would either reinforce the masculine/feminine binary or suggest their biological make-up has given them privileged access to the feminine. While in the Athenian context, 'playing the other' illustrates a fear of the feminine that the male seeks to understand and control, in these contemporary contexts, the actors refuse to play the male 'playing the other' and instead challenge normative views of gender in their society.

Reinforcing Stereotypes in *Lysistrata Jones*

Having discussed the role of butch-femme role playing and cross-gendered casting in the previous section, I now want to consider the role of cross-dressing, or rather the absence of it, in a contemporary production[75] of a comedy. Produced by Callistratus in 411 BCE, when Athens had been involved in the Peloponnesian War for twenty years and was in the midst of a political and military situation that was 'in almost every respect, very bad',[76] Aristophanes' *Lysistrata* dramatizes a wishful solution to the predicament: a sex strike waged by women in order to stop the men from fighting. Although fifth-century Athenian women were marginalized in their society and had no citizen status, in this battle of the sexes, the 'Women' are triumphant; so, despite the comedy's androcentric origins, directors in modern times have often interpreted the play as a powerful statement by women against war.[77]

---

[75] For further reading on this production, see Klein (2014) 127–45.

[76] Sommerstein (1990) 1.

[77] Productions such as the *Lysistrata Project* and the Egyptian Lenin El Ramly's *The Peace of Women* are examples of this typical approach. For a discussion of these works, see Case (2007). On the ambiguous nature of Lysistrata's feminism, see Klein (2014) 5–6.

The musical production I consider here, however, takes a far less political approach. Despite its inclusion of women actors, as opposed to cross-dressed actors, I will argue that *Lysistrata Jones*, unlike *Honey I'm Home* and *Oedipus Rex XX/XY*, strips its ancient precursor of its subversive potential to present instead a commercialized rendition of modern women who have little drive or ambition apart from encouraging their loser boyfriends to win a game.

After successful runs at the Dallas Theater Center, under the title *Give it Up!*, and off-Broadway at the Judson Memorial Church Gym, the pop musical comedy began previews on Broadway at the Walter Kerr Theatre in November 2011 and closed shortly after on 6 January. With a book by the Tony and Drama Desk award nominee Douglas Carter Beane and music and lyrics by Lewis Flynn, the musical adapts Aristophanes' bawdy work into the context of the fictitious Athens University whose losing basketball team has not won a game in thirty years. Fed up with these stats, the Lysistrata character Lyssie J., played by Patti Murin, leads the cheerleading squad on a crusade for abstinence until the team finally wins a game.

Aristophanic comedy,[78] which derives its energy and humour from mocking everyday people[79] and events,[80] aims to present caricatures of the men and women, not realistic depictions. While the characters and performances in *Lysistrata Jones* also exaggerate stereotypes of each gender, unlike in the Aristophanes, women actors, not dressed-up men, play the women roles. In their distorted masks, padded breasts, and body stockings,[81] the ancient male actors may have for comedic purposes

---

[78] On Aristophanes, see Revermann (2006) and (2014); and Kozak and Rich (2006).

[79] Whereas the characters of tragedy are mythological icons, the women of comedy are wives, mothers, flute players, and festival attendees; the men are sausage sellers, farmers, charcoal burners, and even caricatures of real-life people such as Socrates.

[80] As in tragedy, the settings and events can often be extreme or other-worldly, such as travelling to the underworld in *Frogs* or creating Cloudcuckooland in *Birds*, but unlike tragedy, the genre refers to actual people, such as the politician Cleon, and events, such as the Thesmophoria festival.

[81] On the Athenian comic stage, actors costumed themselves in padded body suits that made their figures appear full and disproportionate. Those playing male parts wore full-headed masks with distorted facial features and short chitons or tunics, which exposed an oversized and thus comic phallus. Male actors playing female roles, on the other hand, had full-headed masks with feminine hairstyles and padded breasts that long feminine chitons concealed. On the comic body, see Foley (2002). On costume in Aristophanes, see Compton-Engle (2015).

Figure 3.6 Robin, Myrrinhe, Lyssie J., Lampito, and Cleonice (left to right) in *Lysistrata Jones*, directed and choreographed by Dan Knechtges. 2011.
Photo © 2011 Joan Marcus.

exploited the illusion of cross-dressing (i.e. if in fact cross-dressing could serve the purpose of getting a laugh).[82] However, instead of playing with

---

[82] Arguing against Lauren K. Taaffe (1993), who 'claims that these roles must be played by men, and men who do not attempt to "pass" as women, at that', Reina Erin Callier (2013) has stated:

> Plays with plots that explicitly bring issues of gender and costume to the fore—such as *Ecclesiazusae*, *Thesmophoriazusae*, and, to a lesser extent, *Acharnians*—might be seen as particularly appropriate venues for 'non-illusionary' cross-dressing. Nevertheless, the potential for 'men in drag' humor is everywhere, and a good director could easily utilize costume, gesture, voice, and blocking to emphasize this humor in performance.

To support her point Callier quotes John Gibert's review (1995) of Taaffe's book, which states, 'Aristophanes' comic purposes are...sometimes better achieved if the illusion of "men playing women" remains intact.' As Taaffe has argued, 'true-to-life representation seems not to have been the central aim of comic costumes and masks...A female mask worn by a padded actor in woman's clothes emphasizes, in fact, the theatrical nature of the imitation' (Taaffe 1993: 13). Despite these arguments, the details on such performances are unclear, for the closest instructions on performing in cross-dressed roles come from comedy itself, vase painting, and perhaps the *Bacchae* of Euripides in which Dionysus instructs Pentheus in how best to disguise himself as a woman when he goes to spy on the maenads. The metatheatrical scene is full of references to the theatrical play, but it is

the illusion of a costumed body as on the ancient stage, the actors playing Lyssie J. and her fellow cheerleaders, Cleonice (Kat Nejat), Lampito (Katie Boren), and Myrrhine (LaQuet Sharnell), bare their real-life flesh and bones, and a lot of it (Figure 3.6). For example, in their numbers 'Change the World' and 'No More Giving it Up', the women dance on stage with bare midriffs, but, while their hot pants, miniskirts, and skintight capris are provocative, their knee-highs, pigtails, and Valley Girl diction infantilize them. In this way, although in some cases such costuming could be used as a means to empower women, these particular modern actors play into the 'male gaze'[83] that projects its desire onto female figures and reinforces stereotypes of women as sexualized objects rather than agents; for while Beane and Flynn identify as gay males, gay men are not resistant to the influences of the patriarchy.

Unlike their cinematic doppelgänger Elle Woods, played by Reese Witherspoon in the 2001 film and 2007 musical *Legally Blonde*, these women do not play up a stereotype only to defy it, become Harvard graduates, and spite their underachieving ex-boyfriends, who never believed in their potential. The plot of *Lysistrata Jones* refuses any such statement. Instead, these women look like stereotypical Valley Girls, and act like them too. They want to have a purpose but are too self-absorbed to find a legitimate cause outside their small world. As Emily Klein has discussed:

The young characters are fluent in a hackneyed language of protest, fighting for what they believe in, standing up for something, supporting good causes, and making a difference. But their naïve and self-congratulatory efforts suggest that privilege and nostalgia may play a role in watering down contemporary notions of activism ... *Lysistrata Jones* puts a history of American activism on par with the effort to end a basketball losing streak. In the lyrics 'I hear the ghost of Susan B. Anthony blowing in the wind' and 'they've marched down Pennsylvania Avenue, Plant a tree, make it clean, no more carbon, keep it green', the show's radical leftist blogger conflates suffrage, environmentalism, civil rights, and the antiwar movement (69–70). While

---

important to note that Dionysus is directing Pentheus in how best to disguise himself, not in how to perform on a stage.

[83] Film theory includes a number of critical frameworks that scholars have developed to analyse film in terms of social impact and influence, e.g. the way in which films construct and reflect cultural, national, and gender identities. See, e.g. the classic work of Laura Mulvey (2009), who discusses the masculine subjectivity of film and the operation of the male 'gaze' that projects its desire onto female figures. Males see, while women are to be seen. Judith Butler (1993) has discussed views of the gaze that take into account lesbian subjectivity.

activism is framed as important and meaningful...it isn't always clear that the characters can distinguish between being civically aware and engaged from being an activist.[84]

The characters' confusion about activism works in part as a satire of the 'apathy of a generation that feels it was born to lose',[85] yet consequently has a social-media driven need to have a cause, or rather post about one on social media, while simultaneously updating relationship statuses, 'liking' photos, and announcing parties. However, the attempt at satire comes at the expense of portrayals of women who are subordinate to men and seriously confused about how to change that power relationship.

For, unlike the ancient Lysistrata who shows and even declares her intelligence and leadership (1124) (however paradoxical that may have been to the ancient male audience[86]), Lyssie J. is no intellectual. She has read the *SparkNotes* of Aristophanes, 'unabridged'. But if not exactly smart, Lyssie is driven. She is tired of everyone giving up. She sings that she wants more, but instead of directing these ambitions toward something productive, she focuses her energy on the success of the men.

When she and the other women fail to motivate the men, they use not their brains but their bodies to try again. Siri, the iPhone's famous assistant, sends them to the Eros Motor Lodge to meet the Hetaira,[87] a tall, plus-sized African American sex worker, played by Liz Mikel with a personality to match her size (Figure 3.7). She takes their side and teaches the women how to be provocative and tease the men. Armed with new tricks, the women engage in a battle of the sexes, but unlike the battle in the ancient comedy between the choruses of old men and old women, who use fire and water, here hypersexualized bodies act as weapons. The men take off their shirts and strip to their underwear. Stepping up their game, the women wear lingerie and nurses' outfits with locks around their waists. At this point, neither side wins. The camp[88] confrontation only leads to some couples breaking up and pursuing new love interests.

However, while this adaptation lacks the famous scene when the naked Peace appears and Lysistrata helps the men to carve out a treaty

---

[84] Klein (2014) 138.   [85] Brantley (2011).

[86] As Sommerstein (1990) 212 notes, 'for the implication that intelligence in a woman is something paradoxical, cf. Eur. *Med.* 1081–9, *Or.* 1204, Aesch. *Ag.* 351. See K. J. Dover *Greek Popular Morality in the Time of Plato and Aristotle* (1974) 99.'

[87] The ancient Greek word for a sex worker for elite males. *Hetairai* contrast with the non-elite sexworkers or *pornai*.

[88] As I discuss in Chapter 4, camp is not always employed for subversive purposes.

Figure 3.7 Hetaira with the company in *Lysistrata Jones*, directed and choreographed by Dan Knechtges. 2011. Photo © 2011 Joan Marcus.

on her own body,[89] a major transition does occur at the end of the play. Lyssie discovers that she can play in the final game of Athens University vs Sparta, because under Title 9 rules, if there is no women's team, then a woman can play on a men's team. She joins in the game, finally, and in slow motion runs to the basket, hands the ball to her former jock boyfriend Mick (Josh Segarra), who hands it back to her. The whole team of men then lifts up Lyssie so that she can make the winning basket. Mick and Robin (Lindsay Nicole Chambers), who are now an item, kiss. Lyssie and her new nerdy beau Xander (Jason Tam) kiss. They all exit the stage. Then, with everyone dressed-up in funky, Greek-inspired costumes, the entire company returns to the stage to sing a reprise of 'Give it Up!'.

In this recap of *Lysistrata Jones*, one critical distinction between its plot and that of the Aristophanes becomes clear. Whereas in the Greek, the women are trying to get the men to stop doing something, in *Lysistrata Jones*, the women are trying to inspire the men to do something. This distinction is important, because it raises the question of why Lyssie and her friends focused on encouraging the men to win at all instead of simply forming their own winning basketball team.

If Lyssie is so tired of everyone giving up, why not start her own team and show the men how to do it? She is not, like the ancient Lysistrata, prevented from competing in a man's world. Moreover, when Lyssie finally does realize that she has a right to play too, she does not rush to make the winning basket; instead, she passes the ball to her former boyfriend. He does pass the ball back to her, but she still does not make the final basket on her own. Rather, the team of men lift her up on their shoulders so that she can dunk the ball. Unlike Elle Woods, another comic Valley Girl with a cause, Lyssie J. lacks the inner resources to carve out her own path, start a team, and win a game. Instead, she continues to rely on men to achieve the goals that she does not, or will not, accomplish on her own.

Accordingly, the men remain the focus of the women's attention. Even the smart and independent Robin ultimately winds up dating the jock and becoming more like a Valley Girl in the process. She does not talk about her own passions but instead states that she wants to see her new boyfriend play basketball with passion. As John Given has commented in

---

[89] While a cross-dressed man could have portrayed Peace, it is possible that a *hetaira* could have played the part. On the misogyny of this scene, see Klein (2014) 6.

his review of the musical, 'Although the production deals with race and sexual orientation in progressive (if generally safe) ways, it is far less forceful about gender issues, casting the women as naturally moral creatures who are intuitively able to lead the deficient men to the gardens of goodness.'[90]

Ironically, the only character who seems not to need men is the Hetaira. In her sex scene with one of the basketball players, she shows herself to be powerful and in control. She intimidates her clients, and when she orders one to get busy, the audience laughs, partly at his immaturity and inexperience, but also at the Hetaira's plus-sized, African American woman's body. For it was in the moment that she took off her billowing robe to reveal the curves of her body, which a skintight black bodysuit accentuated, that laughter erupted. At a key moment in the musical when a woman acts not simply for the purpose of bettering her male counterparts, the audience, in this performance at least, showed discomfort with her body and its potential for agency.[91]

Thus, my discussion here suggests a paradox. Aristophanes' *Lysistrata* was produced in a society that severely limited women's political and social power, but feminist productions have demonstrated that the ancient text presents an opportunity for staging an empowering portrayal of women or at the very least a damning portrayal of men. Although we know little about the 411 BCE performance of the comedy, the extant text presents a strong woman character. Her means of 'education' (1127) consist of knowing 'a good deal about the religious institutions of the Greek world (1129–32) and about the history of the last hundred years (1137–56)',[92] and she outsmarts the men. She may have no political power, but she still accomplishes her objective. When the men refuse to listen to her and instead can only drool over the 'Women' and sexually violate Peace/Reconciliation,[93] they, not Lysistrata, appear to be the fools, who insist on waging war, as if it were nothing more than another sexual conquest. Nevertheless, to the men in the ancient audience, Lysistrata may not appear to be smart as much as these warring men

---

[90] Given (2012).

[91] On laughter as an expression of social anxiety, see Bergson (1991).

[92] Sommerstein (1990).

[93] As noted at n. 13 above and n. 89 page 117, it is possible that the part was played not by a dressed-up man but by a *hetaira*.

appear to be more foolish than even a woman. In this way, the comedy becomes not a means to praise women but rather, perhaps, to condemn the men who continue to insist on war.

In any case, the contemporary adaptation *Lysistrata Jones* offers no such political commentary or potential for empowering women. Instead, it presents women characters who continue to cheerlead for losing men, rather than pursuing the countless opportunities that their society presents to women. Thus, despite the performance of actors who identify as women on the stage, *Lysistrata Jones* does not seem to serve women any better than its ancient precursor did nearly 2,500 years ago.

Conclusion

Feminist scholars continue to grapple with a paradox, namely that Greek drama depicts so many strong female characters, but the society excluded women from citizenship and political life.[94] Although this historical debate may remain unresolved, it raises important questions. For practitioners and audiences must determine how the role of women in contemporary revisions relates to the dressed-up 'Women' on the ancient stage. To what extent may productions challenge or inadvertently reinforce stereotypes of women that already exist in these ancient plays? In other words, how can women perform roles originally intended for cross-dressed men without reproducing the male-constructed bias inscribed in the ancient characters?

The three productions I have studied in this chapter have addressed this question, posed by Sue-Ellen Case, in distinct ways. Split Britches and the Faux-Real Theatre Company tackled the issue by casting women in the iconic male roles of Admetus and Oedipus. Although breeches roles are nothing new, Shaw's and Regina's performances are not just cross-dressed; their strategy of playing 'man' has allowed them to criticize the ancient culture that subjugated women and excluded them from the stage. These artistic choices have allowed for a sophisticated feminist 'reclaiming'[95] of 'Women', i.e. the male-constructed, male-performed creations of real-life women on the ancient stage. For if, as Bassi has argued, Athenian cross-dressing functioned as 'appropriative mimesis', then Shaw and

---

[94] On this paradox, see Hall (1997) 126.   [95] On reclaiming, see the Introduction.

Regina have used queer and feminist performance strategies to present in its place a subversive form of cross-gendered role play.

In contrast to these off-off-Broadway companies' productions, the Broadway musical *Lysistrata Jones* excludes cross-gendered casting and does little to empower the women actors performing the women roles. While clearly not all productions that cast women in the male-constructed female roles reinforce stereotypes of women as the subordinates of men, this particular work does. Accordingly, because it is the one example of a Broadway show that I have discussed here, *Lysistrata Jones* raises the question of whether the commercialism of Broadway has influenced its representation of women.

Few productions of Greek drama, let alone Greek comedies, make it to Broadway. Some in recent years include the *Gospel at Colonus* (1988),[96] which set *Oedipus at Colonus* in an African American Pentecostal Church, and the Fiona Shaw–Deborah Warner *Medea* (2012), which 'translated the magnitude of Medea's fury, pain and grief into a commentary on contemporary gender relations, on corporate indifference, on the hypocrisy of community, and on the power of acting and design elements in performance itself'.[97] Despite their limited runs, these shows suggest that the commercialized venue of Broadway does not preclude a progressive approach to the classics, even though the confines of off-off-Broadway theatres more readily attract an audience who welcome and encourage innovative dramaturgy and a socially liberal agenda.[98] Instead, the reason behind the distinct approaches between *Lysistrata Jones* and the work of Split Britches and Faux-Real may simply be the distinction between the competing discourses that exist about women in American society today. The stories that best represent women continue to be in competition with those that depict 'Women'.

---

[96] For a recent discussion of this controversial performance, see McConnell (2015).

[97] Dolan (2005) 30.

[98] On this subject, see Brater et al. (2010) 154–5. They explain, for example, that:

> *Shrek the Musical*'s salute to multiculturalism is not without precedent. In fact, there is a long tradition of liberal musicals with antiracist messages, including *Show Boat* (1927), *South Pacific* (1949), and *West Side Story* (1957), even if most of them, like *Shrek*, end up exoticizing and commodifying the subjugated cultures for which they so eagerly advocate. However, politically progressive musicals are relatively scarce, because the genre historically has catered to upper-middle-class audiences that would prefer for politics to be left at the stage door. Even the vast majority of so-called black musicals, from *A Trip to Coontown* (1898) to *The Color Purple* (2005), employ the same conventions as white musicals, while drawing more explicitly and knowledgably on African-American musical forms.

4

'Disidentification' in Allain Rochel's *Bacchae*, Tim O'Leary's *The Wrath of Aphrodite*, and Aaron Mark's *Another Medea*

This chapter builds on Chapter 3 in its discussion of sex and gender. However, my focus here shifts from women to gay men. During the 1960s in New York, a tradition of gay male Greek drag adaptations began with artists such as H. M. Koutoukas, whose 'tragical camp' *Medea of the Laundromat* was performed at New York's Café Cino in 1965, Ethyl Eichelberger, who performed solo works based on iconic women, such as Jocasta, Clytemnestra, and Medea[1], and Charles Ludlam, founder of the Ridiculous Theatrical Company, who wrote a *Medea* that was only performed later, in 1987, by his partner Everett Quinton and long-time friend and collaborator Black-Eyed Susan.[2] Following in this tradition are contemporary artists such as Bradford Louryk, whose *Klytaemnestra's Unmentionables*[3] was originally created in 2000 and revived in 2001 at New York's HERE Arts Center, Harrison David Rivers, whose *And She Would Stand Like This* was

---

[1] For example, as noted in Macintosh et al. (2005), Eichelberger's *Klytemnestra: The Nightingale of Argos* was performed at P.S. 122 in 1987.

[2] On this production, see Foley (2012b) 225.

[3] For further discussion of this production, see Edgecomb (2008) 63–8 and Foley (2004) 93–8.

produced at A.R.T. Theatre in New York (2017), and Aaron Mark, whose work *Another Medea* I discuss later.

In this chapter, however, I want to focus not necessarily on this particular tradition per se but on three productions by playwrights who reimagined ancient tragedies for the LGBTQ community during a period of US history when the struggle for gay rights and gay marriage was reaching a critical juncture. Allain Rochel's *Bacchae* (2007), Tim O'Leary's *The Wrath of Aphrodite* (2008), and Aaron Mark's *Another Medea* (2013) revised Euripides' *Bacchae*,[4] *Hippolytus*,[5] and *Medea*[6] respectively to challenge heteronormative constructions of gender in the years immediately leading up to the historic 2015 US Supreme Court decision *Obergefell v Hodges* that legalized gay marriage. Anticipating and participating in this movement, these productions have voiced the need for legal and social reform in the US by reimagining Euripidean tragedy to challenge the subjugation of the LGBTQ community.

As I will discuss later in detail, these productions all comment on the popular appropriation of 'camp', i.e. an aesthetic characterized by irony, ostentation, and exaggeration, which has traditionally functioned as a gay male performative counter-discourse, but has also been appropriated

---

[4] Euripides' *Bacchae* dramatizes the conflict between the god of wine, masks, and theatre, Dionysus, and the ruler of Thebes, Pentheus. Dionysus, disguised in mortal form as a priest of his cult, arrives in Thebes from the East with a devout band of his sincere female worshippers, maenads or Bacchae. Because the city has denied Dionysus' divinity, he punishes its women with a madness that leads them to a perverse interpretation of his rites on Mt Cithaeron until he can persuade Thebes and especially Pentheus to respect him. Nevertheless, the stubborn young Pentheus refuses to acknowledge the stranger/foreigner who is a god, so Dionysus convinces him to dress up like a maenad to spy on the women. The god then deludes Pentheus' mother, Agave, into believing her son is a lion, and Agave, her sisters, and the rest of the Theban maenads brutally murder him on the mountain, affixing his head to a stake. The play ends with Dionysus' pronouncement of his punishment for Agave and Cadmus.

[5] Euripides' *Hippolytus* dramatizes the tragedy of the title character's stubbornly pious refusal to acknowledge Aphrodite, the goddess of love, because of his devotion to Artemis, the virgin goddess of the hunt. Aphrodite punishes him for his impiety by having his stepmother Phaedra fall desperately in love with him. When Hippolytus refuses her love, she retaliates by committing suicide and leaving a note stating that he tried to rape her. When her husband, Hippolytus' father, Theseus returns home, he exercises a curse given to him by the sea god Poseidon that leads to his son's death. Hippolytus is brought before his father to die. As he lies there in agony, Artemis appears *ex machina* to explain the truth about what happened with Phaedra.

[6] See Chapter 1, n. 18 for a summary of this tragedy.

to propagate a certain mediatized[7] image of gay men. Questioning this appropriation of camp and highlighting the resulting corruption of camp's subversive potential, these works illustrate an example of what the late performance theorist José Esteban Muñoz has defined as 'disidentification', i.e. 'the survival strategies the minority subject practices in order to negotiate a phobic majoritarian public sphere that continuously elides or punishes the existence of subjects who do not conform to the phantasm of normative citizenship'.[8] Disidentification 'negotiates strategies of resistance within the flux of discourse and powers. It understands that counterdiscourses, like discourse, can always fluctuate for different ideological ends and a politicized agent must have the ability to adapt and shift as quickly as power does within discourse.'[9]

Employing disidentificatory performance styles, the works invoke Greek tragedy to fight for the legal protection of the LGBTQ community. Rochel's *Bacchae* uses a hyper-camp performance style as a dramaturgical device to challenge not only stereotypes of gay men but also the appropriation of camp itself. O'Leary's *The Wrath of Aphrodite* also employs camp in its comparison of Aphrodite's wrath against Hippolytus to that inflicted on the LGBTQ community by those who rally against gay marriage. In contrast, Aaron Mark's *Another Medea* is a minimalist one-man show, featuring the Tony award nominee Tom Hewitt, that avoids camp entirely, but here the absence of camp is as much a statement as is its presence in Rochel's and O'Leary's works. Using a stylized naturalism in place of camp, Mark politicizes the performance in a way that camp could not, as the monologue works to legitimate same-sex families by reframing the traditional male-female family unit into a male-male model that conceives through in vitro fertilization. Reframing traditional narratives in such distinct disidentificatory performance styles, Rochel's, O'Leary's, and Mark's works challenge mediatized representations of gay

---

[7] 'Mediatization' is a concept in media studies that argues that the media frames social and political discourse. According to Darren G. Lilleker (2006) 119, the concept of mediatization suggests:

> that what the public see and hear in the media shapes the way that they view the world and themselves and, subsequently, how they act . . . The fear is that media bias becomes the only real knowledge owned by the public sphere, that access to anything else is limited and reliant on the efforts of individuals.

On live performance in a mediatized culture, see Auslander (1999).

[8] Muñoz (1999) 4.   [9] Muñoz (1999) 4.

men, and the stereotype of the 'tragic or suicidal homosexual' in particular. These productions thus serve not simply to queer classical drama, but also to classicize queer performance and legitimate same-sex love.

Ancient Love and Modern Laws

Greek tragedy gives little explicit indication of same-sex love of any kind.[10] However, the genre belongs to a culture that practised and represented it openly. The details of these practices, and the ancient judgements of them, remain a subject of debate between the so-called 'essentialists', or those who believe in a transcultural or universal practice of 'homosexuality', and the 'social constructionists', who argue that same-sex love (and views of it) must be situated within its distinct social and historical context.

The prevailing view is that of the social constructionists, pioneered by Sir Kenneth Dover, David Halperin, and John J. Winkler.[11] These classicists have helped to formulate an understanding of the Athenian practice of pederasty, or man–boy love, as an active/passive polarity in which 'phallic penetration was an index of sociopolitical empowerment . . . [with] boys, as passive "victims" of penetration . . . parallel to women, slaves, and foreigners as instrumental foils to the adult citizen males who wielded the political franchise and thereby the right to phallic supremacy'.[12] Their scholarship has influenced recent studies that both build upon and depart from such views.[13]

In contrast, for example, Thomas Hubbard has argued that 'one finds little support for this interpretation in the textual evidence, and even the iconographic tradition points toward a different conclusion'.[14] He suggests

---

[10] As with the relationship between Achilles and Patroclus in Homer's *Iliad*, speculation also exists over possible references to same-sex love in Athenian tragedy, such as between Pentheus and Dionysus in Euripides' *Bacchae*, Orestes and Pylades in Euripides' *Iphigenia in Tauris* and *Orestes*, and Neoptolemus and Philoctetes in Sophocles' *Philoctetes*. However, while later works have interpreted these relationships as homoerotic, there is no clear evidence that any such relationship was implied or interpreted by the ancient Athenian audience. Thus, arguments for the presence of homoeroticism in Athenian tragedy rest more in the realm of possibility than probability.

[11] Dover (1978); Halperin (1989); Winkler (1990).

[12] Hubbard (2003) 10.

[13] See, e.g. Masterson, Rabinowitz, and Robson (2015); Blondell and Ormand (2015); and Hubbard (2014).

[14] Hubbard (2003) 10.

instead that 'The widespread notion that a "general acceptance" of homosexuality prevailed is an oversimplification of a complex *mélange* of viewpoints about a range of different practices, as is the dogma that a detailed regimen of protocols and conventions distinguished "acceptable" from "unacceptable" homosexual behaviors.'[15] Translating the critical sources on the topic, he aims to show that 'There was, in fact, no more consensus about homosexuality in ancient Greece and Rome than there is today.'[16]

This point has been reiterated by the controversial study of James Davidson, who has questioned traditional approaches influenced by Foucault and the classical scholar Sir Kenneth Dover.[17] He argues that 'modern work on ancient Greek culture is remarkably obsessed with the ins and outs of homosexual sex acts performed two and a half thousand years ago'.[18] Taking issue in part with Davidson's methodology, Nancy Worman has argued in contrast that the 'literary depictions of classical Greek sexual practices' are in fact 'largely metaphorical'.[19] Carol Atack has described these contrasting methodologies as follows:

Where Dover and Winkler sought to extrapolate actual behaviour from these terms, and Davidson sought to desexualise them, Worman in revising her own earlier views on abusive language offers a criticism of attempts to recover ancient sexual behaviour from rhetorical texts. She develops a persuasive account of the use of sexual language in the assessment of political behaviour among Athenian citizens, providing a route out of now stagnant debates.[20]

The 'stagnant debates' to which Atack refers are ones that David Halperin[21] has attributed to disputes between 'humanism and the new historicism, perhaps explaining why the anti-theoretical Davidson has emerged as the whipping boy for the various post-Foucauldian classicists' of *Ancient Sex: New Essays*.[22]

Whatever the subtleties and nuances of these historical sexual practices may have been, the view of them in popular US culture is what is most significant for this chapter. Because of its pre-Christian view on same-sex love, the Graeco-Roman world has been celebrated and invoked by the LGBTQ community. Several court cases in recent years

---

[15] Hubbard (2003) 7–8.   [16] Hubbard (2003) 8.
[17] Dover (1978); Foucault (1986).   [18] Davidson (2007) 119.
[19] Worman (2015) 39.   [20] Atack (2016).   [21] Halperin (2015).
[22] Atack (2016).

have even referenced Athenian sexuality in their proceedings. *Lawrence v Texas*, decided by the US Supreme Court in 2003; *Romer v Evans*, a 1996 decision; and *Bowers v Hardwick*, a 1986 decision, all included testimony on same-sex relations in antiquity.[23]

The testimony offered in these cases was complicated. Sophisticated classical texts became subject to legal arguments that inevitably strait-jacketed their nuanced discussions.[24] On the one hand, critic and classicist Daniel Mendelsohn has criticized these proceedings, stating that 'there might be a fundamental incompatibility between "the narrow requirements of legal discourse as it actually proceeds" and "the expansive nature of serious humanistic inquiry"'.[25] On the other hand, Brooke Holmes has commented that Mendelsohn may be too pessimistic. For it is important to recognize 'the salutary impact of the Foucauldian line of argument that homosexuality is a category of recent vintage in *Lawrence v. Texas*', even if 'it is undeniable that the complexities of what Plato thought about same-sex desire and behaviours, to say nothing of his views on sex, desire and the body more generally, got lost in the pressure to commit to the record what the ancients thought once and for all about homosexual sex'.[26] However, while Holmes' point is cogent, the simplification of the historical record has not, in all cases, been advantageous.

For example, while *Obergefell v Hodges* declared gay marriage legal, the case presented another example of a simplified view of classical thought. The conservative justices tried to argue that antiquity did not conceive of, let alone approve of, same-sex marriages, even though they accepted same-sex couples. They thus claimed that the definition of marriage has always referenced heterosexual unions, even in cultures where discrimination was not present:

Plato 'wrote approvingly of same-sex relationships, did he not?' Justice Samuel Alito said, musing on the ancient Greeks. 'So their limiting marriage to couples of the opposite sex was not based on prejudice against gay people, was it?' ('I can't speak to what was happening with the ancient philosophers,' Bonauto [the attorney representing the same-sex couples] replied.)[27]

---

[23] Holmes (2012) 105–10.

[24] As discussed in Chapter 3, the categories of homo- and heterosexual are a modern invention and do not appropriately reflect the spectrum of gender that governed relations in antiquity.

[25] Holmes (2012) 109. Mendelsohn (1996), quoted in Holmes.

[26] Holmes (2012) 109.   [27] Justice Alito, quoted in Davidson (2015).

In addition, 'Justice Antonin Scalia insisted that "for millennia, not a single society" supported marriage equality.'[28]

From a classicist's perspective, the use of antiquity in these legal cases makes little sense, for, as David M. Perry argues, 'given that most Americans would find abhorrent the types of marriages of which ancient Athens approved [let alone their phallocentric culture's practice of slavery], why should they care whether they would have disapproved of gay marriage?'[29] However, historical methodology and philosophical inquiry do not seem to be the point. Instead, the conservative justices employ a simplified interpretation of the classical sources to support a predetermined argument. Against such views, the artists discussed in this chapter have aimed to work.

Allain Rochel's *Bacchae*

From the naked hippie romps of Richard Schechner's *Dionysus in 69* to Alan Cumming's gold lamé kilt,[30] Euripides' *Bacchae* has inspired some of the sexiest reperformances of ancient tragedy ever. Although the ancient text suggests the chorus was *sōphrōn*, or balanced, and devoted,[31] modern productions can rarely resist exploiting the alluring appeal of the maenads' passionate cries, leaping limbs, and throats thrust back in ecstasy. The production I discuss here is no exception to this sexy trend. However, unlike most contemporary versions of the *Bacchae*, the Los Angeles-based writer and performer Allain Rochel's 2007 critically acclaimed, award-winning production has staged a chorus of beautiful, youthful, leather-clad, bare-chested men. Instead of simply flirting with the arguably homoerotic undertones of the Dressing-up scene,[32] typical of some stagings such as Joanne Akalaitis' 2009 production at New York's Public Theater, the all-male cast reorientates the play entirely, and even substitutes all of the play's female pronouns with male ones. Thus, while Greek tragedy typically uses 'Woman'[33] in its exploration of male

---

[28] Justice Scalia, quoted in Millhiser (2015).   [29] Perry (2015).

[30] In the National Theatre of Scotland's (2008) production.

[31] See Powers (2014) for further discussion.

[32] On the possible homoerotic connotations of this scene, see Ormand (2003) and Poole (1990).

[33] See Chapter 3 for a discussion of this concept of 'Woman' as the male-construction of real-life women.

subjectivity, Rochel completely writes the women out in order to criticize the gay male community's complicity in propagating mediatized versions of gay men that contribute to the social marginalization of the gay community as a whole.

First performed at the Celebration Theatre in the predominately gay neighbourhood of West Hollywood in Los Angeles, Rochel's *Bacchae*, directed by Michael Matthews, takes place within the larger sociopolitical context of the struggle for gay rights in the US. In the programme notes, Rochel clearly articulates his purpose. He wants to address the politics involved in the debate over gay marriage in the 2004 presidential election by using 'the mythology of the *Bacchae* to represent this marginalization of the gay community as stemming from a societal and governmental denial of the homosexual as a whole person'. In so doing, the production raised questions such as 'What does it mean to be gay outside of a sexual context, in what ways do mediatized versions of gay lives encourage assimilation to them, and what if a gay man does not conform to such images?'[34]

These social and political concerns reflect those of the theatre that staged the play. The Celebration Theatre, located on Santa Monica Boulevard in West Hollywood, better known as WeHo, is an intimate, approximately seventy-seat 'black box theater' that is 'dedicated to presenting innovative, provocative and relevant work that examines the gay, lesbian, bisexual and transgender queer experience. [Such works] endeavor to challenge society's perception of this community and give a vibrant voice to its evolving identity.'[35] Founded in 1982 by the gay-rights pioneer Chuck Rowland, the theatre has typically attracted an audience of gay men in their fifties and sixties from the Silverlake neighbourhood of Los Angeles. However, at the time of this 2007 production, the *Bacchae* attracted a younger crowd of men, and even a few women (like me). Whether this change in demographics was due to the choice of play, the critically acclaimed artistic director Michael Matthews, who joined the theatre in 2005, or the attractive young men in the chorus is uncertain.

However, one thing is certain: the chorus is clearly attractive. The five young multiracial men were described by one reviewer as 'five of the

[34] Programme for Allain Rochel's *Bacchae* at the Celebration Theatre, Los Angeles, 2007.
[35] http://www.celebrationtheatre.com/about.html, accessed 4 November 2009.

Figure 4.1 The set of Allain Rochel's *Bacchae*, directed by Michael Matthews. 2007.

Photo © 2007 Kurtis Boetcher.

hottest young male actors you'll see slithering, writhing, slinking, jumping and dancing in any theater in town'.[36] Yet, as exciting as this comment may be, the image of these gorgeous actors is exactly what Rochel seeks to deconstruct: 'We [i.e. the gay community] must be wary to prevent the images we are inundated with on the covers of "gay" publications and advertisements on Sunset Boulevard from becoming a model that demands assimilations.'[37] Rochel's *Bacchae* aims to deconstruct the billboard image of the hot and sexy gay male in an effort to combat the stereotype that simultaneously evokes desire and fear.[38]

The production does so by employing a performance style that works to comment on the media's appropriation of camp itself. For example, the chorus opens the play by dancing to the tunes of techno music on the club-like set (Figure 4.1) with its spray-painted graffiti that references

---

[36] Stanley (2007).

[37] Programme for Allain Rochel's *Bacchae* at the Celebration Theatre, Los Angeles, 2007.

[38] A 2018 calendar of 'ordinary' gay men published by the London-based *meat magazine* made headlines in the mainstream media for its aim of going against 'the prevailing image of gay men as young, with perfect, porn-ready bodies' (Wong 2017).

the back room of a gay sex club, not unlike the one located directly across the street from the theatre. This context marks a place where dirty things can happen, as suggested by the giant spray-painted image of a penis with the word 'here' written underneath. This graffiti serves as a metaphor for the Dionysian vines that have overrun the city. The young revellers embrace this setting as they continue to dance about with a luxurious large velvet cloth from which a muscular, bare-chested African American Dionysus (Michael A. Shepperd) arises amid the shirtless revellers, who, in a wonderful feat of staging, wrap the shimmering fabric around their libidinous god's waist. Kneeling on a newspaper-littered stage, the Bacchae then direct their painted faces, which look like a cross between a Chinese opera mask and the glam band Kiss, at the crotch of their beloved leader. The tableau highlights Dionysus' power and magnitude, as the god delivers his prologue. In contrast to these boyish, club kid beauties, Dionysus' powerful presence exudes a calm and controlled sensibility. His bald head, goatee, tall frame, and strong, muscular, masculine physicality contrast with his effeminate affectation as he delivers his monologue, while each of his five glamorous devotees extends the fabric away from their proud god and becomes like a point on a black velveteen star, extending Dionysian energy into every point. As a unit, god and followers represent a hyper-sexualized camp cult of desire that becomes almost a caricature of the image of the gorgeous gay male.

In sum, Matthews' staging of the chorus and the principal characters' relationship to it provides a critical framework for his political statement. He does not, as the Euripidean text suggests and as some directors, such as Bill T. Jones,[39] have done, visually depict the distinction between the Theban maenads on the mountain, whom Dionysus has struck mad for failing to recognize him, and the chorus, who are the true Asian worshippers of the god.[40] Rather, the production conflates the Theban maenads with the chorus and portrays the single group as mad, not from their failure to recognize Dionysus, but rather from their society's inability to recognize their sexuality.

As in the Euripides, the city's rejection of the chorus and their god leads to a madness that infects it, so to protect themselves, the two old

---

[39] Bill T. Jones directed a workshop of the play in 2001 at University of California, Davis. See Powers (2009).

[40] On the distinction between the two choruses, see Powers (2014).

men, Cadmus and Teiresias, dress up and dance for Dionysus,[41] despite their ageing limbs. Nevertheless, the rest of the city does not follow them, and the fear projected onto the chorus by the city in turn influences the behaviour of the ostracized chorus and causes them to reject those such as Cadmus, played by Daryl Keith Roach, who have difficulty emulating a hyper-sexualized image. Regarding Cadmus, Rochel has explained that he imagined the character as an older gay man, outside of the social hierarchy who can still go out and have fun with Teiresias. The two are completely open and free in their personal space but do not have a relationship.[42] The reviewer Travis Michael Holder has described, 'The campy Bobby Reed, resembling a fugitive from an old Andy Warhol movie as an aging bare beer-bellied, leather-garbed Tireseas [sic], and Daryl Keith Roach as the eventually hoodwinked Cadmus', as being 'wonderful in scenes together that could be playing out at the French Quarter Marketplace [a popular New Orleans-style restaurant in West Hollywood]'.[43] The duo's raised intonation and elongated vowels mark their speech, as the two jolly old friends frolic about slapstick-style before ending their scene in a tango. Echoing the comic elements of the duo in the Euripides,[44] the actors' antiquated dance and goofy antics show Cadmus especially to be an older gay man of an earlier generation with little hope of conforming to the young hyper-sexed image of the club kids.

The production thus presents an irony. Heterosexist society marginalizes the gay community. However, the community itself can further

---

[41] On the comic elements in this scene in the Euripides, Seidensticker (1978) has argued: 'While it is impossible to prove that this is how Euripides intended the scene to be staged [i.e. with comic overtones], the other evidence under discussion supports the hypothesis that a comic effect is indeed what the dramatist had in mind' (313). On comedy in the *Bacchae*, see also Foley (1985) 217–19, 225–34, 237, 244–5, 250–1, and 257.

[42] Rochel (2007). My grateful thanks to Allain Rochel for kindly granting me an interview.

[43] Holder (2007). However, just as Holder appreciated this scene and understood Rochel's approach, another reviewer, Les Spindle (2007), criticized the scene: 'The production raises more questions than it answers: such as how does a screaming-queen stereotypical character ultimately support Rochel's stated aspirations of delivering a pro-gay message?' While, to my mind, Spindle has misunderstood the ways in which Rochel plays up the stereotype to debunk it, these varying viewpoints nevertheless demonstrate the competing discourses over representation within the community itself, the very discourses which the production examines and questions. The review thus serves as another example of the slippery nature of using stereotypes to critique them.

[44] See n. 41 above on the comedy of this scene in the Euripides.

marginalize those within it by inadvertently assimilating to and propagating an idealized image of a youthful, hyper-sexed, well-dressed, fashion-savvy buff gay man to which few can conform.

Like the elderly Cadmus, the mid-West frat boy Republican closeted Pentheus, played by Bob Simpson, also cannot identify with or assimilate to the chorus' sexualized image. He represses his sexuality and love for Quintus (played by Michael Tauzin), an invented character who, as Pentheus' slave, delivers both messenger speeches. However, this repressed desire metaphorically erupts in the Earthquake scene.[45] In the Seduction scene that soon follows, Dionysus kisses Pentheus, who temporarily slips out of his usual aggressive stance. Then, as if feeling ashamed of his actions, Pentheus becomes angry and pushes Dionysus onto the ground, stepping on the god's crotch.

This power struggle reverses, however, in the Dressing-up scene, where Dionysus convinces Pentheus to dress up as a maenad. They kiss several times, and the chorus arrives with Pentheus' new wardrobe. Emphasizing the ritualistic as opposed to comic elements of the Euripidean version,[46] Rochel has Dionysus stand behind his young cousin, strip him, put on his trousers, a black sash-like girdle, and an evergreen crown that foreshadows the tree on which Pentheus will soon meet his doom. Once Pentheus is appropriately dressed, everyone begins to celebrate in an extended camp dance number. They make provocative eye contact with the audience, as the characters kiss and gyrate their hips to the camp pop beats of 'Paul McCartney' by the Scissor Sisters. Swept up in the moment, Cadmus kisses Dionysus, a moment punctuated by the choreography of the chorus, each one of whom in turn does snap-turn rotations as they turn to look at Cadmus, as if catching their dad in his first male kiss. In the midst of this drunken, amazing bacchanal, the crowned, now shirtless Pentheus finally kisses his inamorato Quintus, who is dressed in an all-white outfit evoking the attire of the well-known LGBTQ community's nationwide White Parties. After drawing the whole room into their rhythm, the dancing abruptly stops as the scene ominously closes before

[45] According to Rochel (2007), the scene was staged by dimming the lights and raining pieces of confetti made from the gay sex ads at the back of the *L.A. Weekly* down onto Pentheus, who lies on the floor in the middle of the scene.

[46] See n. 41 above on the comic elements in the Cadmus and Teiresias and Dressing-up scenes. On ritual in this scene, see Dodds (1960) 194 nn. 935–6 and Seaford (1997) 224–5 nn. 935–8.

the murder of Pentheus, not by his mother Agave, as in the Euripides, but by his grandfather Cadmus.

Covered with blood and holding Pentheus' severed head, the grieving Cadmus physically manifests the violence to the self that erupts from a subject's inability to identify with and conform to a group, whether that group consists of Dionysus and his devotees, the culture at large, or a youthful camp gay subculture. Although Pentheus does finally embrace the Dionysiac revelry, his death symbolizes his inability to complete his rite of passage[47] and to realize fully his identity, because he does not discover his own personal sense of sexuality. Instead, he tries to conform to the image of it projected by the group and thus loses or destroys a part of himself in the process. He becomes limited instead of fulfilled by his sexuality, because, while conforming to the camp chorus allows him to express his sexuality, he does so at the expense of being true to his own personal expression of himself. In this way, the production commented on the sinister effects of a mediatized version of camp that has infected the gay community itself.

This critique of camp functions in terms of what Muñoz has called 'disidentification', for Rochel's *Bacchae* dramatizes the ways in which camp, which started as a disidentificatory practice to challenge hetero-normative culture, can be appropriated to marginalize the very culture it sought to empower. By identifying this appropriation of camp, Rochel 'understands that counterdiscourses, like discourse, can always fluctuate for different ideological ends', and he acts as 'a politicized agent ... [with the] ability to adapt and shift as quickly as power does within discourse'.[48] He makes camp subversive again, while in the process showing the ways in which the gay community can be complicit in allowing popular culture to appropriate camp's potential as a disidentificatory practice.

Like Marga Gomez's *The Life*, Rochel's *Bacchae* aims to help:

us imagine an expansive queer *life*-world, one in which the 'pain and hardship' of queer existence within a homophobic public sphere are not elided, one in which the 'mysteries' of our sexuality are not reigned [*sic*] in by sanitized understand-ings of lesbian and gay identity, and finally, one in which we are all allowed to be drama queens and smoke as much as our hearts desire.[49]

For under Matthews' direction, Rochel's *Bacchae* disidentifies with the cliché image of the fabulous, typically white, gay male character who, as

---

[47] On Pentheus' failed rites of passage, see Foley (1985).
[48] Muñoz (1999) 19.   [49] Muñoz (1999) 34.

Cristy Turner describes in her review of *Sex and The City*, is useful only for his 'color swatches, fashion tips, and cheeky one-liners, as audiences are encouraged to ignore the sexual and gender politics deeply embedded in these social relations'.[50] While gay characters in such shows typically 'exist as accessories for increasing the cultural capital and "cool" of the female characters',[51] Rochel takes back this cliché by hyperbolizing that very camp stereotype which limits the recognition of a gay man as a whole person.

Thus, the hyper-camp performance style of the production simultaneously illustrates homophobia while criticizing it. Fear of the Dionysiac functions as a metaphor for homophobia and the fear that gay rights proponents will infect the cities with social ills such as AIDS and paedophilia. This fear, which drives the chorus into its frenzy, is one that the production (and production notes) present as not only damaging to individuals but also capable of influencing elections, such as that in 2004 between George W. Bush and John Kerry.

In this way, the play connects with politics, just as perhaps did the Euripides, for critics such as Foley have suggested that the Euripidean chorus of Asian maenads 'press the audience to make complex connections and comparisons between the ritualized spectacle of Pentheus' failure to accept the god and the festivities and excesses of contemporary Attic democracy'.[52] If Foley is correct, then the ancient *Bacchae* provoked discussion not solely on the merits of a democracy, as Paul Woodruff has suggested,[53] but also on its inherent dangers. Rochel then transforms such political interpretations of the Euripides into a sociopolitical commentary that revives camp to explore the extent to which the performance technique can successfully function, like the theatre god himself, as a subversive tool to challenge traditional notions of sexual identity.

---

[50] Turner (2004).   [51] Turner (2004).

[52] Foley (1985) 239. She further argues that 'Dionysiac rite and myth can complement the political aims of a democracy and guard against the institution of tyranny' (240). She also states that 'in a city under pressure, pushed to excess, he [Dionysus] appears behind the corrosive pressure of the democratic majority for revenge and for the destruction of outstanding men' (240).

[53] Woodruff (1998), xx. Woodruff has suggested that the chorus objects to Pentheus' autocratic rule and champions the *demos*. He states that 'in writing as if lawful democracy is a real possibility, Euripides is squaring off against those enemies of democracy who slander it as a lawless tyranny by the lower classes over everyone else'.

Tim O'Leary's *The Wrath of Aphrodite*

Directed by Martin Casella, Tim O'Leary's *The Wrath of Aphrodite* was performed in 2008 at a small, approximately fifty-seat, 'black box theater' at GAYFEST NYC, a New York City theatre festival that began in 2007, featuring new work by the LGBTQ community and other minority communities for world stages and film and television production.[54] With a simple set consisting of a brick wall backdrop, framed by a large plant and two Greek statues resting on three-foot columns, *Wrath* departs from its precursor by introducing two gay relationships: Hippolytus and Adonis', and Atalanta (an invented character, who is one of Hippolytus' hunting companions) and Ione's (another invented character, who serves as Phaedra's maid). In both of these cases, the chaste worship of the virgin goddess Artemis that characterizes the ancient Hippolytus and his companions becomes in the modern version a way to ignore and conceal their sexuality. Thus, the Artemis/chastity versus Aphrodite/sexuality struggle of the ancient play becomes a means to explore issues relevant to the LGBTQ community.

For example, Euripides' play on the word *semnos* (pious/proud),[55] which characterizes Hippolytus' devotion to Artemis but also marks him as hubristic in his disrespect of the goddess of desire Aphrodite, becomes a means to explore the risk of suppressing one's passion at the expense of the self-harm that can result from doing so. The theme of *aidōs* (shame/respect), which characterizes the sense of social shame that pressures Phaedra to take her life and accuse Hippolytus of rape rather than suffer disgrace, becomes a means to explore the social pressure and rejection inflicted upon individuals because of their sexual orientation. Like its precursor, *Wrath*'s central narrative focuses on Hippolytus' struggle to

---

[54] http://www.gayfestnyc.com/currentprojects.html, accessed 3 March 2016. As stated in the programme notes, the not-for-profit GAYFEST NYC features:

> Actors' Equity Association casts and a Broadway-calibre creative staff... The mission is to develop new voices for the LGBT community by expanding the reach and accessibility of both emerging and established playwrights. Profits of GAYFEST NYC's fundraising efforts are used to provide scholarships and after school programs for students of Harvey Milk High School in New York City, a public high school focusing on the educational needs of children who are in crisis or at risk of physical violence and/or emotional harm.

[55] On this theme and the theme of *sōphrosynē* in *Hippolytus*, see Halleran (1995) 43–9.

negotiate the two opposing goddesses and in the process maintain *sōphrosynē* (balance/moderation/safe-mindedness),[56] but the conflict between Aphrodite and Artemis in *Hippolytus* is reimagined as one between an LGBTQ identity and the sexual restrictions of one's religion. Fear of social rejection, unrequited love, and religion are all addressed to explore the struggle of negotiating one's religious identity with one's sexual orientation.

To do so, O'Leary, a Los Angeles-based screenwriter, author, and ghostwriter, follows the Euripidean plot in many respects, but one key distinction is in his characterization of Hippolytus. He makes Hippolytus, played by Ryan Serhant (now well known from the popular Reality TV Show *Million Dollar Listing*), 'more likeable',[57] meaning less misogynistic. Like the Euripidean character, he is a handsome prince devoted to the virgin goddess of the hunt, Artemis, but he befriends and hunts with a pack of friends, including a woman Atalanta. Wearing short, revealing white tunics, which are Roman, not Greek, and peppering their speech with anachronisms such as 'Fuck, yeah',[58] Hippolytus, Atalanta, Meleager, Perseus, and Adonis pledge celibacy and enjoy their pious lifestyle of praying and hunting.

However, their idyllic world soon comes under attack, when in a camp moment that betrays the impending doom, 'celestial music fills the air'[59] and two sparkling golden-robed goddesses appear. Whereas Artemis (played by Caroline Strong) believes the men are pure and happy in their chastity, or in this case suppression of their sexuality, the meddling Aphrodite (Tamara Hickey) cannot accept that Hippolytus and Adonis (Will Poston) clearly love each other but will not 'abandon their devotion to virginity and begin their devotion to each other's manly parts' (Figure 4.2).[60] With a camp style of humour that punctuates the first act, Artemis declares, 'Perhaps they have no love for other men,' to which Aphrodite responds, 'This is Greece. Believe me, they have love for other men.'[61]

---

[56] In the Greek world, worshipping and respecting all the gods was a crucial requirement for *sōphrosynē*. On *sōphrosynē*, see North (1966) and Rademaker (2005).

[57] O'Leary (2016). My grateful thanks to Tim O'Leary for his generosity in granting me an interview.

[58] O'Leary (2008) 2. My grateful thanks also to Tim O'Leary for allowing me to quote from his unpublished play.

[59] O'Leary (2008) 4.   [60] O'Leary (2008) 7.   [61] O'Leary (2008) 4–5.

Figure 4.2 Hippolytus and Adonis in Tim O'Leary's *The Wrath of Aphrodite*, directed by Martin Casella. 2008.

Photo © 2008 Carlos Gustavo Monroy.

The scene ends with Aphrodite's placing a bet with Artemis that if she were to give Adonis the courage to declare his love, Hippolytus would reciprocate and break his vow.

Despite the shared attraction, the prince initially rejects his inamorato and in the process curses Aphrodite, calling her the 'whore of

Olympus'.[62] To punish this hubris, the goddess has his stepmother Phaedra fall passionately in love with him. Although Michael Halleran in his commentary on *Hippolytus* has explained that the 'metaphor of mortals as "puppets" of the gods is misleading for this play',[63] O'Leary explores this point for comic purposes by having Aphrodite grab Phaedra and 'use her as a puppet' so that every time Aphrodite touches Phaedra she shrieks in a hilariously comic style of possession:

> PHAEDRA: . . . Yes, it feels like madness . . . You must not tell him
>   [Hippolytus] of this. Please, none but the three of us must know
>   I am so unwell. You will not speak a word!
> ATALANTA: Of course not, my queen.
> (*Aphrodite touches her.*)
> APHRODITE/PHAEDRA: Or I will have your head!
> ATALANTA: I will say nothing, I swear!
> (*Aphrodite releases her.*)[64]

Hickey's camp performance of the goddess, reminiscent of Agnes Moorehead's 'lesbian camp icon'[65] Endora[66] in the hit 1960s TV show *Bewitched*, adds levity to this first act.[67] The 'faux-luxe' costumes, exaggerated performances, and thigh-grazing togas focus the audience's attention on the sensuality and materiality that characterize camp. For the sparkly, supernatural goddess costumes, together with the buff, bare bodies, create an aesthetic that seduces the audience into a joyful, eye-candy-full fantasy, complete with the *Dynasty*-style[68] camp of the bickering goddesses and an Endora-esque, sometimes visible, sometimes invisible glitzy Aphrodite.

The camp production style thus illustrates the joys of life. However, it also represents the pain of those within the LGBTQ community whose

---

[62] O'Leary (2008) 27.   [63] Halleran (1995) 41 n. 26.   [64] O'Leary (2008) 34–5.

[65] Flynn (1999) 453. Flynn describes Endora as a 'side-kick character associated with playing older (that is, older than the star) sisters, aunts, various "spinsters", mothers, and mother-in-laws [*sic*], who invariably are the smartest, and most smart-assed, women around'.

[66] Endora is the witch mother of the character Samantha Stephens on the popular 1964–72 American TV show *Bewitched*, which has been noted for its queer subtext.

[67] O'Leary (2016).

[68] A famous 1980s American prime-time soap opera starring Joan Collins and Linda Evans.

inner reality is not in sync with the youthful, happy, sexy veneer of the mediatized image of gay men. For the party almost immediately stops in Act 2, when the joyful bliss of Adonis' requited love turns into a tragic unfolding of events that begins when Hippolytus rejects Phaedra, and, as in the Euripides, she commits suicide and leaves a note stating her stepson's attempted rape is the cause. When his father Theseus returns to Troezen and hears the news, he banishes all of Hippolytus' friends except Adonis, whose love Hippolytus has finally returned. Thinking that breaking his son's heart was not enough punishment, Theseus then prays to Poseidon to put a curse on Hippolytus, who is soon killed by a wave that pulls him down off a precipice. When the dying Hippolytus is brought to his father, Artemis appears and reveals the truth of her devotee's innocence. Then, to avenge Aphrodite's vindictive scheming against Hippolytus and Phaedra, who had done nothing to deserve the goddess' wrath, Artemis asks Aphrodite's beloved Adonis to join Hippolytus in the Elysian Fields for eternity—an offer which Adonis accepts. The play ends with the tragic death of the lovers but with the comfort of knowing the two will be forever joined in love (Figure 4.3).

In this way, the production depicts Hippolytus' devotion to the virgin goddess Artemis as part of an identity that he cannot at first reconcile with his passion for Adonis, even though nothing prevents the prince from exploring his sexuality but himself. For, while the other characters, such as Phaedra and Theseus, criticize his vow of chastity, they do not criticize same-sex love. For example, Phaedra suggests he might enjoy trying not being chaste,[69] and Theseus states:

THESEUS: Sex is a wonderful part of life, son... Surely at your age you must be feeling desire... that Adonis boy has a handsome shape to him. And you've been close most of your lives. The two of you never...?

HIPPOLYTUS: Adonis? No!

THESEUS: Well, what about one of your other friends? Those boys you're always with. Or one of the palace girls? Any one of them would give their right hand to lie with you.[70]

---

[69] O'Leary (2008) 31.   [70] O'Leary (2008) 14–15.

Figure 4.3 Adonis holding the deceased Hippolytus with Aphrodite (left), Artemis (right), and Theseus (background) in Tim O'Leary's *The Wrath of Aphrodite*, directed by Martin Casella. 2008.

Photo © 2008 Carlos Gustavo Monroy.

Despite this encouragement from his parents, Hippolytus still struggles with accepting his feelings of desire until Adonis shows him the error in his reasoning:

Artemis is a virgin, yes, but Hippolytus, she is also a god! We're mortals, and we're built to need one another. I believe in Artemis as much as you, but I believe she means us to follow the spirit of her path, not mimic it exactly. The lesson of her virginity isn't meant to be taken literally; it's a metaphor for living a pure and wholesome life.[71]

While this argument, which echoes those over the literal interpretation of the Bible, convinces Hippolytus to abandon his vow, Aphrodite would not let him go unpunished for cursing her. Thus, Hippolytus' initial disrespecting of Aphrodite ultimately results in tragedy.

With these revisions of the Euripidean plot structure, *The Wrath of Aphrodite* uses ancient Greek culture to examine the modern struggle between an LGBTQ identity and a Judaeo-Christian religious one. In fact, O'Leary's inspiration for the revision was not only having performed in the play in college but also the struggle he witnessed in gay men attempting to reconcile their sexuality with their religious views. For example, in his interview with me, he referenced the stories of Catholic friends who felt they were not accepted by the Church but would 'swallow it and still attend', and two Mormon men whose journey to accepting their identity was 'tumultuous and violent, not because of other people's cruelty to them but because of how cruel they were to themselves'.[72] Likewise, *Wrath*'s Hippolytus could have loved men or women without his parents' or friends' disapproval, but instead he denies himself love of his own volition, which in the ancient context of the play was unthinkable. Accordingly, the wrath of Aphrodite, which at first results from Hippolytus' refusal to embrace his sexuality, functions as a metaphor for the violence inflicted on the self that is caused by the social and political institutionalization of a Judaeo-Christian taboo against same-sex love. For this reason, Hippolytus suffers Aphrodite's wrath even after he has consummated his love with Adonis. Thus, the work explores the tension between religion and sexuality as a personal struggle, but, in the process, the play also highlights the role that religion has

---

[71] O'Leary (2008) 43.   [72] O'Leary (2016).

played in preventing the LGBTQ community from enjoying the legal rights and protection of marriage.

Aaron Mark's *Another Medea*

In contrast to Rochel's *Bacchae* and O'Leary's *The Wrath of Aphrodite*, Aaron Mark's *Another Medea* avoids camp entirely. The work is a minimalist, one-man, ninety-minute show, written and directed by the New York City-based writer/director and performed by the Tony award nominee Tom Hewitt (*Jesus Christ Superstar*, *The Rocky Horror Show*, *Dracula*). Mark frames the iconic power struggle between Jason and Medea as one between the genders, not the sexes. For in place of the ancient marginalized foreign woman with no family, no home, no rights, and no protection, Mark presents Marcus, a gay man, an actor with no money and no family, except for his estranged homophobic mother. In so doing, he translates the marginalized 'otherness' of Medea into a modern context by creating a character who cannot appeal to the state for help. His Medea is a gay man who, having conceived with his partner's sister through in vitro fertilization (IVF), could be characterized as a sperm donor, with no legal claim over his children.

Medea's 'divided self'[73] (masculine/heroic versus feminine/maternal), which strives for masculine heroic glory (*kleos*)[74] despite her love for her children, is thus reimagined as Marcus' struggle between his need for money, power, respect, and legal protection and his love for the theatre, Jason, and their children.

First performed in 2013 at the Duplex Cabaret, a few doors down from the Stonewall Inn site of the '69 uprising, the show was later produced by All For One Theater in its subsequent runs at New York's Cherry Lane Studio Theatre in 2013 and the Wild Project in 2015.[75] As a self-described student of the work of Charles Ludlam, Mark adapted *Medea* after he read Ludlam's version of it.[76] Also inspired by Koutoukas' and Eichelberger's Greek works, Mark's play continues in this tradition, but his version is quite distinct. In his research, he discovered that although there is a rich history of men cross-dressing as Medea, he could not find a single instance of a script

---

[73] Foley (1989).   [74] Foley (1989).

[75] I attended the production at the Cherry Lane Theatre on 30 October 2013.

[76] Ludlam never performed the part but his partner Everett Quinton and long-time friend and collaborator Black-Eyed Susan did.

Figure 4.4 The anonymous Actor playing Marcus in Aaron Mark's *Another Medea*, directed by Aaron Mark, starring Tom Hewitt. 2013.
Photo © Aaron Mark 2013.

that adapted the iconic figure into a male character; this discovery became the starting point for his adaptation.[77]

Described by Mark as 'Grand Guignol horror in the style of Spalding Gray',[78] the metatheatrical work, which references experiences and locations with which New York actors would be familiar, begins when Hewitt puts on the character of an anonymous Actor, who then puts on the character of Marcus Sharp, the Medea figure (Figure 4.4). This anonymous Actor is fascinated with the news reports about Marcus because he once replaced him in a play. He has visited Marcus in jail to learn about, and now recount to the audience,[79] the chilling tale of the actor's fairy-tale romance that ultimately led to the murders of his partner Jason

---

[77] Mark (2016). My grateful thanks to Aaron Mark for all of his time and generosity in granting me an interview.

[78] Faquet (2013).

[79] Mark (2016) has described his audience as comprised primarily of 'theatre-goers', people who really understood the context of the piece and were interested in *Medea* or Tom Hewitt. At the performance I attended, the audience demographic appeared to be primarily Euro-Americans in their twenties to sixties.

Russell, their two children, and his partner's paramour, the 25-year-old Paris List.

The anonymous Actor recalls that Marcus had given up acting to become a stay-at-home dad, only to become depressed as his relationship with Jason, a wealthy British oncologist, deteriorated. When Jason declares that he is leaving to go to London with his new love Paris and that he is taking the twins, and his sister, their mother, with him, Marcus begins to unravel. His reaction intensifies as Jason explains that he can do so, because legally he is the children's provider and his sister Anjelica is their sole guardian. He tells Marcus that he can take them to court, but that the judge would probably not be impressed with his parental capabilities.[80] When Marcus asks why he would do such a thing, the Actor narrates Jason's response: 'Because you're a bloody fucking crazy person, Marcus! I can't do it anymore, I can't keep up with you! And I don't want the twins around you, it isn't good for them.'[81] In disbelief, the Actor/Marcus reminds him that he is their 'father'. To which the Actor/Jason replies, 'I'm their father. You're the sperm donor.'[82]

Shortly following this exchange, Marcus proceeds to break down, as he realizes that he has abandoned his career for a fairy tale that never really existed. The Actor/Marcus says to Jason, 'So you've conspired against me with the mother of my children . . . Look at me. Look me in the eye! . . . Look me in the fucking eye!'[83] He then narrates to the audience the actions that followed the exchange: 'And I shove him, I whack his shoulder, and he takes a swing at me, like a reflex, and he hits me right in the jaw, and I'm so disoriented, my blood is boiling, all I can say is, "Who *are* you?"' To which the Actor/Jason responds: '"Oh, for once, don't be so fucking dramatic!" before he storms out of the room.'[84] Out of work, with few prospects of getting employed, and no money because Jason has cut him off, he begins to pass the time at Lincoln Center watching videos of various Medeas: Fiona Shaw, Diana Rigg, Zoe Caldwell, Judith Anderson, Maria Callas in Pasolini's film, Lars von Trier's film, a Mexican version *Such is Life*, and so forth. Clearly, it becomes his

---

[80] Mark (2015) 31. My grateful thanks to Aaron Mark for granting me permission to quote from his currently unpublished play. A published version should hopefully be available soon.

[81] Mark (2015) 32.   [82] Mark (2015) 32.   [83] Mark (2015) 32.

[84] Mark (2015) 32.

obsession. And this passion for Medea becomes a critical turning point before the play rolls through the violent recollection of Marcus' brutal murders.

As the content of *Another Medea* functions as a criticism of laws that once limited marriage and still limit paternity rights for gay couples,[85] so too does the play's form. What is especially interesting about the piece is the absence of what Aristotle would call *opsis*, or what theatre historians today might call the *mise en scène*, or spectacle: the costumes, the make-up, the lighting, the set design, etc. Such design elements of performance are those most often exploited to produce a camp aesthetic. Mark, however, rejects this approach entirely. Despite the influence of Ludlam, Eichelberger, and Koutoukas on his work, he avoids camp completely. Rather than commenting on the appropriation of camp, as Rochel and O'Leary do, he totally strips it away, probably to the surprise of those members of his audience who, when they heard Tom Hewitt, well-known for his amazing performance as Frank 'N' Furter in *Rocky Horror*, was performing in a male-Medea, expected the piece to be either 'too serious or too camp'.[86]

Instead, Mark starts with the question: 'How is it possible to scare people in the theatre again?'[87] His interest in reviving the crime fiction genre, to which productions such as *Deathtrap* or *The Mousetrap* belong, has led to his creation of what I call a 'theatre of the mind', a technique that he also explores in his solo horror plays *Empanada Loca*, an adaptation of *Sweeney Todd*, and *Squeamish*. According to Mark, scaring people and staging violence in the theatre without being phony or hokey has become difficult because of the prevalence of violent, graphic cinematic images. Thus, in the manner of an ancient messenger speech, which was performed before an ancient audience who were familiar with violence not through cinematic images but battlefield combat,[88] Mark chooses to narrate rather than stage any violence.

He turns inwards. His trilogy explores a performance style fuelled by its intense, almost meditative concentration on the solo performer that

---

[85] For a recent article on the legal complications faced by same-sex couples, see Harris (2017).

[86] Mark (2016).   [87] Mark (2016).

[88] See Chapter 5 for a discussion of Greek drama and veterans. Most Athenian males would have had some experience of combat. This experience would have surely influenced their reception of the narration of violence in the theatre, although in what ways we cannot know.

seduces the audience into a sort of hypnotic state that inspires their imagination to create or visualize the events being narrated. With no physical representation of the places or events described, the audience must imagine them. 'It's personal,' Mark explained, 'because it all takes place in your head. The images that your mind creates make it personal.'[89] He carefully plants subtle ideas. For example, he uses the framing device of the anonymous Actor playing Marcus whose recollection gives permission to the audience to imagine. He also dims the lights in the intimate seventy-seat theatre to make the audience feel isolated despite the people around them. In doing so, Mark carefully prepares the audience psychologically. Their minds become open to imagining the horrors of the murders and getting lost in the drama, because the production strips away everything that could remind them they are sitting in a theatre.

To achieve this effect, the charming and charismatic Hewitt, who is well known for his portrayal of villains, sits absolutely still behind a desk for nearly the entire ninety-minute performance. Within this period, he makes only a few movements. For example, at the beginning of the show, he takes off his glasses, in an action that serves as the inverse of a Greek actor putting on a mask, to signify the moment when he is no longer the anonymous Actor but rather the anonymous Actor embodying the role of Marcus. It is nearly an hour into the performance before the next significant movement occurs. Hewitt, with great physical virtuosity and technical control, stages a fight between Marcus and Jason, just after Marcus' realization that Jason has decided to take everything from him by moving back to London with his sister, the twins, and Paris. The brilliant choreography of Hewitt's schizophrenic fight between the two characters played by him becomes a metatheatrical moment that symbolizes the mental breakdown of the character, for, following this moment, he describes his obsession with Medea that leads to the murders. Apart from a few key movements such as these, Hewitt stays painfully still, until the end of the play, when the actor playing Marcus 'returns to his neutral self', 'gets up from the table', and 'walks abruptly off the stage'.[90]

[89] Mark (2016).   [90] Mark (2015) 48.

The result of this minimalist approach is that the audience, who have no visual imagery fed to them, become actively engaged in creating visual imagery. During the anonymous Actor's recollection of Marcus' harrowing description of dropping a hairdryer in the bath to electrocute the children,[91] for instance, the 'audience would look down and cover their eyes as if there was something to see'.[92] After the show, people would describe this murder differently to Mark, because they had imagined it differently, and actors, whose training attunes them to such visualization, would be especially disturbed.[93]

What I personally found so interesting about this performance was how vivid my memory of it seemed to be years after seeing it. Two years after attending the performance, while I was interviewing Mark, I could recall with detail the flat where the murders took place, even though there is no image of it, either portrayed through the set design or described by a character. As Mark has explained, 'when we are producing these images, we are participating in and creating this violence. It's a psychological process.'[94] Having actively participated in the creation of this image, I could remember it that much better.

Mark's method, however, stems not from any motivation to present an alternative discourse to camp. Rather it is a coincidental by-product of his interest in creating a form that will work to 'scare people in the theatre again'.[95] At the same time, perhaps because of the appropriation of camp for commercial purposes, Mark has had to invent this new pared-down, bare-bones, yet dynamic performance style in order for his work to convey the same fresh political impetus of Ludlam, Eichelberger, and Koutoukas.

---

[91] Mark (2015) 44.   [92] Mark (2016).   [93] Mark (2016).

[94] Mark (2016). According to Mark, the psychological dimension of the piece also left an impression on Hewitt, who during rehearsals felt emotionally drained with the process of having to relive the horror. Once the show opened, however, he found the performance to be more demanding physically than emotionally, as if the audience somehow shared the pain with him and dispersed it among them. He then began to discover what it meant to be still, to focus on one spot, and to look into the dark for ninety minutes, an experience that Hewitt described as like going into a time warp—perhaps something like a sort of prolonged, meditative messenger speech of the ancient tradition, in which his voice functioned almost like a Greek mask. Mark described the experience as being 'a power rush for an actor: to do so little while doing so much at the same time, and have such power over the audience'.

[95] Mark (2016).

For Mark's interest in directing attention inwards works not only to frighten his audience but also to challenge their preconceived ideas about gender and the power relations between the sexes. He casts Hewitt, who frequently plays strong masculine villains such as Pontius Pilate in *Jesus Christ Superstar*, Dracula in *Dracula*, and Scar in Disney's *Lion King*, as Marcus, who, as an actor, especially a struggling ageing actor with no money, is a feminized male. The idea that someone, a doctor no less, could save Marcus from a life of struggle further feminizes the character by creating a Cinderella effect. For Jason is a wealthy, successful doctor who 'tastes like Montepulciano and some kind of safety',[96] someone who is capable of saving lives, but who instead destroys Marcus'. His profession, success, and money give him a masculine power, whereas Marcus' profession and poverty marginalize him.

Yet despite the feminization of the character, Hewitt resists performing him as such. He wears simple all-black clothes, maintains his strong physicality, and speaks in a rich, deep voice, free of any affectation. At the same time, this stereotypically masculine performance is feminized through the circumstances of the character, to the point where Marcus always refers to sex with Jason as 'He fucks me.'[97] Hewitt's playing an actor who is playing a feminized character in a way that is not stereotypically effeminate thus suggests that gender is a creation or a construct or performance that is linked to power.

In this way, the form of the performance works symbiotically with the content of the play, which depicts a woman as having more power than Marcus does. Anjelica is a wealthy and beautiful painter who has 'never sold a painting in her life, but it doesn't matter cause she's fucking rich'.[98] She has power not only because of her money but also because she has legal protection and rights as the birth mother of Marcus' child. In contrast, the only real power that Marcus has is his charm, which, of course, is a feminized trait.

Mark thus explores the idea of the connection between money and gender in a power game. How do Marcus' income and choice of profession feminize him and further contribute to his marginalized status? Thus, in substituting a male character for the iconic scorned 'Woman',[99] *Another*

---

[96] Mark (2016) 9.   [97] Mark (2016) 9, 17, 19.   [98] Mark (2016) 10.
[99] See Chapter 3, n. 12 on the idea of 'Woman' or the male-constructed female character.

Medea challenges essentialist figurations of gender identity by framing the showdown between Medea and Jason as a power struggle between two men. In this way, through form and content, the production challenges normative constructions of gender as well as mediatized versions of what it means to be a gay man.

For, like Rochel's *Bacchae* and O'Leary's *The Wrath of Aphrodite*, the work questions the image of the socially acceptable, TV-version of the happy gay male with a buff physique and a keen fashion sense. Instead, it 'disidentifies' with such media images and constructs an altogether different story of an ageing and struggling individual whose wealthy, accomplished partner can exploit him because at the time no laws existed to protect the finances or paternity rights of gay men whose same-sex partnerships had dissolved. With a lack of clear legal protection and a lack of financial resources to challenge Jason in court, Marcus breaks down. His murder-suicide thus suggests the moral culpability of a state that discriminates against individuals based on their sexuality and refuses to offer the legal protections that serve in part to mitigate the type of 'eye for an eye' retribution that Marcus, like his precursor Medea, exacts.

Stereotypes of Gay Men in the US

In all three of these productions that cast same-sex lovers in the canonical male-female relationships of the classical tragedies, camp, or the absence of it, works as a performative counter-discourse to the mediatized versions of campy gay men. However, despite their aims of legitimating same-sex love, the productions cannot escape a troubling problem. By following the plot of the Euripidean tragedies, the gay male heroes must die. Thus, the productions raise the question of whether they blindly reinforce or instead challenge the 'gay suicide trope' or the stereotype of the 'tragic homosexual'.

As Stanford doctoral student Samuel Clowes Huneke has explained, the gay suicide trope began at least as early as nineteenth-century Germany, when, in response to German laws that 'banned unnatural acts', many gay Germans committed suicide rather than face persecution under the new laws. Artists and writers at first began to depict the association between 'homosexuality' and suicide as a way to protest, but later writers, under the influence of the neo-romanticists, 'used the suicides of their characters not to show the suffering caused by the

German legal code, but rather as a cathartic catastrophe with which to seal the tragedy of their art'.[100] Huneke hypothesizes that with the emigration of gay intellectuals from Germany to the United States during the Second World War came the importation of the gay suicide trope to American literature.

The medium that now garners the most attention for the propagation of this trope is television, where:

Fictional representations of LGBT characters are important because, in the lonely world of the closet, they might be the only models young people have. Depictions of romantic suicides are particularly insidious because populations confronted with suicide—whether illusory or real—are more prone to it themselves. Gay, lesbian and transgender youth are between twice and four times as likely as their straight peers to attempt suicide.[101]

Despite this problem, the long-standing practice of killing off gay characters continues. It has become known as 'Bury Your Gays', i.e. when 'LGBT characters are frequently killed off—often in tragic ways, following a happy event'.[102] As the *Washington Post* has recently reported, 'In 2016 alone, 10 characters identifying as lesbian or bisexual have been killed, on shows such as CW's *Jane the Virgin*, AMC's *The Walking Dead* and Syfy's *The Magicians*.'[103] When the CW channel's programme *The 100* killed off the openly gay character Lexa, viewers took to Twitter and Tumblr to express their outrage. 'During the episode following Lexa's death, fans tweeted with the trending topic LGBT Fans Deserve Better, which has since become an international fan-led initiative . . . [and] Bury Tropes Not Us, sending the topic trending nationally.'[104] As Bethonie Butler has explained:

GLAAD's 2015 'Where We Are Now on TV' report cited that 35 regular characters in the 2015–2016 television season identified as gay, lesbian or bisexual—just 4 percent of a projected 881 characters. Gay TV characters are important because 'younger gay people don't necessarily know other gay people or have gay friends,' said Autostraddle's founder Marie Lyn Bernard (who goes by Riese). 'It's so instrumental it just ends up being a lifeline.'[105]

TV attracts attention regarding this issue in part because of the teen audience it engages. However, the genre also functions as a powerful

---

[100] Huneke (2016).   [101] Huneke (2016).   [102] Butler (2016).
[103] Butler (2016).   [104] Butler (2016).   [105] Butler (2016).

identificatory apparatus in that viewership takes place in the home, where characters are invited to return repeatedly over a period of time, a practice that often results in intense relationships between viewers and characters.

Thus, while the debate over the purpose of art and whether it reflects or affects social behaviour is at least as old as Aristophanes' *Frogs* and Plato's *Republic*,[106] viewers, scholars, and activists such as Huneke have declared an end to the argument: art does influence society and should depict representations that are socially responsible. According to Huneke:

This gay suicide trope is a grotesque and farcical reality that still causes suffering, a literary device perpetuated by a romantic sensibility that absurdly insists that the most fitting end to any gay life is premature, self-inflicted death. The 'tragic homosexual' is a stereotype we can live without.[107]

However, despite the frightening statistics on gay suicide, particularly among the teenage population, each work of art must be evaluated in its own context and on its own terms.

Such is the case with the three productions described in this chapter. Artists have a problem in revising Greek tragedy with LGBTQ characters, because simply by following the plot of most tragedies they risk reiterating the gay suicide trope. However, despite the deaths at the end of each production, these three works do not reinforce the narrative but in fact challenge or rather 'disidentify' with it by working 'on, with, and against a cultural form'.[108] In other words, the performances allow for reflection instead of identification. In so doing, they use Greek tragedy as a means to challenge the trope of the so-called 'tragic homosexual'.

For example, in the three works, the death of the principal characters results not from their families', friends', or their own inability to accept a LGBTQ identity, but rather from homophobia itself. They die from the pressure of the social rules and regulations that prevent them from living their lives as multifaceted human beings with full citizen rights. In Rochel's *Bacchae*, Pentheus dies in the midst of a frenzied chorus who represents a mediatized image of gay men to which he and Cadmus

---

[106] In *Frogs* (405 BCE), the comic characters 'Aeschylus' and 'Euripides' debate over whose tragedy better serves the city. In Book X of *Republic* (c.380 BCE), Socrates declares that theatre should be banned from the ideal city (*kallipolis*) because of its power to encourage undesirable behaviour among citizens.

[107] Huneke (2016).   [108] Muñoz (1999) 12.

cannot conform. *The Wrath of Aphrodite* uses the image of the mytho-logical Elysian Fields to represent not death but a utopian existence with which Artemis rewards Hippolytus and Adonis for their undying love for each other, as she punishes Aphrodite for inflicting her wrath on them. *Another Medea* depicts Marcus' murders not as an act of despair over his sexuality but as the only means he feels that he has to acquire justice in a society that offered him no opportunity to enjoy marriage or any other legal protections as a biological father conceiving through IVF with a woman to whom he is not married or with whom he had no legal arrangement. Rather than aestheticizing the deaths of gay men and encouraging an audience to identify with the image, each work instead politicizes it, as did the original authors of the gay suicide motif in Weimar Germany whom Huneke describes. Thus, the deaths in these productions do not reiterate the trope but rather subvert it through each performance's recycling of 'encoded meaning', i.e. by using the code of the majority 'as raw material for representing a disempowered politics or positionality that has been rendered unthinkable by dominant culture'.[109]

In this way, these productions have participated in a march toward positive representations of the LGBTQ community in the media. In 2007, for example, when Rochel's production was first performed, 1.3 per cent of prime-time network television represented a gay, lesbian, or bisexual couple, but by 2015, that number had tripled to 4 per cent.[110] Considering that the Motion Picture Association of America codes from the 1930s to 1968 dictated that 'no sympathy for the violation of human, natural, and divine laws be presented',[111] these numbers suggest pro-gress. Nevertheless, despite the increase of LGBTQ characters on scripted cable TV (84 in 2015 versus 64 the previous year) and the advent of reality programmes such as *RuPaul's Drag Race*, *I Am Cait*, and *The Real L Word*, such statistics are still meagre.

More importantly, the type of representation is often problematic, for GLAAD's statistics on representation do not exclude negative portrayals,[112]

---

[109] Muñoz (1999) 31.   [110] GLAAD (2016).   [111] Cover (2016) 192.

[112] Moreover, some of these representations, while not completely negative, are contro-versial, such as Caitlyn Jenner's reality show *I Am Cait*, which documents the Olympic decathlon gold medal winner's transition from her identity as Bruce. For, while Jenner has undoubtedly been helpful for trans visibility, she has not done so without criticism. Her financial resources can afford her a version of trans and a level of protection that many in

such as those films and programmes that reiterate the gay suicide trope and controversial gay characters, such as *Sex and the City*'s Stanford, *Glee*'s Kurt, and *Ugly Betty*'s Marc. As Ramin Setoodah has argued:

if we accept that... [some gay characters on television, such as Will from *Will and Grace*] once fostered acceptance, it's fair to ask if *Glee* may be hurting it, especially because the Kurt model [of the cliché gay male diva] is everywhere. There's Marc (Michael Urie), the flaming fashion assistant on *Ugly Betty*; Lloyd (Rex Lee), Ari's sassy receptionist on *Entourage*; the gay couple on *Modern Family* (one guy still pines for his ice-skating career; the other wears purple in every episode)... Lesbians face a different problem. They are invariably played by gorgeous, curvy women straight out of a straight man's fantasy—Olivia Wilde on *House*, Sara Ramirez on *Grey's Anatomy*, Evan Rachel Wood on *True Blood*—they're usually bisexual. How convenient.[113]

As Setoodeh also notes, the purpose of TV is to entertain, not lecture or even educate, but the images propagated on these programmes and in the culture at large are undeniably powerful and inevitably influence popular thinking and politics.

Conclusion

On the contrary, the theatrical productions that I have discussed in this chapter defy such 'mediatized' stereotypes. Through the medium of live theatre, they provide a critical distance that allows for a 'disidentification' with not only majoritarian views of gender but also the 'mediatized' representation of the LGBTQ community in popular culture that often serves a commercial purpose. These off-off-Broadway theatrical productions may not have the same mass impact as television and may not necessarily change people's minds and attitudes.[114] However, even if individually they do not change the culture overnight, collectively their voices foster activism by providing a crucial alternative image to mainstream views.

---

the community find unattainable, so she has put forward a 'mediatized' image of transitioning that does not fully reflect the difficulty of the process. As one critic has commented, despite Caitlyn's strong desire to 'get it right', she has become a media phenomenon 'that always seemed crafted for the curiosities and pleasures of a non-trans audience' (Cross 2015).

[113] Setoodeh (2009).   [114] See Román and Miller (2002).

In my follow-up interviews with Rochel,[115] O'Leary,[116] and Mark,[117] all of which took place several years after their productions were mounted, a common thread emerged: how much the world has changed since we first met at the time of their productions in 2007, 2008, and 2013. Indeed, much progress has been made for LGBTQ rights in these years, especially with the US Supreme Court's historic 2015 decision that legalized gay marriage nationwide.[118]

Almost overnight, these playwrights' works were no longer part of a movement toward marriage equality. Instead, they were period pieces of a sort. Thus, as quickly as the mass media has appropriated images and representations of the LGBTQ community for its own corporate marketing purposes, theatre artists such as Rochel, O'Leary, and Mark have presented new strategies of resistance by using the medium of Greek tragedy as a way to challenge stereotypes of gay men and the gay suicide trope in particular.

---

[115] Rochel (2016).   [116] O'Leary (2016).   [117] Mark (2016).

[118] O'Leary (2016) recalled working on a sci-fi play to make a commentary on the prohibition of gay marriage, a premise that suddenly became irrelevant overnight.

5

Challenging the Stereotype of the 'Disabled Veteran' in Aquila's *A Female Philoctetes* and Outside the Wire's *Ajax*

My focus in this chapter is on veterans who, now that military enlistment is voluntary, are a minority community in the US with 'less than .5 percent of the population serv[ing] in the armed forces, compared with more than 12 percent during World War II'.[1] Many tragedies relate to veterans, but three, Sophocles' *Ajax* (*c.* 440 BCE[2]) and *Philoctetes* (409 BCE) and Euripides' *Heracles* (*c.* 416 BCE), are often associated with vets.[3] Although these plays are not as popular as classics such as *Oedipus*, *Medea*, and *Trojan Women*, in recent years various American artists have staged these works or versions of them. For example, in New York City, Blue Heron Arts staged Seamus Heaney's adaptation of *Philoctetes*, titled *The Cure at Troy*,[4] in 2002, Soho Rep staged *Philoktetes*[5] in 2007, and in Los Angeles, the Theater Lab at the Getty Villa staged *Philoktetes*

---

[1] Eikenberry and Kennedy (2013). The article continues: 'even fewer of the privileged and powerful shoulder arms. In 1975, 70 percent of members of Congress had some military service; today, just 20 percent do, and only a handful of their children are in uniform.'

[2] As with *Heracles*, the exact date is uncertain.

[3] Whereas *Philoctetes* dramatizes the abandonment and deception of a wounded veteran, *Heracles* and *Ajax* stage the madness and suicide of two great Greek warriors and thus provide an ancient parallel for post-traumatic stress disorder.

[4] *The Cure at Troy* (2002), http://www.apgrd.ox.ac.uk/productions/production/6047, accessed 15 September 2016.

[5] *Philoktetes* (2007), http://www.apgrd.ox.ac.uk/productions/production/13783, accessed 15 September 2016.

Fragments[6] in 2008. New York's Flux Theatre Ensemble produced *Ajax in Iraq*[7] in 2011, and Target Margin Theater put on *Ajax: A Furious Study on Humanity*[8] in 2007. Perhaps one of the most famous productions of *Ajax* was directed in 1986–7 by Peter Sellars, who cast a deaf actor in the title role and set the play in front of the Pentagon.[9] American Repertory Theatre (ART) staged *The Madness of Herakles*[10] in 1997, and a rock and roll version of the play, *Hercules in High Suburbia*,[11] was staged at La MaMa E.T.C. in 2004, as well as an adaptation *Home Front* by Daniel Algie in 2006.[12] Among these varied works are those of the two nationally recognized theatre companies on which I focus in this chapter: Aquila Theatre and Outside the Wire.

Both of these companies have been using Greek tragedy as a means to raise awareness about concerns of veterans, from post-traumatic stress (PTS) issues to reintegration into civilian life to conflicts between leaders and subordinates. However, sitting in a post-performance discussion at one Outside the Wire event, I found myself thinking that the subject that kept arising without actually being named was disability. At that point, I began to understand more clearly the connection between the veteran and disabled communities and the persistence of the stereotypical image of the 'disabled veteran' in American society. Thus, instead of thinking of these theatre companies, as others have done,[13] solely in terms of

---

[6] *Philoktetes Fragments* (2008), http://www.apgrd.ox.ac.uk/productions/production/11145, accessed 15 September 2016.

[7] *Ajax in Iraq* (2011), http://www.apgrd.ox.ac.uk/productions/production/12125, accessed 15 September 2016.

[8] *Ajax: A Furious Study on Humanity* (2007), http://www.apgrd.ox.ac.uk/productions/production/10135, accessed 15 September 2016.

[9] *Ajax* (1986–7), http://www.apgrd.ox.ac.uk/productions/production/3147, accessed 15 September 2016. For a thorough discussion of this play, see MacDonald (1992).

[10] *The Madness of Heracles* (1997), http://www.apgrd.ox.ac.uk/productions/production/3340, accessed 15 September 2016.

[11] *Hercules in High Suburbia* (2005), http://www.apgrd.ox.ac.uk/productions/production/9799, accessed 15 September 2016.

[12] *Home Front* (2006), http://www.apgrd.ox.ac.uk/productions/production/9913, accessed 15 September 2016. *Home Front*, performed before a civilian audience at La MaMa E.T.C., was a pioneering performance that used Greek drama to address the concerns of veterans and the violence of war. The production adapted its Euripidean predecessor to dramatize a fictional account of a Vietnam veteran, a former prisoner of war, named Harrison, who, suffering from PTSD, returns home to his Midwest family in 1972 after being away for eight years.

[13] See Adamitis and Gamel (2013) and Lodewyck and Monoson (2015).

'applied theatre',[14] 'engaged theatre',[15] or 'social theatre',[16] I began to think about them also in terms of 'disability theatre'.

Like Lodewyck and Monoson, I agree that Aquila and Outside the Wire 'democratize' (to use their term) Greek drama in the sense that they address a non-theatre-going elite, 'mobilize interpretations of texts to address unseen or neglected public interests, disrupt the format of traditional full-length performances of Greek texts, amplify certain voices in the sources, and occasion public discourse and moments of commonality'.[17] Elaborating on these observations, I here want to study the ways in which these companies may also 'democratize'[18] Greek drama by challenging stereotypes of the 'disabled veteran'.

In other words, I want to explore how the critical lens of disability studies can help to demonstrate the ways in which these theatre companies have been using the performance of Greek tragedy to generate important national conversations that combat the social stigmas and stereotypes surrounding the mental health of veterans. In doing so, I will investigate the ways in which the companies distinctively employ the ancient tragedies *Philoctetes*[19] and *Ajax*[20] to serve their purposes. How do these tragedies help communities to 'name' the emotions and experiences of war? How does presenting a historical model of the mental and physical distress of veterans work to destigmatize these conditions in the present? How does providing a public forum for discussing the military experiences that affect mental health help to 'normalize' and promote as 'natural and inevitable' conditions such as PTS, and thus make them a problem of war, a problem and product of society, as opposed to a failure of any individual?

---

[14] Theatre that seeks to effect social change. See Blatner (2007); Prentki and Preston (2009).

[15] Theatre that 'includes, but is larger than, applied theatre', Cohen Cruz (2010) 5, quoted in Adamitis and Gamel (2013) 285.

[16] Theatre that 'refers to events that may forge partnerships among artistic and civic groups and address specific issues of importance to these communities', Lodewyck and Monoson (2015) 653.

[17] Lodewyck and Monoson (2015) 652.

[18] Greek drama was, of course, already democratized in the sense that it was the hallmark art form of the Athenian democracy.

[19] See the section 'Aquila's *A Female Philoctetes*' later in this chapter for a summary of this tragedy.

[20] See the section 'Outside the Wire/Theater of War's *Ajax*' later in this chapter for a summary of this tragedy.

At the same time, I will also investigate the ways in which the companies risk inadvertently reinforcing stereotypes, even though their aim is to challenge them. How do they use ancient tragedy to 'name' emotions without implying that the suffering of veterans is universal and thus inevitable? How do they manage the fine line between discussing trauma and exploiting it?

Exploring questions such as these, I will examine the methods of each of these companies. For, while they are often grouped together because of their similar subject matter, the companies' approaches are quite distinct. Ultimately, I will suggest that, while both companies work in the interest of veterans, Aquila's not-for-profit status, employment of veterans, and expert-led discussions are a model that successfully avoids many of the potential problems that the for-profit Outside the Wire risks by hosting events that feature celebrity as opposed to veteran-led readings of the plays.

The Stereotype of the 'Disabled Veteran'

The connection between veterans and the disabled community has a long history. Many Vietnam veterans were in the vanguard of the fight for the passage of the Americans with Disabilities Act (ADA) of 1990, and the image of the disabled veteran in Western culture has a long history, dating back at least to Sophocles' *Philoctetes* and *Ajax*. Beginning with these ancient tragedies and continuing into modern-day Hollywood films, the physically and mentally wounded veteran has long worked as a cultural image that defines and is defined by a culture's social and political attitudes toward masculinity and war.

For example, when *Philoctetes* premiered in the Theatre of Dionysus, the wounded Philoctetes would have been a feminized character, unable to act or perform as a male citizen should. To the primarily, if not exclusively, male citizen audience,[21] experienced in combat warfare, his screams of pain would have been a familiar sound. They probably produced 'mixed feelings of pride and pity, admiration and repulsion... Without the social positioning of the disabled veteran that we have in the twentieth

---

[21] For a discussion of the scholarly debates over the presence of women at the performances in the Theatre of Dionysus, see Powers (2014).

century, the ancient disabled soldier starkly represents the very real horrors of war.'[22]

In the US, where the categories of disability and veteran do exist, and do allow for a social positioning of veterans, representations of disabled veterans have been used for various purposes, from reinforcing gender roles to mitigating societal guilt over war. In the twentieth century, the fictional construction of the disabled veteran began in the post-war era with narratives such as those in Ernest Hemingway's novel *A Farewell to Arms* (1929) and Hollywood films such as *Pride of the Marines* (1945), in which:

disabled veterans with compromised manhood because of injury or illness are rescued by a female savior, in the form of nurse, wife, or girlfriend, who functions simultaneously as both Mother and nurturer and mistress and sex object. In such dramas, the responsible woman's role is to coax and to manipulate the man into becoming 'his old self' again, or in Jeffords's phrase, *remasculinized*. At the center of these dramas, however, are not such day-to-day aspects of living with a disability as mobility, accessibility, or work, but instead symbolic male dominance and heterosexual intimacy. Reclaiming manhood is thus conceived within the framework of a melodrama in which men and women ultimately sort themselves out by conventional gendered categories in their emotional and sexual relationship.[23]

Such narratives are typical of the early and mid-century, but they change in the Vietnam era.

The Vietnam veterans have had the 'double stigma' of 'disabled status and involvement in an unpopular war'.[24] Society has 'thus coded them to be among its most Otherized and potentially troublesome people. In response, filmmakers working on behalf of mainstream society have mostly advocated the "cure" option ... these highly marginalized figures are eventually reabsorbed into mainstream society.'[25]

Most recently, Hollywood films such as *Jarhead* (2005), *The Hurt Locker* (2008), *Zero Dark Thirty* (2012), and *American Sniper* (2014) have received both praise and criticism for their attempts to depict the experience of Iraq and Afghanistan War veterans. Unlike the Hollywood of previous generations, this current generation of film-makers has begun to work together with veterans with the aim of producing authentic representations of them in film and on television. Organizations such

---

[22] Edwards (2000) 66.   [23] Gerber (2000) 10–11.
[24] Norden (2000) 110.   [25] Norden (2000) 109.

as Got Your Six (a military term for 'got your back'), a spin-off of the former first lady Michelle Obama's Joining Forces, have worked to change and strengthen the image of post-9/11 veterans as 'broken heroes' to one of 'community leaders'.[26] In 2015, the organization launched '6 Certified', a sort of seal of approval that will be awarded to film and television programmes that attempt to portray veterans accurately and responsibly. Reality TV producer Charlie Ebersol (USA Network's *NFL Characters Unite* and CNBC's *The Profit*), who suggested the idea of certification, told *The Hollywood Reporter*, 'We've gotten to this point where the depictions of veterans are so extreme: They are either heroes or they're victims. There is nothing in-between.'[27]

Through initiatives such as these the veteran community has been working to gain control over the narratives that in the past have marginalized and stereotyped them as either the 'uneducated Joe Six-Pack',[28] the disabled, disgruntled, homeless, mentally ill alcoholic, or the superhuman Chris Kyle-esque hero.[29] They understand and appreciate the physical and psychological traumas and the opportunities for heroism created by war. However, they take umbrage at the cultural perception that war inevitably leads to the creation of either victims or superhumans. As one of Aquila's actors who is a veteran has explained, 'I don't need to be called a hero. You know? I'd much rather have you . . . not put . . . a yellow ribbon on your car—[but] just reach out. And really invest yourself, and be interested. Invite us over . . . And have a beer and hot dog with us.'[30] Whatever their experiences, veterans often just want to be treated like anybody else.

Another misperception about veterans is that all 'returning veterans are more likely [than the civilian population] to be dealing with significant problems'.[31] For example, as Got Your Six has reported, 83 per cent of US civilians polled believe that Iraq War veterans are more likely

---

[26] https://gotyour6.org/impact/cultural-perceptions-of-veterans/, accessed 25 September 2016.

[27] Daunt (2015).

[28] Shay (1994) xxii. According to the *Merriam-Webster Dictionary*, the first known use of the disparaging term 'Joe Six-Pack' was in 1973. It comes from the stereotype of beer as a working-man's beverage.

[29] Chris Kyle was the Navy SEAL whose book became the basis for the Academy Award-nominated film *American Sniper*. He has been called the deadliest sniper in American history with 160 confirmed kills.

[30] Lawrence (2014).

[31] https://gotyour6.org/impact/cultural-perceptions-of-veterans/, accessed 25 September 2016.

to suffer from mental illness than the civilian community, 75 per cent believe that they are more likely to commit suicide, and 60 per cent that they would be more prone to unemployment. However, Got Your Six states that more than 95 per cent of Americans dealing with PTS are civilians; veterans are no more likely to commit suicide than civilians in their same age range are, and a higher proportion of veterans have been in employment than civilians in ninety-six of the last ninety-nine months that Got Your Six surveyed. Although the 'twenty-two veterans commit suicide every day' statistic has been much touted by politicians and the media, the figure is misleading, both because of how the statistic is calculated and because it lacks context. For example, the number is not representative of the suicide rate of Iraq War veterans, which appears to be closer to one a day, most of which have occurred during the first three years after returning home.[32] Accordingly, these misperceptions are 'not based on data' but rather are 'correlated to the way veterans are inaccurately portrayed in popular culture'.[33]

Thus, on the one hand, statistics such as one in three servicemen and women lives with PTS and one in five lives with traumatic brain injury, cited by the now infamous Wounded Warriors organization,[34] may be helpful in raising public awareness and public funds to help veterans. On the other hand, such decontextualized statistics may not only present an inaccurate picture[35] but also cause the public to project onto veterans already existing stereotypes about people with mental illness as being 'dangerous and unpredictable, to blame for their illness, and incompetent to achieve most life goals'.[36]

As Sergeant John Eubanks, a US Marine who has worked with Outside the Wire's Theater of War programme, has explained:

The biggest problem is the stigma when you come back... whether you are considered weak... the rumors that go around... If you go seek psychological

---

[32] https://gotyour6.org/impact/cultural-perceptions-of-veterans/, accessed 25 September 2016. On the inaccuracy of the twenty-two suicides per day statistic, see Bare (2015).

[33] https://gotyour6.org/impact/cultural-perceptions-of-veterans/, accessed 25 September 2016.

[34] The organization is one of the largest veterans' charities in America. In 2016, its CEO and top executives were accused of wastefully spending approximately 40 per cent of its donations on overheads that included expensive business-class flights, hotel rooms, and conferences. See Philipps (2016).

[35] On some of the problems with diagnosing PTS in veterans, see Dobbs (2012).

[36] Corrigan, Druss, and Perlick (2014).

help, you'll ruin your career, because you can't get a security clearance ... or if you want to be a cop when you get out. And some people even say if you want to go to college, they won't accept you because you're crazy ... you have PTSD just because you went to see a psychologist one time which is not true ... but people feel it ... but even if you are diagnosed with PTSD there are laws that prevent against discrimination ... That's just the mass amount of rumors that go around the ranks.[37]

Eubanks' words poignantly describe the ways in which the social stigmas surrounding mental health care prevent those in need from seeking care.[38] Thus, educating the public and destigmatizing disability and mental illness are essential to destigmatizing veterans.

By giving modern veterans the opportunity to respond to ancient narratives about their historical counterparts (and, in Aquila's case, to create and be in control of their own modern narratives), Aquila's and Outside the Wire's programmes bridge the civilian–military gap and foster the 'knowledge, culture, and social networks [that] can influence the relationship between stigma and access to care ... [For] social networks, including family members, friends, and co-workers, can also have a big impact on people's decisions to pursue treatment, serving either to enhance feelings of stigma or to encourage care seeking.'[39]

Disability Studies and Disability Theatre

It is important to make clear, however, that neither Aquila nor Outside the Wire identifies as a disability theatre company working in disability theatre specifically. Yet, while these theatre companies may not identify with disability theatre per se, their work still intersects with the genre. For:

Disability theater ... does not designate a single pattern, model, site, disability experience, or means of theatre production. Rather, the term has emerged in connection to the disability arts and culture movement at a particular moment in the re-imagining of the term 'disability' in many different geographical, socio-economic, and otherwise diverse cultural contexts. Different artists have embraced and resisted both sides of the term. Some have sought to highlight specific disability experiences while others favor kinds of performance that lie outside the scope of theatre's more traditional framings.[40]

---

[37] Brown (2010).   [38] Corrigan, Druss, and Perlick (2014).
[39] Corrigan, Druss, and Perlick (2014).   [40] Johnston (2016) 35.

While Aquila's and Outside the Wire's primary aims are to work with veterans of all abilities, my critical lens of disability studies will highlight and explain each company's approaches to mitigating the stigma of mental illness that has infiltrated the veteran community and contributed to the creation of the stereotypical image of the 'disabled veteran'.

To understand better the process of combating such social stigmas and stereotypes, it will be helpful to define and explain disability studies and disability theatre. In general, the field approaches disability as a social construct rather than a medical condition.[41] Disability studies 'approaches the phenomenon of disability by assuming that there is nothing inherently wrong with the disabled body and that the reaction of a society to the disabled body is neither predictable nor immutable'.[42] Disability theatre is 'broadly connected to impulses for social justice in the face of ableist ideologies and practices as well as a profound recognition of disabled lives and experiences as inherently valuable'.[43]

Phamaly, Back to Back Theatre, Apothetae, and Theater Breaking Through Barriers are some examples of key US theatre companies that have created opportunities for artists with a variety of physical, emotional, and intellectual abilities.[44] Of these companies, only Theater Breaking Through Barriers has produced a Greek drama.[45] Under its former name Theater By the Blind, the company staged Ted Hughes' richly imagistic version[46] of Seneca's *Oedipus* with the title character played by the blind actor J. Martin McDonough.[47]

In productions such as these, companies have aimed to challenge common stereotypes and preconceptions about disability. In some cases, theatre companies' efforts to destigmatize people with disabilities have 'involved reclaiming words found to be limiting and stigmatizing by

---

[41] Rose (2003) 16.   [42] Rose (2003) 16.   [43] Johnston (2016) 25.

[44] For contemporary plays by disabled playwrights, see Lewis (2006).

[45] Other contemporary productions that have engaged with disability are Teatro Patologico, an Italian company whose *Medea* has been performed at La MaMa E.T.C., and perhaps Peter Sellars' *Ajax*, in which the deaf actor Howie Seago played the title role, although it is important to note that many members of the deaf community do not identify themselves as disabled. In addition, the Five Blind Boys of Alabama shared the role of Oedipus in *The Gospel at Colonus* (1983). See Padden and Humphries (2006).

[46] The National Theatre Company first staged Hughes' *Oedipus* at the Old Vic Theatre in 1968. Peter Brook directed and Sir John Gielgud and Irene Worth starred.

[47] The production received strong reviews. Honor Moore (2005) of the *New York Times* commented on its 'Strong clear performances . . . Vividly contemporary and shocking . . . Uncanny power . . . An extraordinary troupe designed to defy expectations.'

persons with disabilities'.[48] For example, by mobilizing the term 'crip' to take back the long-standing term 'cripple', some of these disability artists, much like artists in the LGBTQ community, have aimed to 'appropriate and rearticulate labels that the mainstream once used to silence or humiliate them and that the liberal factions of their subcultures would like to suppress'.[49]

However, despite such debates over the use of words within the field, one aim that unites most disability theatre scholars and practitioners is to replace the medical model of disability that considers the disabled population as a 'problem' to be fixed, corrected, or healed. This medical model of disability prevalent in the US today offers an 'understanding of impairment that "renders disability as a series of physiological, psychological and functional pathologies originating within the bodies of individuals"'.[50] Disability studies scholars have argued that 'impairment is distinguished from disability. The former is individual and private, the latter is structural and public.'[51] The medical model reduces 'the complex problems of disabled people to issues of medical prevention, cure or rehabilitation'.[52]

From this critique of the medical model emerged the social model. 'Social model thinking', explains Shakespeare, 'mandates barrier removal, anti-discrimination legislation, independent living and other responses to social oppression. From a disability rights perspective, social model approaches are progressive, medical approaches are reactionary.'[53] This social constructivist approach views disability as a 'disjuncture between the body and the environment' and 'locates disability within a society built for nondisabled people'.[54] The 'minority model', which is an extension of the social constructivist perspective, argues that 'disability is a mutable category by self-consciously crafting a new disability identity. In this view, the disabled become a distinct minority community that has been excluded from full participation in society because of discrimination

---

[48] Johnston (2016) 32.
[49] Sandahl (2003) 36, quoted in Johnston (2016) 33. As Kirsty Johnston has explained, 'whether using the term "disabled people" or "people with disabilities", the word "disability" itself has therefore been remobilized by advocates for its power to reference disabling social and economic conditions, building connections among an otherwise strikingly diverse and vast complement of people through their shared experience of oppression' (2016: 17).
[50] Longmore (2003), quoted in Johnston (2016) 18.
[51] Shakespeare (2006) 198.   [52] Shakespeare (2006) 199.
[53] Shakespeare (2006) 199.   [54] Sandahl and Auslander (2005) 7–8.

in education, employment, and architectural access.'[55] These models 'accept impairments as natural, inevitable human differences that should be accommodated. Activists persuasively point out that medical advances have not eliminated impairments, but proliferated them.'[56]

The social constructivist approach, as opposed to the medical model:

lifts the disabled veteran out of the haze of ideology and technical knowledge by which he [she, or they] has been obscured in the past and gives him [her, or their] a voice in influencing how he [she, or they] is seen. At the least, we become aware that we cannot take for granted that he [she, or they] is represented in what others have said about him [her, or them], or in the public policies and medical therapies developed in his [her, or their] behalf.[57]

Such social constructivist views were crucial in the passage of the Americans with Disabilities Act (ADA) of 1990, for which the veteran community were instrumental in lobbying. Thus, the connection between veterans and the disabled community has been not only long-standing but also important from a political perspective.

Breaking the Silence

By giving veterans a platform to speak about their first-hand experiences, including issues such as PTS, Aquila and Outside the Wire help to demonstrate the social constructivist view that disability is not a 'series of physiological, psychological and functional pathologies originating within the bodies of individuals'.[58] Rather, the issue rests not with the individual but with the environment. Impairments 'as natural, inevitable human differences' should be accommodated.[59] In this way, the theatre companies function in terms of disability theatre.[60] They do not aim to 'heal' or 'correct' any disabilities, but rather simply to provide an opportunity for veterans to 'name' and discuss their experiences, for 'naming and speaking about traumatic experiences is fundamental to

---

[55] Sandahl and Auslander (2005) 8.   [56] Sandahl and Auslander (2005) 129.
[57] Gerber (2000) 4.   [58] Longmore (2003) 1, quoted in Johnston (2016) 18.
[59] Sandahl and Auslander (2005) 129.
[60] For example, although it may not identify as a disability theatre company, Outside the Wire nevertheless functions in terms of disability theatre through its stated aims to 'de-stigmatize psychological injury' and 'increase awareness of post-deployment psychological health issues', http://www.outsidethewirellc.com/projects/theater-of-war/overview, accessed 10 July 2016.

processing them. Turning them into explicit conscious intentional recollections rather than reliving them through unconscious unintentional remembrances. This telling is part of the healing process.'[61]

The ability to talk is important, because, as Sergeant Eubanks has explained, veterans often encounter silence when they most need to talk:

For a while there I was very angry all the time, but at the same time, I didn't want to talk to anyone. Then I tried talking to the people, and it was just...I tried telling my friends, but they were going through the same things. So they didn't want to talk...Then I tried talking to my civilian friends, and they just either didn't get it, or they did not want to touch those issues at all. It became more of a burden, and it seemed that it bothered them any time I brought it up. So I became more isolated myself, and then it just became a cycle.[62]

This 'silencing' of the talk that is necessary for healing often results from social stigmas and stereotypes:

These displays of discrimination can become internalized, leading to the development of self-stigma: people with mental illness may begin to believe the negative thoughts expressed by others and, in turn, think of themselves as unable to recover, undeserving of care, dangerous, or responsible for their illnesses. This can lead them to feel shame, low self-esteem, and inability to accomplish their goals. Self-stigma can also lead to the development of the 'why try' effect, whereby people believe that they are unable to recover and live normally so 'why try?' To avoid being discriminated against, some people may also try to avoid being labeled as 'mentally ill' by denying or hiding their problems and refusing to seek out care.[63]

As Sergeant Eubanks has suggested, the stereotypical image of the mentally ill veteran contributes to a self-perpetuating cycle that intimidates many veterans into maintaining a fearful silence that results in further psychological wounds; for, according to Jonathan Shay, 'Unhealed war trauma can leave men as speechless as victims of prolonged political torture.'[64] Accordingly, because speaking about trauma contributes to and is a major sign of healing, the social taboos and stereotypes about mental health that prevent veterans from talking can exacerbate, if not in part cause, the disability itself.

Thus, if Aquila and Outside the Wire provide any healing, it is not (in the manner of a medical model approach to disability) the healing of any

---

[61] Smith (2002), quoted in Tomm (2013) 76.   [62] Brown (2010).
[63] Corrigan, Druss, and Perlick (2014).   [64] Shay (1994) xxii.

individual's disability, but rather the healing of the social stereotypes and stigmas that contribute to the silence that demoralizes veterans. Meredith Kleykamp, an associate professor of sociology at the University of Maryland, who is working on a study that looks at how the media and society often portray veterans as victims, has explained that:

> while a permanent, overarching 'fix' may never be found, there are ways to change perceptions [of veterans]... starting with perhaps the simplest solution of all: familiarity... People should get to know someone in the military— befriend your military neighbor... The best thing that can happen is for people to have natural, human relationships with one another.[65]

By fostering this familiarity between veterans and civilians, and fostering awareness about the physical and psychological costs of war, these theatre companies take a social constructivist approach to disability. In the process, they help to educate the public, the armed forces, and the veteran community at large to recognize and combat the social and cultural taboos about mental health that have contributed to the stereo-type of the 'messed-up', 'out of luck', 'out of control' veteran that in turn leads to the self-perpetuating cycle of self-stigma and silence.

A closer look at the distinct approaches of these two companies will demonstrate the methods they use to heal not individuals but rather a society whose stereotypes about veterans, disability, and mental health have prevented it from fully understanding and appreciating the valour, heroism, and contributions of those who serve in the armed forces. Distinguishing between these two companies and their approaches is important, because their shared interest in veterans often results in their being conflated, even among classical scholars. Such is the case, for example, in James Romm's review of Aquila's *Our Trojan War* (2017).

For, despite the critical distinctions in these two companies' work with veterans, Romm haphazardly groups them together and dismissively describes them as the 'heirs' of clinical psychiatrist Jonathan Shay's approach, which has famously argued that Greek theatre was 'a theater of combat veterans, by combat veterans, and for combat veterans'.[66] Romm questions Shay's comparison of the ancient and modern experi-ence of PTS stating that ancient warfare, and by extension the hoplite

---

[65] Pawlyk (2015).   [66] Shay (2002) 152.

soldier, had little in common with any modern counterpart.[67] Fearful that Aquila and Theater of War will diminish the 'noble old poems' of the Greeks (as if that were possible), he argues:

With its universality and range of meaning, the *Iliad* has gripped readers in many ages and societies, both peaceful and belligerent. It is not, in the end, a poem about war but rather about life and death, which stand out in starker relief on the battlefield than in any other setting. One can read it with great feeling and insight without having taken part in war oneself, though the implied assumptions of 'Our Trojan War' and similarly Shay-inspired productions seems [*sic*] to argue otherwise. The sight of Achilles in a flak jacket, searching for I.E.D.s with shaky hands and a twitchy trigger finger, gives us too simple and reassuring a peg on which to hang these noble old poems. Veterans need to read and discuss them, but so do we all.[68]

Although questioning the cultural specificity of PTS is an important point, what is odd about Romm's review is that he first criticizes Shay's approach for its ahistorical reading of PTS (a view which he then applies to Aquila with no regard for the post-show event), but, as this quotation demonstrates, he himself hearkens to the 'universality' of the *Iliad*. He also closes with the statement, 'Veterans need to read and discuss them [the noble old poems], but so do we all', a statement which ignores the fact that the 'we all' of the ancient audience was in fact veterans. This final sentence which separates, or segregates, 'veterans' from the 'we all' who can read the ancients 'with great feeling and insight without having taken part in war oneself' reveals exactly the mindset against which Aquila and Theater of War are working.

Aquila Theatre Company

Although founded in 1991 by Dr Peter Meineck (the company's translator and lighting designer, who holds the endowed chair of professor of Classics in the Modern World at New York University), Aquila, since 2011, has been under the artistic directorship of Desiree Sanchez, a former principal dancer with the Metropolitan Opera Ballet whose study of movement therapy at the New School for Social Research has influenced her directing and her work with veterans in particular. Aquila is now one of the foremost producers:

---

[67] Romm (2017). On this point, Romm references Crowley (2012).
[68] Romm (2017).

of touring classical theater in the United States with an international reach, visiting 50–60 American cities per year and traveling abroad with a program of two plays, workshops and educational programming. The company is regularly funded by the National Endowment for the Arts, the National Endowment for the Humanities, the New York State Councils for the Arts and Humanities, and the New York City Department of Cultural Affairs, and has performed at the White House on two separate occasions. Aquila has also received a Chairman's Special Award from the National Endowment for the Humanities for its innovative applied theater public programming.[69]

Although the company has staged national tours and critically acclaimed performances for such prestigious audiences as the president and first lady of the United States and members of the US Supreme Court, and at venues such as Lincoln Center and Carnegie Hall, the heart of Aquila's work takes place at schools and local public libraries.[70] Aiming to bring 'the greatest theatrical works to the greatest number', Aquila has earned accolades for providing 'the only chance many areas get to see serious plays' and for taking 'the classics off their pedestals' and presenting them as 'live action, flesh and blood adventures'.[71]

Although the company has a diverse array of projects, its National Endowment for the Humanities-funded public programmes Page and Stage Ancient Greeks/Modern Lives, You|Stories: Ancient and Modern Narratives of War, and Warrior Chorus (all of which I have participated in as a local programme scholar) have focused on using Greek drama to educate the public about the needs and concerns of US veterans. Each grant programme is distinct and builds on the knowledge and experience of the previous programmes. Whereas Ancient Greeks/Modern Lives had one module which addressed veterans, You|Stories and Warrior Chorus[72] have been developed in response to requests for more work with veterans.

---

[69] http://www.aquilatheatre.com/history/, accessed 25 September 2016.

[70] For example, Aquila has programmes such as Theatre Breakthrough, which gives school-age children the opportunity to witness professional live theatre, Workshop America, where people of all backgrounds and ages can explore the creative process of theatre, and Shakespeare Leaders and Greek Drama, a project in which students learned the skills of responsibility, professional conduct, and self-worth in the process of staging full performances of Shakespeare and Greek theatre in local communities and at a New York City theatre.

[71] Press quotes from the *New York Times* and *Dramatics Magazine* respectively, quoted in http://www.aquilatheatre.com, accessed 5 July 2016.

[72] Developing a way to provide jobs, artistic control, and funding directly to veterans, in 2016 Aquila began a new two-year National Endowment for the Humanities-funded initiative titled Warrior Chorus, which provides a new model for veteran engagement.

Like Outside the Wire's Theater of War programme, Aquila makes no claims to be a disability theatre company or to work with or for the disabled community. However, through my study here, I want to demonstrate the ways in which the company's work, by and for veterans, engages with concerns crucial to combating stereotypes, particularly those about the mental health of veterans. In order to do so, I here focus on a performance that was part of the You|Stories programme: *A Female Philoctetes*, directed and adapted by Desiree Sanchez and advised by Kristen Rouse, an Afghanistan veteran.[73]

Aquila's *A Female Philoctetes*

'You|Stories has been a national program aimed at members of the Veteran community and the public that uses ancient stories about war to inspire new stories ... [It] has visited over 120 towns in 34 states

The programme is 'a national initiative that trains veterans to present innovative public programs based on ancient literature. Programming performed by veterans will focus on critical social issues including war, conflict, comradeship, home, and family and will include veteran-led readings, discussions and the innovative use of New Media', http://www.aquilatheatre.com/warrior-chorus/, accessed 5 July 2016. The performers are veterans, who are assisted by scholars, and 'members of the chorus will develop their own area of artistic/humanities interest within the program to present unique events reflective of their particular skills. These can be, but are not limited to, acting, directing, dramaturgy, producing, writing, visual arts, photography, dance, etc.', http://www.warriorchorus.org/-what-we-do, accessed 5 July 2016.

[73] In April of 2016, Aquila presented *Philoctetes* with the acclaimed actor and veteran Richard Chaves in the title role. The mixed-gender cast were all veterans who had served in Vietnam, Iraq, and Afghanistan and in the Marines, Army Rangers, Navy, and Air Force. The actors rewrote the words of the chorus with their own words based on their own experiences. Jacquelyn Claire's (2016) review of the work commended Desiree Sanchez's direction: 'Her extensive background in dance allows her to draw exquisite physicality from the performers. She has shone a blinding light onto the personal atrocities of war with this clean, uncluttered production.' And Tim O'Brien (2016) commented:

> This is no gimmick; the performers are also accomplished actors and writers, many of them have been trained at the best institutions and acted onstage, in film and on television. Among them are published poets, produced playwrights and teachers. Highly skilled, they are the cream of the crop, like the author of *Philoctetes* himself, the highly educated war veteran who may have been the greatest playwright who ever lived, Sophocles.

Marcina Zaccaria (2016) said that Sanchez's direction 'sways toward the operatic. Taking advantage of every skill of the veterans, Sanchez very carefully asks these former soldiers to make sense of every word. Ideas in text find universality, as the Warrior Chorus comments on the action.'

reaching over 120,000 people.'[74] The programme has included performances, staged readings, reading groups, and public talks; and also an
award-winning app and web platform (www.youstories.com) through
which people are able to upload their own video stories to be archived
at the Library of Congress. As part of this programme, Aquila staged
A Female Philoctetes to generate a public discussion about women
veterans by casting a woman in the title role of Sophocles' ancient
tragedy about the mythological hero Philoctetes.[75]

Philoctetes, the Greeks' greatest archer, has an incurable festering,
stinking wound to his foot caused by a snakebite in a sanctuary. Because
his comrades cannot bear his cries of pain or the stench of his festering
wound, they abandon the injured warrior on a distant island until ten
years later, when they discover that the war cannot be won without the
soldier's magical bow. While other ancient dramatists had also staged
versions of the Philoctetes myth, one of Sophocles' innovations[76] was to
focus on dramatizing the conflict of Neoptolemus, the young son of
Achilles, who must choose between honouring the hero or following
the orders of his scheming commander Odysseus, who has commanded
the young man to trick Philoctetes into giving him the bow. What
Neoptolemus ultimately decides is ambiguous, for the play ends with
the appearance of Heracles *ex machina*, who orders Philoctetes to return
to Troy and predicts that he will be cured and that his help will make the
Greeks victorious.

As Paul Woodruff's commentary for You|Stories explains, the play:

raises questions and leaves them hanging for us to answer. As a society we should
ponder these questions as we continue to prepare for war, and especially before
we enter a new war: can we teach youngsters the arts of war, including subterfuge,
without destroying their ethical character? Can we overcome the isolation of
veterans who have been wounded in body and soul? Is victory important enough
to warrant the whole cost of war?[77]

---

[74] http://www.aquilatheatre.com/youstories/, accessed 5 July 2016.

[75] In recent times, some have interpreted the story of Philoctetes as a metaphor for
AIDS, with Philoctetes as a plagued outcast. See, e.g. James (2007).

[76] According to Woodruff (2014), Sophocles' innovations include placing Philoctetes on
a deserted island, introducing Neoptolemus, and ending the play with Heracles as the *deus
ex machina*.

[77] http://youstories.com/public/uploads/resources/documents/9DDB642B-AA28-E9DA-
F376-E659EF65AD31.pdf, accessed 5 July 2016.

Such complex questions are ones that Aquila explores at its events under the guidance of Classics professors, who serve as moderators to explain historical context and offer their expert insights. After the production of *A Female Philoctetes*, which was advertised as a staged reading but premiered in sold-out performances in April 2014 at Brooklyn Academy of Music's (BAM) Fisher Hillman Studio, Meineck moderated the post-performance discussion together with American combat veterans and the Aquila artists who performed the roles.[78]

In this production, the script followed the Sophocles closely apart from referencing the title character as 'she'. This artistic choice, as opposed to one that would adapt the text significantly, could have frustrated some women in the audience, for such was the case when Outside the Wire presented a female *Ajax*. The women veterans in the audience, who were:

unfamiliar with the Greek play or myth and were not prompted at the outset to recognize that this was an imagined rewrite of an ancient source ... [were] ... struck by the absence of any mention of sex-related belittling and other tensions, including sexual violence, inflicted on female soldiers by their fellow troops, as well as the particular kind of stigmas female veterans suffer in civilian life.[79]

Perhaps because of its academic approach which I later discuss, Aquila avoided such criticism with its presentation of *A Female Philoctetes*, which demonstrates how the simple substitution of casting an actor

---

[78] The following year, on 18 June 2016, Aquila produced The Warrior Chorus: Arts and Humanities in Action, a veteran-led national initiative hosted by Aquila Theatre with New York University, Columbia University, the University of Texas at Austin, and the University of Southern California. The programme trains veterans to present innovative public programmes to Americans based on classical literature. It uses readings from ancient Greek and Roman drama, accompanied by modern works created by veterans and inspired by the readings. Guided by Dr Peter Meineck, a public discussion follows, as the programme aims 'to foster meaningful dialogue between the veteran and civilian communities', www.warriorchorus.org, accessed 25 September 2016.

[79] Lodewyck and Monoson (2015) 658. According to Bryan Doerries, other women identified with the performance and made comments, as he recalled, such as:

How profoundly sad [one woman] thought it was that it required Ajax's killing herself for people to finally come out of the woodwork to fight over her respect and honour and to acknowledge that they respected and honoured her. She said I walk through the halls along with my female colleagues on a daily basis and it feels sometimes that we would have to die before anyone would ever acknowledge or respect us in a way that Ajax was respected at the end of the play. And for me that was a profoundly different perspective on what this play had to say to an audience.   (Cohen and Rogers 2011)

who identifies as a woman in the title role would affect the play's reception. By preserving the language and plot of the classical tragedy, the audience could draw its own conclusions about the connections between the gendered experiences of ancient and modern veterans; and these topics have been the subject of the post-performance discussions at the various productions in locations such as New York, London, and Athens.[80]

Although *A Female Philoctetes* was not reviewed, it received some attention in the media. On *The Diane Rehm Show*, the National Endowment for the Humanities Chairman and Vietnam veteran William Adams mentioned that the show 'deeply moved' him.[81] National Public Radio also ran a story about it on its 'All Things Considered' programme, where Sanchez explained that the play is about post-traumatic stress: 'Her [Philoctetes'] wound is more of a psychological wound. And you really get the sense that it's something that not only she has to deal with, but other people don't want to deal with.'[82]

Unlike theatre reviews, this type of media coverage, limited though it was, gave the veterans performing in the show a platform with direct access to speak to a wider audience about their concerns. For example, Kristin Rouse, the Afghanistan veteran who advised on the production, commented that the play:

is not just about—is war a good idea? Is war a bad idea? Here's how Sophocles really got it that long ago—to really communicate—to bridge that divide between people who have been to war and people who have not—or to—rather, to the people who sent us to war. To really communicate the seriousness of what all that means.[83]

Ken Goode, a former Marine, both in this interview and on a video uploaded through the You|Stories app, made a comparison between Philoctetes' nine-year abandonment, during which he suffered excruciating pain on the island of Lemnos, and US veterans' inability to receive medical care in a timely manner because of the inordinately long waits at the Veterans Affairs hospitals.[84] In addition to this media coverage, Aquila's

---

[80] The performance in July 2015 was staged at the Michael Cacoyannis Foundation's Cultural Centre in Athens, Greece, with support from Theatre Communications Group as a Global Connections grant recipient.

[81] Rehm (2014).   [82] Lawrence (2014).   [83] Lawrence (2014).

[84] Lawrence (2014); Goode (2014); https://vimeo.com/93654610, accessed 5 July 2016.

Michael Castelblanco, who served eight years on active duty and two years in the reserves, attaining the rank of Staff Sergeant in the Marines, published an article in Theatre Communications Group's magazine about his experience of performing in *A Female Philoctetes* while working with refugees in Athens.[85]

Seeing, hearing, and reading the words of veterans such as these helps civilians learn about and understand the experience of war from an unfiltered first-hand perspective. Moreover, hearing veterans, such as Castelblanco, who is a linguist fluent in four languages, conversant in an additional nine, and a musician who plays eight instruments, speak intelligently and passionately about classical literature also helps to debunk the pernicious 'uneducated, Joe Sixpack' stereotype that contributes to the division between the veteran and civilian communities. In the words of Kleycamp, 'You get a sense of what veterans are as a group sometimes through their unfiltered perspectives.'[86] These perspectives challenge stereotypes at each of Aquila's events in a variety of communities across the country.

To illustrate this work more specifically, I here focus on a You|Stories event in which key scenes from *A Female Philoctetes* were performed on 13 June 2015 at the John Jay Homestead in Katonah, in the state of New York. In the ballroom of the historic homestead and before about one hundred audience members comprised primarily of white middle-aged Westchester residents, the company presented scenes, complete with musical accompaniment and choral song and dance. The actors, all veterans, wore black combat trousers and black vests. In contrast, the female Philoctetes wore a cropped white vest and green combat shorts that left her injured foot exposed (Figure 5.1). The movement in the performance gave the scenes a 'masculine' physicality, as Sanchez incorporated military movement and worked with all the veterans to incorporate their physicality into the choreography. Like their performance in the premiere of *A Female Philoctetes* at BAM, the chorus' exquisite movement and choreography, performed by young men in the peak of physical condition, while singing an emotional score, were a highlight

---

[85] http://www.tcgcircle.org/2015/07/veteran-performance-in-a-female-philoctetes/, accessed 5 July 2016.

[86] Pawlyk (2015).

Figure 5.1 Philoctetes with bow and the chorus in Aquila Theatre Company's *A Female Philocetes*, directed by Desiree Sanchez at the Brooklyn Academy of Music. 2014.

Photo © 2014 Richard Termine.

of the evening (Figure 5.2).[87] If the skill, artistry, and intellectual and emotional depth of these choral movements could not succeed in debunking the 'uneducated Joe Sixpack' stereotype of veterans, then the veteran-led conversation following the performance surely did.

After an hour's presentation of key scenes from the play and a standing ovation from the audience, Meineck presented a quick intro-duction that explained the key differences between ancient veterans and those of today. He provided historical context, such as that *Philoctetes* is the only Greek tragedy without a woman, but in Greek terms, the wounded hero was a feminized character. He used historical detail to raise complex questions about the play, for example, how the fact that the

---

[87] For scenes of the play, see https://vimeo.com/95354175, accessed 5 July 2016.

Figure 5.2 The chorus in Aquila Theatre Company's *A Female Philocetes*, directed by Desiree Sanchez at the Brooklyn Academy of Music. 2014.
Photo © 2014 Richard Termine.

same ancient actor who played Odysseus would probably have played the role of Heracles raises the question of whether Odysseus is pretending to be the god and tricking Philoctetes into coming to Troy. While continuing to contextualize and complicate the ancient material in this way, he kept the focus of the evening on veterans and their families by also making statements such as that America now has 2.5 million returning veterans who are bringing back experiences that could in fact lead to another golden age of the arts, as happened in ancient Greece.

After these remarks, Meineck introduced Aquila's director Desiree Sanchez and the company's actors, many of whom are veterans and members of the Society for Artistic Veterans, such as Michael Castelblanco, who played the Chorus Leader, and Caleb Wells, a Marine deployed to Iraq and former Director of the Marine Corp Shooting Team, who played Odysseus. Before the actors took the lead, Sanchez explained that the company typically has more women veterans, but they were unavailable for this particular performance. Nevertheless, the male veterans, together with the women in the audience, and Julia Crockett, who played Philoctetes, added their particular insights into this ancient work while also sharing various anecdotes from women in the armed forces.

For example, although Crockett is not a veteran, she spoke on issues affecting veterans who identify as women. She explained that those who had seen this production often talked about how they had had to prove they had a right to be in combat. 'When you put a woman in this role,' Crockett stated, 'there are so many immediate political issues that arise . . . Seeing a woman with all of these men . . . thinking of sexual assault . . . What is the wound? . . . [It's] not just a physical wound but also a psychological wound.' Her remarks prompted an audience member who grew up in a military family to share her own experience with psychological abuse that derived not from sexual trauma but from simply being a woman. 'The wound for women', she stated, 'was just being a woman, because everything always revolved around men . . . women lived in isolation . . . during Vietnam especially, they were real social outcasts too.' Philoctetes' wound thus took on a variety of meanings for women in the armed forces, not just sexual violence.

Like Philoctetes, women and transgender veterans can be abandoned. They struggle with a lack of recognition, for, whereas men are acknowledged as 'true veterans', not all vets get respect. Sarah Blum, a decorated nurse and Vietnam veteran has stated, 'Many women complain that when they are waiting to be served in line at the VA, the person taking down information will literally look past the woman in line to the men, as though, in their mind, only men are veterans.'[88] According to Gayle Tzemach Lemmon, 'Whether you're male or female transitioning out of the military is challenging . . . But from what I've seen, it's just that much harder when you're female. People don't think you've seen combat and that couldn't be further from the truth in some cases.'[89] Lemmon has also spoken about the 'dismissive mentality and invisibility women experience at VA centers. On a regular basis, I'm mistaken for a spouse of a male veteran, completely overlooked by healthcare staff, or cut in line by male patients oblivious to my presence.'[90] Lemmon attributes this invisibility, in part, to the dearth of women in the armed forces represented in popular culture, for 'at a time when so few Americans serve, movies often offer people's only exposure to combat, shaping the way they see who fights the nation's battles'.[91] Moreover, when people do see women veterans

[88] Dolsen (2015). [89] Dolsen (2015).
[90] Dolsen (2015). [91] Lemmon (2015).

represented, 'the victim narrative has overtaken all others in recent years when it comes to the story of women in uniform'.[92]

Aquila has helped to replace this stereotype of victimized women veterans with an image of them as heroes by giving real-life women veterans a public platform to speak about their experiences on the battlefield. By presenting the strong but lithe Crockett (Figure 5.1) in the midst of the masculine energy of the chorus, it raises questions about the ways in which the gendered behaviour in the armed forces contrasts with the gendered behaviour to which women in civilian life are expected to conform. At the same time, while addressing a variety of concerns specific to women veterans, the discussion does not shy away from the problem of sexual assault. Instead, Aquila 'names' the problem, discusses it, but also does not present the issue as the only one, or even the primary one, affecting the armed forces.

For example, without dwelling on the specific issue of sexual violence, the actors/panellists presented the play's theme of 'moral injury'[93] that can result from soldiers taking orders from dishonourable superiors. Castelblanco raised awareness about this type of injury by commenting on Neoptolemus' struggle in dealing with commanders who are not honourable. Wells followed up by stating that as an officer he would not tell his men to do something that he would not do, and he wished that the president had served in the armed forces because then he would have a better idea of what it means to send people to war.

This discussion of moral injury raised in the context of *A Female Philoctetes* acknowledged the disabilities that can result not only from suffering sexual trauma but also from reporting it. For 'sometimes veterans develop post-traumatic stress disorder more from the retaliation that occurs when they report the crime than from the sexual assault itself. This is especially

---

[92] Lemmon (2015).

[93] Jonathan Shay, a retired Veterans Affairs psychiatrist and author of the acclaimed *Achilles in Vietnam*, has explained 'moral injury' as:

> when there has been (a) a betrayal of 'what's right'; (b) either by a person in legitimate authority (my definition), or by one's self—'I did it' (Litz, Maguen, Nash, et al.); (c) in a high stakes situation. Both forms of moral injury impair the capacity for trust, and elevate despair, suicidality, and interpersonal violence. They deteriorate character. (Shay 2014: 182)

For further reading on the moral wounds of soldiers, see Sherman (2015).

true for those veterans who served in prior wars, such as Vietnam, before there were any resources or recognition of these types of crimes.'[94]

Thus, by generating a conversation about women veterans specifically, Aquila engages in 'naming' and thus destigmatizing the wounds of sexual trauma and moral injury, and in educating the public about the mental and physical disabilities that can be caused by them. Such work is important because: 'For service members managing the effects of unwarranted and unwanted sexual violence and trauma, recent research by the Service Women's Action Network shows only 32 per cent of military sexual trauma-related post-traumatic stress claims are approved compared to 54 per cent of other post-traumatic stress claims.'[95]

In the words of Meineck:

By using these ancient stories and discussing them, what happens is we discuss . . . subjects people sometimes are uncomfortable talking about . . . What then happens is we ask the vets to contribute their knowledge and their experience, and now we're having a conversation about the 'uncomfortable' themes in our culture—but it never gets political. It only validates the conversation.[96]

By providing a forum for these veteran-led conversations, Aquila replaces the Hollywood stereotype of the victimized 'disabled veteran' with an image of veterans as strong, artistic, intellectual, emotional, healthy—in fact, beautiful—but also vulnerable, breakable, and ultimately human.

Outside the Wire's Theater of War

Unlike Aquila events, which always invite a civilian and military audience, some of Outside the Wire's Theater of War events have been closed to military personnel on bases. In addition, while Aquila is a non-profit professional theatre company that stages critically acclaimed productions, in addition to its local library projects, Outside the Wire, in its function as a for-profit social-impact company, offers only readings of the Greek material. Although the company now addresses a variety of

---

[94] http://www.nolo.com/legal-encyclopedia/getting-disability-compensation-military-sexual-trauma.html, accessed 10 July 2016.

[95] Dolsen (2015). This discrepancy may be due in part to the 'higher burden of proof the Veterans Benefits Administration imposes on service members in order to attach military sexual trauma to a claim for disability benefits'.

[96] Pawlyk (2015).

social issues, such as addiction, end of life, acts of violence, and incarceration, Theater of War was the company's first outreach programme.

The project was inspired by an article in the *Washington Post* on 18 February 2007 that described the mouldy, cockroach- and rodent-infested Walter Reade facility. There, veterans suffering from 'brain injuries, severed arms and legs, organ and back damage', and various degrees of post-traumatic stress were released from hospital beds but 'awaiting bureaucratic decisions before being discharged or returned to active service duty'.[97] From a motivation to improve such social conditions rather than simply create theatre, Outside the Wire was born.[98]

Since receiving its initial opportunity to present a reading before a military audience at the United States Marine Corps Combat Stress Conference in 2008:

Theater of War Productions has presented over 300 performances of Sophocles' *Ajax* and *Philoctetes* for military and civilian audiences throughout the United States, Europe, and Japan ... at military sites as diverse as the Pentagon, Guantanamo Bay, Army posts throughout Germany, VA Hospitals, Walter Reed Army Medical Center, homeless shelters, high school auditoriums, theaters, and churches ... [before] service members and veterans from the US Army, Navy, Air Force, Marine Corps, Coast Guard, Special Forces, National Guard, and Reserves, as well as high-ranking officials from the Department of Defense and the Department of Veterans Affairs.[99]

From June 2016, Outside the Wire received generous grants from the Pentagon, the Stavros Niarchos Foundation, and the Bristol-Myers Squibb Foundation. It has collaborated with institutions such as Massachusetts General Hospital Academy, National Council for Behavioral Health, and Points of Light. The company has performed for 'over

---

[97] Priest and Hull (2007).

[98] According to Wyatt Mason (2014: 63), after facing many closed doors initially, Doerries introduced himself to Captain William P. Nash, a combat- and operational stress-control coordinator for the Marines, who was quoted in the *New York Times* as telling carers in the US that if they wanted to understand their new ex-military patients, they needed to read Sophocles' *Ajax*. With Captain Nash, Doerries brokered his first performance presenting his translations of *Ajax* and *Philoctetes* to 400 Marines and their spouses at a military conference. In the process, Doerries attracted the attention of General Sutton, who subsequently hired him to present a hundred performances on bases around the world.

[99] http://www.outsidethewirellc.com/projects/theater-of-war/overview, accessed 17 June 2006.

80,000 service members, veterans, and their families [who] have attended and participated in Theater of War performances and discussions'.[100]

At these events, not veterans but professional actors perform. Some even include Hollywood stars such as Frances McDormand, Paul Giamatti, Jake Gyllenhaal, Jesse Eisenberg, and Adam Driver,[101] who sit behind a table and microphone to deliver select speeches from Sophocles' *Ajax* or *Philoctetes*. Following these readings, typically four panellists, who are affiliated with the armed forces in some way, offer their unprepared, gut responses before the moderator and Outside the Wire's founder Bryan Doerries opens the discussion to the audience.

As Doerries has explained, this audience discussion, not the readings, is the highlight of the performance; and the actors' and panellists' jobs are in effect to make the audience feel comfortable or 'give them permission' to speak about their emotional experience of serving and returning home. In this sense, the events work almost like group therapy without the label of psychological counselling that so many members of the armed forces fear will stigmatize them or prevent them from getting security clearance, jobs, or even admission to higher education.[102] However, Doerries is careful to clarify that these events are not therapy. For example, after his work was advertised as 'Using Sophocles to Treat PTSD',[103] Doerries commented that he was uncomfortable with that title because 'we don't characterize Theater of War as therapy'.[104]

However, while the company does not provide psychological counselling per se, the events have surely done much to encourage audiences to consider the possibility of seeking counselling or even simply speaking about their emotions to their spouses and families. For the company's core concepts and values are not primarily to produce theatre but rather to use dramatic readings to 'create safe environments for open dialogue about difficult and sometimes divisive subjects'.[105] In this way, Doerries aims not to entertain but to 'elicit open and honest emotional responses' and 'engender empathy, humility, and understanding in diverse audiences' while empowering 'community members, from a variety of

---

[100] http://www.outsidethewirellc.com/projects/theater-of-war/overview, accessed 28 February 2018.
[101] Driver is a veteran.   [102] Brown (2010).
[103] Mason (2014).   [104] Decaul (2015).
[105] http://www.outsidethewirellc.com/about/mission, accessed 16 September 2016.

perspectives . . . about community-based public health and social issues to respond directly to the issues raised by our performances'.[106]

His Theater of War project in particular aims to 'de-stigmatize psychological injury, increase awareness of post-deployment psychological health issues, disseminate information on available resources, and foster greater family, community, and troop resilience'.[107] In other words, as he has stated, he is something like the Phil Donahue[108] of ancient Greek drama. His interest rests in using the readings as a catalyst for discussion. He claims that 'These ancient plays timelessly and universally depict the psychological and physical wounds inflicted upon warriors by war' and that they can 'forge a common vocabulary for openly discussing the impact of war on individuals, families, and communities'.[109]

Outside the Wire/Theater of War's *Ajax*

A closer look at a Theater of War event will demonstrate the ways in which the company works specifically to combat stereotypes about veterans both among civilians and within the armed forces themselves. As with Aquila's staging in Katonah, the event took place in what (compared to New York City) seemed like the middle of nowhere, this time on a dark, rainy winter's night at Fort Tilden, in Rockaway, New York. There, in the off-the-beaten track places that make up Theater of War's home, television and stage actors Zach Grenier and Marin Ireland read Doerries' translation of key scenes from Sophocles' *Ajax*, such as Tecmessa's pleas to Ajax to protect her safety and their child's, and the hero's famous suicide speech. They delivered a powerful reading of these scenes to a mixed military and civilian audience consisting of about sixty Euro-Americans, primarily, of a variety of ages.

Ajax depicts the suicide of the great warrior Ajax, who, driven mad by the goddess Athena, violently slaughters, in a frenzied state of mind,

---

[106] http://www.outsidethewirellc.com/about/mission, accessed 16 September 2016.

[107] http://www.outsidethewirellc.com/about/mission, accessed 16 September 2016.

[108] A popular American media personality whose television programme *Donahue* was the first US chat show to include audience participation. The programme was broadcast nationwide between 1970 and 1996.

[109] http://www.outsidethewirellc.com/projects/theater-of-war/overview, accessed 16 September 2016.

livestock, instead of his intended target of the Greek generals who had disrespected him by awarding the armour of his dear friend, the great hero Achilles, to the wily politician Odysseus instead of him. The second half of the play deals with the aftermath of the suicide. It depicts a debate between Ajax's half-brother Teucer and the Greek leaders Agamemnon and Menelaus over whether the soldier's corpse should be buried or dishonoured. Finally, Odysseus steps in and persuades the Greeks to bury Ajax, so even though he does not receive the hero's burial he would have otherwise received, Ajax can still be laid to rest.

As is the format with all of Theater of War's productions, Doerries introduced the programme and summarized the play up to the point of the actors' readings. Then, when the actors had finished, Doerries summarized the play's ending before he introduced panellists who offered their spontaneous, gut responses before Doerries moderated an audience discussion that he centred on questions that he said he asked at all events across the globe.

He asked why General Sophocles wrote this play and staged it. The audience members at Fort Tilden responded with comments such as that the general was trying to prepare soldiers for the reality of war and that he wanted to explore the gulf between the politicians and the people they were sending to war. In between such comments, Doerries kept the discussion moving by responding to the audience with comments, such as *Ajax* is the play that says this is the experience that we should make a communal experience.

Doerries' next question was about Tecmessa's line 'Twice the pain is twice the sorrow.' He asked the audience what she meant and what that line meant to them, as he quickly followed the question with an explanation of a RAND Corporation study which reported that military spouses were becoming carers for the more than 40,000 servicemen suffering from injuries that would have killed them in any other war. Doerries commented that women said that they had spent sixty years of their lives as carers for different generations of their family. To which an audience member responded, 'It seems like a 1,000 years of pain.' Another audience member then introduced the idea of moral injury, which Doerries defined before stating that *Ajax* is a play about moral injury because the hero's anger over losing Achilles' armour is connected to the overwhelming grief he felt for the loss of his friend.

This point led to Doerries' third question about the number of times we might have left people alone on sand dunes like Ajax. A panellist responded by speaking about a friend who lost one of his legs and whose wife later left because of his alcoholism. His friend told the story as he was cleaning the 45-calibre pistol he had wondered about using to kill himself. To which another panellist responded that, upon returning from war, people do not recognize you. In the midst of this audience discussion, Doerries continued to interject comments that helped to frame the conversation and connect it to *Ajax*.

The event continued by touching on topics such as boosting morale, healing the spirit of units, the effect of victory parades, and developing rituals that would help veterans to heal, before Doerries ended with his fourth and final question, asking the audience what they would do if Ajax were their friend and they were with him on the sand dune? To which one audience member responded by sharing a story about when his friend confided in him about his thoughts of suicide and he responded by beating his friend up until blood came from his nose and they looked at each other and laughed. With his charming, low-key style and cheerful sense of humour, Doerries quipped that this approach might not be for everyone! After the audience shared a laugh, one member reminded everyone of the suicide hotline number: 1-800-273-Talk.

At 8.00 p.m., after two hours, Doerries closed with what he referred to as his 'benediction'—that if he had one message to deliver from General Sophocles it would be that you are not alone and that Sophocles wanted to help. He then shared that this was Theater of War's 281st performance.

Doerries has described the direction of such events as coming from the audience. At the same time, he considers the term 'talkback' to be:

kind of a dirty word. We're trying to change the relationship between theatre and audience, and by doing so we're actually privileging the discussion, the town-hall discussion, over the performance. We're not privileging the audience over the performers; everyone has a role to play . . . The performers come out of their element . . . and they take a risk . . . because they go for broke . . . and then we have community members who come up and they respond in the moment from their guts to what they heard and saw, and they take a huge risk. And they're our chorus. They're mediating the event between the audience and the actors . . . And then we ask the audience to take a much huger risk which is to get up and bear witness to the truth of what they just heard as it relates to their own experiences individually and as a community. We all have a role to play in this equation, but unfortunately in the theatre, where you go to see plays performed and then to hear people expound about them afterward, during talkbacks or panel discussions, that fluid relationship between all of us, that sort of equality in our relationship that we're trying to create in Theater of War, we don't see represented. So one of the first things we do after the performance is get them [the actors] off the stage, because it's about the community... Most of the time the community is grateful for the opportunity to speak, and to have been given permission by way of the actors' performances to express emotions that were taboo and anathema prior to that moment.[110]

Through this model, Doerries aims to generate the type of social conversations that puncture the silence surrounding the subject of mental health, the very silence that results from the stigmas, taboos, and stereotypes surrounding those who seek mental health care.

The authority of the classical text and its ability to express the pain, sorrow, and suffering of heroes and their families mitigate the stigma and social shame associated with emotions that seem to find little place in a culture that thrives on a love for the happy ending. According to Doerries, 'the text becomes the language that people use to connect.'[111] The words of the text work to shatter the silence surrounding these feelings and emotions, a silence that Sergeant Eubanks has described as contributing to the vicious cycle of isolation and anger.[112] By encouraging the social conversations and the bonds that prevent isolation, Theater of War, like Aquila, functions in the manner of disability theatre by using classical drama to break the silence that fosters the myths and stereotypes surrounding the mental health care of veterans. Thus, the therapy that these companies offer is not for any individual per se but rather for a society that does not yet fully understand and accept the importance of mental health and the effect of war upon it.

Reinforcing the 'Disabled Veteran' Stereotype

The benefits of Aquila and Theater of War in educating the public about veterans' affairs are clear. However, despite the advantages of these programmes, it is important to examine the possibility that this work could also be counterproductive, a point which veterans and their

---

[110] Cohen and Rogers (2011).   [111] Cohen and Rogers (2011).
[112] Brown (2010).

families have sometimes made about Theater of War events. For example, one viewer of a Theater of War YouTube video commented:

In my opinion, they are making a mockery out of PTSD and something like PTSD is no joking matter. The very first time I saw this was in my Ancient Greek Literature class and I immediately became offended by it because I have family members that have PTSD and when I showed them and other military service men/women all of them got offended by this because it is NOT a good representation of PTSD.[113]

The viewer explained that the programme offended her because 'it is NOT a good representation of PTSD', so she seemed to take issue not with the audience discussion at an event but with the comparison made between Ajax's mania and PTS. In other words, she seemed to question the notion, often iterated at Theater of War gatherings, but avoided by Aquila, that the experience of PTS is somehow 'universal'.

For Outside the Wire's website claims that 'these ancient plays *timelessly and universally* [my italics] depict the psychological and physical wounds inflicted upon warriors by war',[114] and panellists and audience members also sometimes echo these claims. For example, one panellist at a Theater of War event I attended commented, 'The pain, the suffering, the sorrow is universal.' Moreover, the series of four questions that Doerries asks at each event frames the discussion of veterans' experiences in a way that erases the historical difference between ancient and modern.

By framing the modern-day veterans' experiences in terms of Ajax's, the questions do not encourage the audience to maintain a critical intellectual distance but rather to identify emotionally with the ancient character by asking, for example, what would we do if Ajax were our friend? Because of the nature of these questions and the programme encouraging the audience to identify emotionally with the material (in the manner of Aristotle) instead of maintaining an intellectual and critical distance (in the manner of Brecht), I disagree with Lodewyck and Monoson's claim that Theater of War operates in the manner of Boal's Theatre of the Oppressed,[115] for more is required of Boal's approach than simply serving a social, as opposed to an aesthetic, purpose.

---

[113] https://www.youtube.com/watch?v=Fus0JYIxFtk, accessed 25 September 2016.
[114] http://www.outsidethewirellc.com/projects/theater-of-war/overview,   accessed   25 September 2016.
[115] Lodewyck and Monoson (2015).

As Helen Morales has suggested, questions such as these are excellent for packaging material, making it accessible, or 'marketing' it for for-profit purposes, like Doerries' books, which are on display for sale at each event, but the approach risks simplifying the material.[116] It erases the complex meanings and historical specificity that provide a vantage point from which the modern world can learn. Instead of leading a discussion informed by current scholarship and inviting audience-led debates on a variety of topics, in the manner of Aquila events, Theater of War limits the historical perspective by framing the discussion and predetermining answers by narrowing the choice of questions.

One combat veteran who deployed to Afghanistan and was in the audience at a Theater of War event nervously expressed this opinion:

> People aren't going to want to hear this but... This is not a collective pain... The war they [the Greeks] fought was over a woman [Helen] who was considered chattel... The war they fought runs counter to our values of democracy... At the same time as this play revered veterans, it also muted and subordinated the voices of women and committed moral injury to the civilian population.

This veteran's comments challenged the entire premise of Theater of War, or at least the appropriateness of making claims that the emotions recorded in the drama of an androcentric, xenophobic culture form a sort of universalized template from which veterans can learn today.

In response, Doerries thanked the veteran for his insights, but he did not ask a follow-up question to explore further the comment and see where it led the discussion. As a result, the event did not provide the time or space for audience members to think carefully and critically about the distinctions between the past and present. Instead, perhaps because Doerries' interest rests in the universality of 'psychological and physical wounds inflicted upon warriors by war',[117] he proceeded with his mission to use theatre as 'a public health tool' by encouraging people to 'let down

---

[116] See Morales (2016), who in her review of Doerries' *Theater of War* comments on Theater of War's privileging of the emotional over the intellectual and the programme's use of tragedy to validate distress rather than offer political responses which, while true to the spirit of tragedy, could jeopardize funding opportunities. Doerries' 'true genius', according to Morales, is 'his entrepreneurial skills, his orchestration of A-list actors to read his work, and his enabling of people who feel discounted to be given a voice'.

[117] http://www.outsidethewirellc.com/projects/theater-of-war/overview, accessed 25 September 2016.

their guard and to acknowledge that they themselves have felt some of the things they hear on stage'.[118] Moving toward that goal, after Doerries expressed thanks for the comment, he then called on another audience member, who moved the conversation back to a comparison of Ajax's anger to modern-day veterans' PTS.[119]

In this way, Theater of War takes a 'drama therapy' approach,[120] because it asks the audience to connect emotionally with the characters at the expense of acknowledging the historical specificity not only of the play but of emotions themselves. The emotions of the present-day actors serve as a catalyst to evoke the audience's emotions, and these emotions, not the historical content or context, guide the event. This style is in contrast to an educational approach such as Aquila takes, which encourages the audience to see similarities such as those Shay points out, but also to appreciate and think critically about historical distance.[121]

The Disabled Veteran in Context

In her study of physical (as opposed to psychiatric and cognitive) disability in the ancient world, Martha L. Rose has explained that the concept of disability is not universal: 'there is no Greek equivalent for the modern, overarching term "disabled", with its many social and political connotations.'[122] Moreover, 'There was no military, social, or economic

---

[118] Cohen and Rogers (2011).

[119] Doerries eventually returned to the first comment by reiterating that the Athenians were a xenophobic culture in which men wrote the voices of women. However, instead of opening it up to the audience for debate, he countered the point, before quickly moving on to his next question by stating that, despite the culture's anti-democratic views on women and foreigners, Sophocles assigned as many lines in his tragedy to the foreign woman Tecmessa as he did to the Greek hero Ajax. He thus echoed Edith Hall's (1997: 126) comments when she stated that 'Athenian tragedy's claim to having been a truly democratic art-form is . . . paradoxically, far greater than the claim to democracy of the Athenian state itself.'

[120] On drama therapy, see e.g.: http://www.nadta.org/what-is-drama-therapy.html, accessed 14 June 2017.

[121] Of course, emotions and intellect are always intertwined, but my distinction here means not to separate the emotions from the mind but rather to clarify the distinct type of responses that Theater of War and Aquila events aim to elicit.

[122] Rose (2003) 11. As Rose explains, there is, however, 'an extensive list of Greek terms that describe conditions of being maimed, blind, and so on' (11). For further reading on disability in the ancient world, see Ogden (1997), Dasen (2013), and Kelley (2015).

category of the wounded veteran',[123] nor does any 'discussion of disability survive that is composed by a person who identifies himself or herself as disabled',[124] and the Greek material rarely overtly mentions or depicts physical disability at all.[125] Even if one could argue that the effects of combat on the human psyche are 'universal', a culture's attitudes toward trauma and those who experience the physical and psychological effects of war are surely culturally determined. Rose makes this point, stating that 'an inaccurate picture of disability in Greek society results from imposing the models of pity, charity, and categorization of disability onto the ancient Greek material'.[126] Contextualizing disability, as Rose suggests, instead of presenting it as a universal concept, is important not only for improving an understanding of the ancient world, but also for revealing modern-day stereotypes and prejudices about people with disabilities.[127]

Despite these points, Theater of War takes a popular as opposed to an academic approach. Sentimental expressions of universalized emotion replace any post-structuralist scholarly perspective that would scoff at claims that tragedies have the power to 'transcend time'[128] and criticize the use of outdated historical details, such as that the audience consisted of 17,000 citizen soldiers (current studies suggest the number is probably closer to 6,000 and that certain women may have in fact been present) and that the generals sat in the front row with the hoplite cadets at the back of the theatre (exactly when the *prohedria* was instituted is uncertain).[129] The question thus becomes whether the ends justify the means. Does the positive impact of Theater of War events on the thousands of civilians, veterans, and their families who have witnessed them supersede the importance of scholarly rigour and historical accuracy?

[123] Edwards (2000) 66.   [124] Rose (2003) 4.   [125] Rose (2003) 17.
[126] Rose (2003) 6.
[127] Johnston (2016) 15. While some still argue that disability 'has existed throughout human history, cutting across time and space', others such as Rose locate its emergence 'as an idea in western modernity' (4). On the subject of historically and culturally contextualizing the bodily experience of pain, see Scarry (1985).
[128] Doerries (2015) 8.
[129] See Powers (2014) for a discussion of the debates in recent scholarship over such issues. At the events I attended, Doerries made such references. For an example of Doerries stating these outdated details, see the video of an event on 14 November 2011, https://www.youtube.com/watch?v=bAfOgmUUprI, accessed 14 June 2016.

The risk, to me at least, is not necessarily the distortion of the historical record or the missed opportunity of using historical difference as a critical tool in combating stereotypes. The real risk, I would argue, is the inadvertent reinforcement of stereotypes about veterans. By encouraging a universalized sense of emotional 'identification' with Tecmessa's agony and Ajax's suicide, the event focuses on the pity and fear that 'In Western cultures . . . are responses to disability and to the disabled veteran that are continuous over many centuries.'[130]

Emphasizing similarity instead of difference in this way may be an excellent way to encourage people to share their emotions and experiences about war and its effects and to generate the much-needed talk that is a necessary process for so many. However, in choosing to approach the material in this way, Theater of War loses the opportunity to encourage a critical discussion about the ways in which stereotypes about disabled veterans ultimately depend on this same evocation of pity and fear.[131] Thus, in working to combat stereotypes about veterans, Theater of War inadvertently risks employing the very tropes of pity and fear which lead to misrepresentations of veterans in the media.

For Doerries does not ask his audience to think critically about the ways in which historical context influences depictions of mental illness, veterans, and the emotional responses to them, or how conjuring sympathy for disabled veterans and their families can be 'publicly manipulated for instrumental purposes',[132] such as the parade of war orphans at the City Dionysia festival in ancient Athens. He instead asks questions which universalize the experience of Ajax and Tecmessa at the expense of the insights provided by questioning the narrative itself and situating it within its dramatic and historical context, pointing out, for example, that madness in Greek tragedy comes not from any internal inexplicable chemical imbalance, but rather from the gods.[133] The power of tragedy to teach the modern world rests in such critical cultural differences, for they bring into relief contemporary views and prejudices that have been used to reinforce the stereotypes that marginalize US veterans.

---

[130] Gerber (2000) 6.   [131] Gerber (2000) 11.   [132] Gerber (2000) 8.
[133] For an excellent study of the distinction between ancient and modern conceptions of madness, see Padel (1992).

Conclusion

Short of stopping war itself, there is little anyone can do to limit or prevent war from damaging human life, but a culture can change the social stigmas and stereotypes that further the harmful effects of combat. To mitigate these effects on their lives and health, veterans have encouraged civilians not to pity them or laud them as heroes, but instead to work tirelessly to eradicate the stigmas and stereotypes surrounding them. Educating audiences about mental health and veterans' affairs is one key way to achieve this goal, and both Outside the Wire and Aquila have made excellent progress in this direction.

At the same time, despite the well-publicized benefits of Outside the Wire's Theater of War programmes, the critical lens of disability studies has helped to reveal shortcomings in the company's approach. For a disability studies perspective elucidates the risks of discussing PTS in public forums, the fine line between 'exposure and exploitation', between a therapeutic sharing and 'trauma porn', and the questions that arise when money is being made from it.[134] Like the famous Jerry's Kids telethon that has raised money for children with muscular dystrophy, programmes with the best of intentions can also work against the very community they seek to help by appealing to viewers' pity and fear and thus reinforcing stereotypes about disability.

Claims that PTS is as old as Sophocles provide comfort. However, emphasizing universality at the expense of historical difference can obscure the ways in which health and illness are not strictly biological phenomena but are also reflective of culturally and historically constructed ideas and attitudes about the body. On the contrary, a focus on difference, which a study of the ancient world so readily offers, can be a powerful tool in the fight to reveal current cultural trends that contribute to the stigmatization of veterans.

By defining disability as a socially constructed phenomenon dependent upon an unrealistic, culturally constructed concept of an idealized body, the field of disability studies helps to frame a conversation about how to serve veterans better. In the words of Gerber, 'Stereotypes ultimately dependent

---

[134] *The Economist* (2007). As *The Economist*'s 'Democracy in America' column has pointed out, this is the same fine line that the American media must negotiate when covering trauma such as the Virginia Tech mass shooting.

on pity and fear remain', but feminist and disability criticism has the ability to widen the representational field.[135] For the field's emphasis on a culturally specific view of disease, disability, and the body, as opposed to a universal human one, allows for the opportunity to recognize and thereby change the ways in which American cultural attitudes, stereotypes, and stigmas limit the potential and opportunities of US veterans.

[135] Gerber (2000) 11.

Works Cited

Adamitis, J. and Gamel, M.-K. (2013), 'Theaters of War', in D. Lateiner, B. K. Gold, and J. Perkins, eds., *Roman Literature, Gender, and Reception: Domina Illustris: Essays in Honor of Judith Peller Hallett*, Routledge Monographs in Classical Studies 13 (New York: Routledge), 284–301.

Alfaro, L. (1998), 'Downtown', in H. Hughs and D. Román, eds., *O Solo Homo: The New Queer Performance* (New York: Grove Press), 313–48.

Alfaro, L. (2006), '*Electricidad* Playscript', *American Theatre Magazine* 23/2: 63–85.

Alfaro, L. (2011), 'Oedipus El Rey' (unpublished manuscript, 3 March 2011).

Alfaro, Luis (2014), 'Oedipus el Rey Playwright Luis Alfaro Talks with Woolly Mammoth Production Dramaturg John M. Baker about Sophocles, Recidivism, and South Central LA grocery stores', Program for Luis Alfaro's Oedipus el Rey at the Dallas Theater Center, Dallas, 2014, pp. 14–15.

Alfaro, L. (2015), 'From Ancient Greece to Modern L.A.: Why the Classics Still Matter', Talk at J. Paul Getty Villa, Malibu, CA, 3 October 2015.

Allport, G. W. (1948), *ABC's of Scapegoating* (New York: Anti-Defamation League of B'Nai B'rith).

Anderlini-D'Onofrio, S. (1998), *The 'Weak' Subject: On Modernity, Eros, and Women's Playwriting* (Madison, NJ: Fairleigh University Press).

Andreas, J. R., Sr. (1998), 'Signifyin' on *The Tempest* in Mama Day', in C. Desmet and R. Sawyer, eds., *Shakespeare and Appropriation* (New York: Routledge), 103–18.

Aquila Theatre (2014), '"A Female Philoctetes" Scenes—Aquila 2014', Vimeo video, 6:05, Scenes from Aquila Theatre's workshop performance of *A Female Philoctetes* at Brooklyn Academy of Music (BAM), 19 April 2014, https://vimeo.com/95354175, accessed 22 October 2016.

Armstrong, L. (2010), '"Pecong" Brings Classic Tale to Modern Times', *New York Amsterdam News* 101/13: 21.

Atack, C. (16 March 2016), 'Review of Ruby Blondell, Kirk Ormand (ed.), *Ancient Sex: New Essays. (Classical Memories/Modern Identities)*', *Bryn Mawr Classical Review*, http://bmcr.brynmawr.edu/2016/2016-03-16.html, accessed 29 May 2017.

AUDELCO (2014), 'About Us', http://www.audelco.net/aboutus.html, accessed 13 August 2014.

Auslander, P. (1999), *Liveness: Performance in a Mediatized Culture* (New York: Routledge).

Baker, R. (1994), *Drag: A History of Female Impersonation in the Performing Arts* (New York: New York University Press).

Banks, D. and Rankine, P. (2015), 'On Remixing the Classics and Directing Countee Cullen's *Medea* and Law Chavez's *Señora de la pinta*: An Interview with Theater Director Daniel Banks', in K. Bosher, F. Macintosh, J. McConnell, and P. Rankine, eds., *The Oxford Handbook of Greek Drama in the Americas* (Oxford: Oxford University Press), 683–98.

Bare, S. (2015), 'The Truth about 22 Veteran Suicides a Day', *Task & Purpose*, 2 June 2015, http://taskandpurpose.com/truth-22-veteran-suicides-day/, accessed 16 July 2016.

Bassi, K. (1998), *Acting like Men: Gender, Drama, and Nostalgia in Ancient Greece* (Ann Arbor, MI: University of Michigan Press).

Benjamin, J. (1998), *Shadow of the Other: Intersubjectivity and Gender in Psychoanalysis* (New York: Routledge).

Bennett, S. (1997), *Theatre Audiences: A Theory of Production and Reception*, 2nd edn (London: Routledge).

Bergson, H. (1991), 'Laughter', trans. by C. Brereton and F. Rothwell, in W. Sypher, ed., *Comedy* (Baltimore, MD: Johns Hopkins University Press), 61–146.

Bernal, M. (1987), *Black Athena: The Afroasiatic Roots of Classical Civilization: The Fabrication of Ancient Greece, 1785–1985*, vol. 1 (New Brunswick, NJ: Rutgers University Press).

Bernal, M. (2001), *Black Athena Writes Back: Martin Bernal Responds to His Critics*, ed. D. C. Moore (Durham, NC: Duke University Press).

Bernal, M. (2006), *Black Athena: The Afroasiatic Roots of Classical Civilization: The Linguistic Evidence*, vol. 3 (New Brunswick, NJ: Rutgers University Press).

Berrios, R. (2006), *Cholo Style: Homies, Homegirls and La Raza* (Los Angeles: Feral House).

Blair, R. (1993), 'The Alcestis Project: Split Britches at Hampshire College', *Women and Performance: A Journal of Feminist History* 6/1: 147–50.

Blatner, A. and Wiener, D. J., eds. (2007), *Interactive and Improvisational Drama: Varieties of Applied Theatre and Performance* (New York: iUniverse).

Blau, H. (1990), *The Audience* (Baltimore, MD: Johns Hopkins University Press).

Blondell, R. and Ormand, K., eds. (2015), *Ancient Sex: New Essays* (Columbus, OH: Ohio State University Press).

Blundell, S. (1991), *Helping Friends and Harming Enemies: A Study in Sophocles and Greek Ethics* (Cambridge: Cambridge University Press).

Bogle, D. (1973), *Toms, Coons, Mulattoes, Mammies, and Bucks: An Interpretive History of Blacks in American Film* (New York: Bantam Books).

Bosher, K., Macintosh, F., McConnell, J., and Rankine, P., eds. (2015), *The Oxford Handbook of Greek Drama in the Americas* (Oxford: Oxford University Press).

Bradley, M., ed. (2010), *Classics and Imperialism in the British Empire* (Oxford: Oxford University Press).

Brantley, B. (2011), 'Yes, Even Sexting Is Off Limits', *The New York Times*, 14 December 2011: http://www.nytimes.com/2011/12/15/theater/reviews/lysistrata-jones-at-walter-kerr-theater-review.html, accessed 16 February 2018.

Brater, J., Del Vecchio, J., Friedman, A., et al. (2010), '"Let Our Freak Flags Fly": *Shrek the Musical* and the Branding of Diversity', *Theatre Journal* 62/2: 151–72.

Bratton, J. and Peterson, G. T. (2013), 'The Internet: History 2.0?', in D. Wiles and C. Dymkowski, eds., *The Cambridge Companion to Theatre History* (Cambridge: Cambridge University Press), 299–313.

Brittain, V. (2000), 'Criminal Diamond Trade Fuels African War, UN Is Told', *The Guardian*, 13 January 2000, http://www.guardian.co.uk/world/2000/jan/13/sierraleone.unitednations, accessed 11 December 2012.

Brooks, D. A. (2006), *Bodies in Dissent: Spectacular Performances of Race and Freedom, 1850–1910* (Durham, NC: Duke University Press).

Brown, J. (2010), *Theater of War on PBS Newshour: Extended Interview with Marines*, Public Broadcasting Service, 2 February 2010, https://www.youtube.com/watch?v=w-ph-fbRJQs, accessed 26 September 2016.

Broyles-González, Y. (1994), *El Teatro Campesino: Theater in the Chicano Movement* (Austin, TX: University of Texas Press).

Bulman, J. C. (2008), 'Introduction', in J. C. Bulman, ed., *Shakespeare Re-Dressed: Cross-Gender Casting in Contemporary Performance* (Madison, NJ: Fairleigh Dickinson University Press).

Burnett, A. P. (1998), *Revenge in Attic and Later Tragedy* (Berkeley, CA: University of California Press).

Butler, B. (2016), 'TV Keeps Killing Off Lesbian Characters. The Fans of One Show Have Revolted', *The Washington Post*, 4 April 2016, https://www.washingtonpost.com/news/arts-and-entertainment/wp/2016/04/04/tv-keeps-killing-off-lesbian-characters-the-fans-of-one-show-have-revolted/, accessed 2 May 2016.

Butler, J. (1993), *Bodies that Matter: On the Discursive Limits of 'Sex'* (New York: Routledge).

Butler, J. (1996), 'Burning Acts: Injurious Speech', *The University of Chicago Law School Roundtable* 3/1, Article 9, http://chicagounbound.uchicago.edu/roundtable/vol3/iss1/9, accessed 1 October 2016.

Byrd, D. A. (2009), Interview by Melinda Powers. Personal interview by telephone, 8 November 2009. New York.

Cairns, D. (2014), '*Medea*: Feminism or Misogyny?', in D. Stuttard, ed., *Looking at Medea: Essays and a Translation of Euripides' Tragedy* (New York: Bloomsbury Academic), 123–38.

Callier, R. E. (2014), 'Men in Drag Are Funny: Metatheatricality and Gendered Humor in Aristophanes', *Didaskalia* 10/13, http://www.didaskalia.net/issues/10/13/, accessed 9 October 2016.

Carlisle, T. (2000), 'Reading the Scars: Rita Dove's *The Darker Face of the Earth*', *African American Review* 34/1: 135–50.

Carlson, M. (1989), 'Theater Audiences and the Reading of Performance', in T. Postlewait and B. McConachie, eds., *Interpreting the Theatrical Past: Essays in the Historiography of Performance* (Iowa City, IA: University of Iowa Press), 82–98.

Carlson, M. (2001), *The Haunted Stage: Theatre as Memory Machine* (Ann Arbor, MI: University of Michigan Press).

Carter, S. (1993), *Pecong* (New York: Broadway Play Publishing).

Case, S.-E. (1985), 'Classic Drag: The Greek Creation of Female Parts', *Theatre Journal* 37/3: 317–27.

Case, S.-E. (1988), *Feminism and Theatre* (New York: Routledge).

Case, S.-E., ed. (1996), *Split Britches: Lesbian Practice/Feminist Performance* (London: Routledge).

Case, S.-E. (1999), 'Towards a Butch-Femme Aesthetic', in F. Cleto, ed., *Camp: Queer Aesthetics and the Performing Subject—A Reader* (Ann Arbor, MI: University of Michigan Press), 185–201.

Case, S.-E. (2007), 'The Masked Activist: Greek Strategies for the Streets', *Theatre Research International* 32/2: 119–29.

Catanese, B. W. (2011), *The Problem of the Color[Blind]: Racial Transgression and the Politics of Black Performance* (Ann Arbor, MI: University of Michigan Press).

Chamberlain, K. (2008a), 'Review: *Medea*', *New York Theatre*, 23 February 2008, http://www.nytheatre.com/Review/kat-chamberlain-2008-2-23-medea, accessed 4 June 2014.

Chamberlain, K. (2008b), 'Review: *Trojan Women*', *New York Theatre*, 16 January 2008, http://www.nytheatre.com/Review/kat-chamberlain-2008-1-16-trojan-women, accessed 11 December 2012.

Chang, E. (2010), 'Why Obama Should not Have Checked "Black" on his Census Form', *The Washington Post*, 29 April 2010, http://www.washingtonpost.com/wp-dyn/content/article/2010/04/28/AR2010042804156.html, accessed 8 June 2014.

Chin, F. and Chan, J. P. (1972), 'Racist Love', in R. Kostelanetz, ed., *Seeing through Shuck* (New York: Ballantine Books), 65–79.

Christiansen, R. (1990), '*Pecong* Replays Greek Tale amid the Mystique of a Caribbean Island', *Chicago Tribune*, 30 January 1990, http://articles.chicagotribune.com/1990-01-30/news/9001090044_1_carter-greek-jason, accessed 1 June 2014.

Claire, J. (2016), 'Theater Review: Sophocles' *Philoctetes* by Aquila Theatre at the GK Arts Center', *New York Theater Guide*, 10 April 2016, http://nytheatreguide.com/2016/04/theater-review-sophocles-philoctetes-by-aquila-theatre-at-the-gk-arts-center/, accessed 16 July 2016.

Coates, T. P. (2007), 'Is Obama Black Enough?', *Time*, 1 February 2007, http://www.time.com/time/nation/article, accessed 7 April 2013.

Cohen, A. R. and Rogers, B. M. (2011), *Theater of War, Part II*, Interview with Bryan Doerries, *Didaskalia: The Journal for Ancient Drama*, 28 September 2011, https://www.youtube.com/watch?v=hwj3-6EIYDk, accessed 25 September 2016.

Cohen-Cruz, J. (2010), *Engaging Performance: Theatre as Call and Response* (London: Routledge).

Conacher, D. J., ed. and trans. (1988), *Euripides'* Alcestis, with introduction and notes (Warminster: Aris and Phillips).

Cook, W. and Tatum, J. (2010), *African American Writers and Classical Tradition* (Chicago: University of Chicago Press).

Corrigan, P. W., Druss, B. G., and Perlick, D. A. (2014), 'The Impact of Mental Illness Stigma on Seeking and Participating in Mental Health Care', *Association for Psychological Science* 15/2 (3 September 2014): 37–70, http://journals.sagepub.com/doi/abs/10.1177/1529100614531398?journalCode=psia, accessed 25 September 2016.

Corti, L. (1998), 'Countée Cullen's *Medea*', *African American Review* 32/4: 621–34.

Cover, R. (2016), 'Queer Youth Suicide: Discourses of Difference, Framing Suicidality, and the Regimentation of Identity', in J. White, I. Marsh, M. J. Kral, and J. Morris, eds., *Critical Suicidology: Transforming Suicide Research and Prevention for the 21st Century* (Toronto: University of British Columbia Press), 188–208.

Croally, N. T. (1994), *Euripidean Polemic:* The Trojan Women *and the Function of Tragedy* (Cambridge: Cambridge University Press).

Cross, K. (2015), 'I Am Cait Panel Review—Five Trans Writers Give Their Verdict', *The Guardian*, 27 July 2015, http://www.theguardian.com/tv-and-radio/2015/jul/27/i-am-cait-panel-review-trans-writers, accessed 6 May 2016.

Crowley, J. (2012), *The Psychology of the Athenian Hoplite: The Culture of Combat in Classical Athens* (Cambridge and New York: Cambridge University Press).

Cullen, C. (1935), *The Medea and Some Poems* (New York: Harper & Brothers).

Curtis, S. (2015), 'An Archival Interrogation', in K. Bosher, F. Macintosh, J. McConnell, and P. Rankine, eds., *The Oxford Handbook of Greek Drama in the Americas* (New York: Oxford University Press), 17–29.

D'Aponte, M. G. (1991), '*The Gospel at Colonus* (And Other Black Morality Plays)', *Black American Literature Forum* 25/1: 101–11.

Dasen, V. (2013), *Dwarfs in Ancient Egypt and Greece* (Oxford: Oxford University Press).

Daunt, T. (2015), 'Michelle Obama, Bradley Cooper to Promote Accurate Hollywood Portrayal of Vets', *The Hollywood Reporter*, 30 January 2015, http://www.hollywoodreporter.com/news/michelle-obama-bradley-cooper-promote-768466, accessed 11 July 2016.

Davidson, J. (2007), *The Greeks and Greek Love: A Bold New Exploration of the Ancient World* (New York: Random House).

Davis, J. and Emeljanow, V. (2001), *Reflecting the Audience: London Theatre-going, 1840–1880* (Iowa City, IA: University of Iowa Press).

Davis, R. (2015), 'Barbarian Queens: Race, Violence, and Antiquity on the Nineteenth-Century United States Stage', in K. Bosher, F. Macintosh, J. McConnell, and P. Rankine, eds., *The Oxford Handbook of Greek Drama in the Americas* (New York: Oxford University Press), 112–32.

Davy, K. (1994), 'Fe/Male Impersonation: The Discourse of Camp', in M. Meyer, ed., *The Politics and Poetics of Camp* (New York: Routledge), 130–48.

Decaul, M. (2015), *Theater of War: PTSD and Sophocles.* 'Bryan Doerries in Conversation with Maurice Decaul', Interview with Bryan Doerries, 26 December 2015, https://www.youtube.com/watch?v=cMLOmkI7m-0, accessed 30 June 2016.

Diamond, E. (1997), *Unmaking Mimesis: Essays on Feminism and Theatre* (London: Routledge).

Dobbs, D. (2012), 'The PTSD Trap: Our Overdiagnosis of PTSD in Vets Is Enough to Make You Sick', *Wired*, 22 March 2012, https://www.wired.com/2012/03/the-ptsd-trap/, accessed 12 November 2016 (originally published in *Scientific American*, April 2009).

Dodds, E. R., ed. (1960), *Bacchae*, 2nd edn (Oxford: Clarendon Press).

Doerries, B. (2015), *Theater of War: PTSD and Sophocles.* 'Conversation with M. Decaul'. The Aspen Institute at the Scholastic Auditorium, New York, 2 December 2015.

Dolan, J. (1988), *The Feminist Spectator as Critic* (Ann Arbor, MI: University of Michigan Press).

Dolan, J. (2005), *Utopia in Performance: Finding Hope at the Theater* (Ann Arbor, MI: University of Michigan Press).

Dolsen, J. (2015), 'The Mistreatment of Female Veterans Is Not Just a Women's Issue', *Task and Purpose*, 11 August 2015, http://taskandpurpose.com/mistreatment-female-veterans-not-just-womens-issue/, accessed 9 October 2016.

Dover, K. J. (1974), *Greek Popular Morality in the Time of Plato and Aristotle* (Oxford: Oxford University Press).

Dover, K. J. (1978), *Greek Homosexuality* (Cambridge, MA: Harvard University Press).

Drouin, J. (2008), 'Cross-Dressing, Drag, and Passing: Slippages in Shakespearean Comedy', in J. C. Bulman, ed., *Shakespeare Re-Dressed: Cross-Gender Casting in Contemporary Performance* (Madison, NJ: Fairleigh Dickinson University Press), 23–56.

Du Bois, W. E. B. (2007), *The Souls of Black Folk* (New York: Cosimo Classics) (1st edn 1903).

Durell, S. (2010), 'Scorn Hath No Fury like Granny Root', *NiteLifeExchange.com*, March 2010, http://nitelifeexchange.com/theatre/theatre-reviews/1060-pecong-scorn-hath-no-furylike-granny-root.html, accessed 1 June 2014.

Easterling, P. E. (1977), 'The Infanticide in Euripides' *Medea*', *Yale Classical Studies* 25: 77–91.

'East Meets West' (31 October 1997), *In Theater* 31, 6.

Economist, The (2007), 'Trauma Porn', 20 April 2007, http://www.economist.com/blogs/democracyinamerica/2007/04/trauma_porn, accessed 25 September 2016.

Edgecomb, S. F. (2008), '"Not Just Any Woman": Bradford Louryk: A Legacy of Charles Ludlam and the Ridiculous Theatre for the Twenty-First Century', in J. Fisher, ed., *'We Will Be Citizens': New Essays on Gay and Lesbian Theatre* (Jefferson, NC: McFarland), 56–78.

Edwards, L. P. E. (2003), 'Alcestis: Euripides to Ted Hughes', *Greece & Rome* 50/1: 1–30.

Edwards, M. (2000), 'Philoctetes in Historical Context', in D. A. Gerber, ed., *Disabled Veterans in History*, enlarged and revised edn (Ann Arbor, MI: University of Michigan Press), 55–69.

Eikenberry, K. W. and Kennedy, D. M. (2013), 'Americans and Their Military, Drifting Apart', *The New York Times*, 26 May 2013, http://www.nytimes.com/2013/05/27/opinion/americans-and-their-military-drifting-apart.html, accessed 18 February 2018.

Epstein, H. (1994), *Joe Papp: An American Life* (Boston, MA: Little, Brown and Company).

Eschen, N. (2006), 'Review of *The Hungry Woman: A Mexican Medea*', *Theatre Journal* 58/1 (March): 103–6.

Faquet, J.-S. (2013), 'A Conversation with *Another Medea's* Aaron Mark', *Huffington Post*, 16 April 2013, http://www.huffingtonpost.com/johnstuart-fauquet/another-medea-aaron-mark-interview_b_3087353.html, accessed 15 March 2016.

Faux-Real Theatre Company (n.d.), 'About', http://www.fauxreal.org/mission/, accessed 9 October 2016.

Fienup-Riordan, A. (1990), *Eskimo Essays: Yup'ik Lives and How We See Them* (New Brunswick, NJ: Rutgers University Press).

Fischer-Lichte, E. (2008), *The Transformative Power of Performance: A New Aesthetics*, trans. S. I. Jain (Abingdon: Routledge).

Fleetwood, N. R. (2011), *Troubling Vision: Performance, Visuality, and Blackness* (Chicago: University of Chicago Press).

Flinn, C. (1999), 'The Deaths of Camp', in F. Cleto, ed., *Camp: Queer Aesthetics and the Performing Subject—A Reader* (Ann Arbor, MI: University of Michigan Press), 433–57.

Foley, H. P. (1981), *Reflections of Women in Antiquity* (New York: Routledge).

Foley, H. P. (1985), *Ritual Irony: Poetry and Sacrifice in Euripides* (Ithaca, NY: Cornell University Press).

Foley, H. P. (1989), 'Medea's Divided Self', *Classical Antiquity* 8/1 (April): 61–85.

Foley, H. P. (1999), 'Modern Performance and Adaptation of Greek Tragedy', *Transactions of the American Philological Society* 129: 1–12.

Foley, H. P. (2001), *Female Acts in Greek Tragedy* (Princeton, NJ: Princeton University Press).

Foley, H. P. (2002), 'The Comic Body in Greek Art and Drama', in B. Cohen, ed., *Not the Classical Ideal: Athens and the Construction of the Other in Greek Art* (Leiden: Brill), 275–314.

Foley, H. P. (2004), 'Bad Women: Gender Politics in Late Twentieth-Century Performance and Revision of Greek Tragedy', in E. Hall, F. Macintosh, and A. Wrigley, eds., *Dionysus Since 69: Greek Tragedy at the Dawn of the Third Millennium* (New York: Oxford University Press), 77–112.

Foley, H. P. (2012a), 'Greek Tragedy on the American Stage', *Atene e Roma* 6/3–4: 314–21.

Foley, H. P. (2012b), *Reimagining Greek Tragedy on the American Stage* (Berkeley, CA: University of California Press).

Foley, H. P. and Mee, E. B., eds. (2011), Antigone *on the Contemporary World Stage* (Oxford: Oxford University Press).

Foster, S. L., ed. (1996), *Corporealities: Dancing Knowledge, Culture and Power* (London: Routledge).

Foucault, M. (1986), *The Use of Pleasure: The History of Sexuality*, vol. 2, trans. Robert Hurley (New York: Vintage).

Fraden, R. (2001), *Imagining Medea: Rhodessa Jones and the Theater for Incarcerated Women* (Chapel Hill, NC: University of North Carolina Press).

Freud, S. (1989), *Jokes and Their Relation to the Unconscious*, ed. and trans. J. Strachey (New York: W. W. Norton & Company).

Gamel, M.-K. (1999), 'Staging Ancient Drama: The Difference Women Make', *Syllecta Classica* 10: 22–42.

Gamel, M.-K. (2010), 'Revising "Authenticity" in Staging Ancient Mediterranean Drama', in E. Hall and S. Harrop, eds., *Theorising Performance: Greek Drama, Cultural History, and Critical Practice* (London: Duckworth), 153–70.

Gates, H. L., Jr. (1988), *The Signifying Monkey: A Theory of African-American Literary Criticism* (Oxford: Oxford University Press).

Gerber, D. A., ed. (2000), *Disabled Veterans in History*, enlarged and revised edn (Ann Arbor, MI: University of Michigan Press).

Gibert, J. (1995), 'Review of *Aristophanes and Women* by Lauren K. Taaffe', *Bryn Mawr Classical Review*, 7 May 1995: (n.p.).

Gill, G. E. (2005), 'The Transforming Power of Performing the Classics in Chocolate, 1949–1954', *Theatre Journal* 57/4: 592–6.

Gilroy, P. (1993), *The Black Atlantic: Modernity and Double Consciousness* (Cambridge, MA: Harvard University Press).

Giltz, M. (2011), 'New Broadway Musical *Lysistrata Jones*: An Airball', *Huffington Post*, 17 December 2011, http://www.huffingtonpost.com/michael-giltz/lysistrata-jones-review-_b_1155436.html, accessed 27 February 2016.

Given, J. (2012), '*Lysistrata Jones*, Review', *Didaskalia* 9, https://www.didaskalia.net/issues/9/2/, accessed 20 February 2018.

Given, J. (2015), '*The Alcestis*—Slater (N.W.) Euripides' *Alcestis*', *The Classical Review* 65/1: 34–6.

GLAAD (2016), 'Where We Are on TV Report', http://www.glaad.org/whereweareontv15, accessed 11 October 2016.

Goff, B., ed. (2005), *Classics and Colonialism* (London: Duckworth).

Goff, B. (2009), *Euripides: Trojan Women* (New York: Bloomsbury Academic).

Goff, B. (2013a), '*Your Secret Language': Classics in the British Colonies of West Africa* (New York: Bloomsbury Academic).

Goff, B. (2013b), *Euripides: Trojan Women* (New York: Bloomsbury Academic).

Goff, B. and Simpson, M. (2007), *Crossroads in the Black Aegean: Oedipus, Antigone, and Dramas of the African Diaspora* (New York: Oxford University Press).

Goldberg, E. (2014), '80% of Central American Women, Girls Are Raped Crossing into the U.S.', *Huffington Post*, 12 September 2014, http://www.huffingtonpost.com/2014/09/12/central-america-migrants-rape_n_5806972.html, accessed 23 December 2015.

Gooch, W. (2010), '*Pecong* by Steven Carter–Off Broadway Theater Review: Classic Greek Heroine Goes Sepia', *Stage and Cinema*, 28 March 2010, http://old.stageandcinema.com/pecong.html, accessed 1 June 2014.

Gottschild, B. D. (1996), *Digging the Africanist Presence in American Performance and Other Contexts* (Westport, CT: Greenwood Press).

Gray, T. (2016), 'Academy Nominates All White Actors for Second Year in a Row', *Variety*, 14 January 2016, http://variety.com/2016/biz/news/oscar-nominations-2016-diversity-white-1201674903/, accessed 5 September 2016.

Green, A. S. (1994), *The Revisionist Stage: American Directors Reinvent the Classics* (New York: Cambridge University Press).

Greenblatt, S. (1991), *Marvelous Possessions: The Wonder of the New World* (Chicago: University of Chicago Press).

Greenwood, E. (2009), *Afro-Greeks: Dialogues between Anglophone Caribbean Literature and Classics in the Twentieth Century* (New York: Oxford University Press).

Griffith, M. and Most, G. W., eds. (2013), *Sophocles I: Antigone, Oedipus the King, Oedipus at Colonus* (Chicago: Chicago University Press).

Gross, B. (2015), 'First Major Sign of Gentrification Arrives in South-Park-Adjacent Pico-Union', *Curbed Los Angeles*, 21 January 2015, https://la.curbed.com/2015/1/21/10000550/first-major-sign-of-gentrification-arrives-in-south-park-neighbor, accessed 29 June 2018.

Haas, L. (1995), *Conquests and Historical Identities in California, 1769–1936* (Berkeley, CA: University of California Press).

Hall, E. (1997), 'The Sociology of Athenian Tragedy', in P. E. Easterling, ed., *The Cambridge Companion to Greek Tragedy* (Cambridge: Cambridge University Press), 93–126.

Hall, E. (2012), *Adventures with Iphigenia in Tauris: A Cultural History of Euripides' Black Sea Tragedy* (Oxford: Oxford University Press).

Hall, E. (2015), 'The Migrant Muse: Greek Drama as Feminist Window on American Identity, 1900–1925', in K. Bosher, F. Macintosh, J. McConnell, and P. Rankine, eds., *The Oxford Handbook of Greek Drama in the Americas* (New York: Oxford University Press), 149–65.

Hall, E. and Macintosh, F. (2005), *Greek Tragedy and the British Theatre: 1660–1914* (Oxford: Oxford University Press).

Hall, E., Macintosh, F., and Taplin, O., eds. (2000), *Medea in Performance 1500–2000* (London: Legenda).

Hall, E. and Vasunia, P., eds. (2010), *India, Greece, and Rome, 1757 to 2007*, special issue, *Bulletin of the Institute of Classical Studies Supplements* 53/S108 (June).

Hall, E. and Wrigley, A., eds. (2007), *Aristophanes in Performance 421 BC–AD 2007: Peace, Birds, and Frogs* (London: Legenda).

Halleran, M. K., ed. and trans. (1995), *Euripides' Hippolytus* (Warminster: Aris and Phillips).

Halperin, D. M. (1989), *One Hundred Years of Homosexuality and Other Essays on Greek Love* (New York: Routledge).

Halperin, D. M. (2015), 'Not Fade Away', in R. Blondell and K. Ormand, eds., *Ancient Sex: New Essays* (Columbus, OH: Ohio State University Press), 308–28.

Hamilton, S. (1993), 'Split Britches and the *Alcestis* Lesson: ("What Is This Albatross?")', in E. Donkin and S. Clement, eds., *Upstaging Big Daddy: Directing Theater as if Gender and Race Matter* (Ann Arbor, MI: University of Michigan Press), 133–50.

Hardwick, L. and Gillespie, C., eds. (2007), *Classics in Post-Colonial Worlds* (New York: Oxford University Press).

Hardwick, L. and Harrison, S. (2013), *Classics in the Modern World: A Democratic Turn?* (Oxford: Oxford University Press).

Harmon, J. (2008), 'Luis Alfaro: "Electricidad" Playwright Speaks to Students at CSUDH', *CSUDH News*, 23 October 2008, www.csudhnews.com/2008/10/luis-alfaro/, accessed 11 October 2016.

Harris, E. A. (2017), 'Same-Sex Parents Still Face Legal Complications', *The New York Times*, 20 June 2017, https://www.nytimes.com/2017/06/20/us/gay-pride-lgbtq-same-sex-parents.html, accessed 25 June 2017.

Hartigan, K. (1995), *Greek Tragedy on the American Stage: Ancient Drama in the Commercial Theater, 1882–1994* (Westport, CT: Greenwood Press).

Haskell, M. (1974), *From Reverence to Rape: The Treatment of Women in the Movies* (New York: Holt, Rinehart and Winston).

Herrera, B. E. (2015), *Latin Numbers: Playing Latino in Twentieth-Century U.S. Popular Performance* (Ann Arbor, MI: University of Michigan Press).

Hill, L. M. (2015), 'A New Stage of Laughter for Zora Neale Hurston and Theodore Browne: *Lysistrata* and the Negro Units of the Federal Theatre Project', in K. Bosher, F. Macintosh, J. McConnell, and P. Rankine, eds., *The Oxford Handbook of Greek Drama in the Americas* (New York: Oxford University Press), 286–300.

Holder, T. M. (2007), 'Euripedes [*sic*] in the Weho: *The Bacchae* at the Celebration Theater', *Entertainment Today* 39/5 (1 February 2007): 5, http://www.entertainmenttoday.net/backissues/ET.2007.02.01.Compact.pdf, accessed 4 November 2009.

Holmes, B. (2012), *Gender: Antiquity and Its Legacy* (Oxford: Oxford University Press).

Hubbard, T. K., ed. (2003), *Homosexuality in Greece and Rome: A Sourcebook of Basic Documents* (Berkeley, CA: University of California Press).

Hubbard, T. K., ed. (2014), *A Companion to Greek and Roman Sexualities* (Oxford: Wiley-Blackwell).

Huneke, S. C. (2016), 'The Gay-Suicide Stereotype Kills Gay People and Must End', *Aeon*, Opinions, https://aeon.co/opinions/the-gay-suicide-stereotype-kills-gay-people-and-must-end, accessed 11 October 2016.

Hunsaker, D. (1987), '*Yup'ik Antigone*', International Meeting of Ancient Greek Drama, Delphi 8–12 April 1984 and Delphi 4–25 June 1985, European Cultural Center of Delphi, Athens, 175–9.

Hutcheon, L. (2006), *A Theory of Adaptation* (New York: Routledge).

Jaggi, M. (2007), 'Beats of the Heart', *The Guardian*, 31 March 2007, http://www.theguardian.com/books/2007/mar/31/poetry.tonyharrison, accessed 27 April 2017.

James, C. (2007), 'Chill, Warrior Outcast, the Gods Are with You', *The New York Times*, 23 October 2007, http://www.nytimes.com/2007/10/23/theater/reviews/23phil.html, accessed 16 July 2016.

Jefferson, M. (2004), 'After Defeat, before the Slavery, Steeping in Civilization's Tatters', *The New York Times*, 7 April 2004, http://www.nytimes.com/2004/04/07/theater/theater-review-after-defeat-before-slavery-steeping-civilization-s-tatters.html, accessed 11 December 2012.

Johnson, C. (2006), '*Electricidad*. Interview with Luis Alfaro', *American Theatre Magazine* 23/2: 64–5.

Johnson, E. P. (2003), *Appropriating Blackness: Performance and the Politics of Authenticity* (Durham, NC: Duke University Press).

Johnston, K. (2016), *Disability Theatre and Modern Drama: Recasting Modernism* (New York: Bloomsbury Methuen).

Kelley, N. (2015), 'Deformity and Disability in Greece and Rome', in H. Avalos, S. J. Melcher, and J. Schipper, eds., *This Abled Body: Rethinking Disability in Biblical Studies* (Atlanta, GA: Society of Biblical Literature), 31–46.

Kershaw, B. (2015), 'Performance as Research: Live Events and Documents', in T. C. Davis, ed., *The Cambridge Companion to Performance Studies* (Cambridge: Cambridge University Press), 23–45.

Klein, E. (2014), *Sex and War on the American Stage:* Lysistrata *in Performance 1930–2012* (London: Routledge).

Knox, B. (1957), *Oedipus at Thebes: Sophocles' Tragic Hero and His Time* (New Haven, CT: Yale University Press).

Kozak, L. A. and Rich, J. W., eds. (2006), *Playing Around: Aristophanes Essays in Honour of Alan Sommerstein* (Oxford: Oxford University Press).

Krebs, K., ed. (2013), *Translation and Adaptation in Theatre and Film* (New York: Routledge).

Kristof, N. (2016), 'Is Donald Trump a Racist?', *The New York Times*, 23 July 2016, http://www.nytimes.com/2016/07/24/opinion/sunday/is-donald-trump-a-racist.html, accessed 15 September 2016.

Kubzansky, J. (2015a), Director's Note. Programme for Luis Alfaro's *Mojada: A Medea in Los Angeles* at the Barbara and Lawrence Fleischman Theater at the Getty Villa, Malibu, CA.

Kubzansky, J. (2015b), Interview by Melinda Powers. Personal interview by telephone, 15 January 2015. New York.

Kudlick, C. (2004), '"Disability" and "Divorce": A Blind Parisian Cloth Merchant Contemplates His Options in 1756', in B. G. Smith and B. Hutchison, eds., *Gendering Disability* (New Brunswick, NJ: Rutgers University Press), 134–44.

La Rocco, C. (2008), 'Bridging Civilizations to Make Sense of Slaughter', *The New York Times*, 23 January 2008, http://theater.nytimes.com/2008/01/23/theater/reviews/23troj.html, accessed 11 December 2012.

Lauretis, Teresa de (1984), *Alice Doesn't: Feminism, Semiotics, Cinema* (Bloomington, IN: Indiana University Press).

Lawrence, Q. (2014), 'Veterans' "Philoctetes" Puts Modern Spin on an Ancient Play', *The Diane Rehm Show*, National Public Radio, 29 May 2014, http://www.npr.org/2014/05/29/317127131/veterans-philoctetes-puts-modern-spin-on-ancient-greek-play, accessed 25 September 2016.

Lee-Brown, E. (2002), 'Performativity, Context, and Agency: The Process for Audience Response and the Implications for its Performance', *Text and Performance Quarterly* 22/2: 138–48.

Leguizamo, J. and Katz, D. B. (1997), *Freak: A Semi-Demi-Quasi-Pseudo Autobiography* (New York: Riverhead).

Lemmon, G. T. (2015), 'Missing in Action? Why Are There so Few Cultural Portrayals of Women in Combat?', *The Atlantic*, 4 August 2015, http://www.theatlantic.com/entertainment/archive/2015/08/missing-in-action/400235/, accessed 11 October 2016.

Lewis, V. A., ed. (2006), *Beyond Victims and Villains: Contemporary Plays by Disabled Playwrights* (New York: Theatre Communications Group).

Lilleker, D. G. (2006), *Key Concepts in Political Communication* (London: Sage Publications).

Lippmann, W. (1997), *Public Opinion* (New York: Free Press).

Llewellyn-Jones, L. (2005), 'Body Language and the Female Role-Player in Greek Tragedy and Japanese Kabuki Theatre', in D. L. Cairns, ed., *Body Language in the Greek and Roman Worlds* (Swansea: Classical Press of Wales), 73–105.

Lodewyck, L. and Monoson, S. S. (2015), 'Performing for Soldiers: Twenty-First Century Experiments in Greek Theater in the U.S.A.', in K. Bosher, F. Macintosh, J. McConnell, and P. Rankine, eds., *The Oxford Handbook of Greek Drama in the Americas* (Oxford: Oxford University Press), 651–70.

Longmore, P. K. (2003), *Why I Burned My Book and Other Essays on Disability* (Philadelphia, PA: Temple University Press).

Loraux, N. (1987), *Tragic Ways of Killing a Woman*, trans. A. Forster (Cambridge, MA: Harvard University Press).

McClure, L. K., ed. (2002), *Sexuality and Gender in the Classical World: Readings and Sources* (Oxford: Blackwell).

McConachie, B. (2008), *Engaging Audiences: A Cognitive Approach to Spectating in the Theatre* (New York: Palgrave Macmillan).

McConnell, J. (2013), *Black Odysseys: The Homeric* Odyssey *in the African Diaspora since 1939* (Oxford: Oxford University Press).

McConnell, J. (2015), 'Lee Breuer's New American Classicism: *The Gospel at Colonus*'s "Integration Statement"', in K. Bosher, F. Macintosh, J. McConnell, and P. Rankine, eds., *The Oxford Handbook of Greek Drama in the Americas* (Oxford: Oxford University Press), 474–94.

McDonald, M. (1992), *Ancient Sun, Modern Light: Greek Drama on the Modern Stage* (New York: Columbia University Press).

McDonald, M. (2003), *The Living Art of Greek Tragedy* (Bloomington, IN: Indiana University Press).

Macintosh, F. (2009), *Sophocles*: Oedipus Tyrannus (Cambridge: Cambridge University Press).

Macintosh, F., McConnell, J., and Rankine, P. (2015), 'Introduction', in K. Bosher, F. Macintosh, J. McConnell, and P. Rankine, eds., *The Oxford Handbook of Greek Drama in the Americas* (Oxford: Oxford University Press), 3–16.

Macintosh, F., Michelakis, P., Hall, E., and Taplin, O., eds. (2005), Agamemnon *in Performance: 458 BC to AD 2004* (Oxford: Oxford University Press).

Maddaus, G. (2015), 'Villaraigosa's New Girlfriend Played the Villain in "Terminator 3"', *L.A. Weekly*, 6 May 2015, http://www.laweekly.com/news/villaraigosas-new-girlfriend-played-the-villain-in-terminator-3-5551743, accessed 11 October 2016.

March, J. (2001), *Sophocles*: Electra (Warminster: Aris and Phillips).

Mark, A. (2015), 'Another Medea' (unpublished manuscript, 5 April 2015).

Mark, A. (2016), Interviews by Melinda Powers. Personal interviews by telephone on 7 and 29 April 2016. New York.

Marrero, M. (2000), 'Out of the Fringe? Out of the Closet: Latina/Latino Theatre and Performance in the 1990s', *TDR: The Drama Review* 44/3: 131–53.

Marshall, C. W. (2000), 'Alcestis and the Problem of Protosatyric Drama', *The Classical Journal* 95/3: 229–38.

Mason, W. (2014), 'You Are Not Alone across Time: Using Sophocles to Treat PTSD', *Harpers Magazine* 329/1973 (October): 57–68.

Masterson, M., Rabinowitz, N. S. and Robson, J. A., eds. (2015), *Sex in Antiquity: Exploring Gender and Sexuality in the Ancient World* (New York: Routledge).

Mendelsohn, D. (1996), 'The Stand: Expert Witnesses and Ancient Mysteries in a Colorado Courtroom', *Lingua Franca* 6/6: 34–46, http://linguafranca.mirror.theinfo.org/9609/stand.html, accessed 11 October 2016.

Mercer, K. (1997), 'Interculturality Is Ordinary', in R. Lavrijsen, ed., *Intercultural Arts Education and Municipal Policy* (Amsterdam: KIT Publishers), 33–44.

Millhiser, I. (2015), 'The Lawyer Defending Discrimination in the Supreme Court May Have Just Talked Himself out of a Victory', *Think Progress*, 28 April 2015, http://thinkprogress.org/justice/2015/04/28/3652122/lawyer-defending-discrimination-supreme-court-may-just-talked-victory/, accessed 15 March 2016.

Moore, H. (2005), 'The Oedipal Anguish Illuminates the Darkness', *The New York Times*, 14 June 2005, http://www.nytimes.com/2005/06/14/theater/reviews/the-oedipal-anguish-illuminates-the-darkness.html, accessed 25 September 2016.

Morales, H. (2016), 'Timeless Classics', *The Times Literary Supplement*, 31 August 2016, http://www.the-tls.co.uk/articles/public/timeless-classics/, accessed 8 November 2016.

Moritz, H. E. (2008), 'Luis Alfaro's *Electricidad* and the "Tragedy of Electra"', *Text and Presentation*, Series 4: 122–37.

Mossman, J. (1995), *Wild Justice: A Study in Euripides'* Hecuba (Oxford: Clarendon Press).

Mulvey, L. (2009), 'Visual Pleasure and Narrative Cinema', in L. Braudy and M. Cohen, eds., *Film Theory and Criticism: Introductory Readings*, 7th edn (Oxford: Oxford University Press), 711–22.

Muñoz, J. E. (1999), *Disidentifications: Queers of Color and the Performance of Politics* (Minneapolis, MN: University of Minnesota Press).

Muñoz, J. E. (2000), 'Memory Performance: Luis Alfaro's "Cuerpo Politizado"', in C. Fusco, ed., *Corpus Delecti: Performance Art of the Americas* (New York: Routledge), 97–114.

Murnaghan, S. (2012), 'Sophocles' Choruses', in K. Ormand, ed., *A Companion to Sophocles. Blackwell Companions to the Ancient World* (Malden, MA, Oxford, and Chichester: Wiley-Blackwell), 220–35.

Norden, M. F. (2000), 'Bitterness, Rage, and Redemption: Hollywood Constructs the Disabled Vietnam Veteran', in D. A. Gerber, ed., *Disabled Veterans in History*, enlarged and revised edn (Ann Arbor, MI: University of Michigan Press), 96–116.

North, H. (1966), *Sophrosyne: Self-Knowledge and Self-Restraint in Greek Literature* (Ithaca, NY: Cornell University Press).

Nyong'o, T. (2009), *The Amalgamation Waltz: Race, Performance, and the Ruses of Memory* (Minneapolis, MN: University of Minnesota Press).

Obama, B. (2008), 'A More Perfect Union', Campaign Speech in Philadelphia, PA, transcript from National Public Radio, 18 March 2008, http://www.npr.org/templates/story/story.php?storyId=88478467, accessed 9 April 2013.

O'Brien, M. (2008), 'The Tragedy of the Issue Play', *Off Off Online: What's on Off Off Broadway*, 11 January 2008, https://www.offoffonline.com/offoffonline/3323, accessed 7 April 2013.

O'Brien, T. (2016), 'Review: Aquila Theatre's "Philoctetes"', *StageBuddy*, 11 April 2016, http://stagebuddy.com/reviews/review-aquila-theatres-philoctetes, accessed 16 September 2016.

Ogden, D. (1997), *The Crooked Kings of Ancient Greece* (London: Bristol Classical Press).

O'Leary, T. (2008), 'The Wrath of Aphrodite' (unpublished manuscript, 6 July 2009 version).

O'Leary, T. (2016), Interview by Melinda Powers. Personal interview by telephone, 6 May 2016. New York.

Orgel, S. (1996), *Impersonations: The Performance of Gender in Shakespeare's England* (Cambridge: Cambridge University Press).

Ormand, K. (2003), 'Oedipus the Queen: Cross-Gendering without Drag', in 'Ancient Theatre', special issue, *Theatre Journal* 55/1 (March): 1–28.

Padden, C. and Humphries, T. (2006), 'Deaf People: A Different Center', in L. Davis, ed., *The Disability Studies Reader*, 2nd edn (New York: Routledge), 331–8.

Padel, R. (1992), *In and Out of Mind: Greek Images of the Tragic Self* (Princeton, NJ: Princeton University Press).

Paley, P. (2009), Interview by Melinda Powers. Personal interview by telephone, 3 December 2009. New York.

Pao, A. C. (2001), 'Changing Faces: Recasting National Identity in All-Asian(-) American Dramas', *Theatre Journal* 53/3: 389–409.

Pao, A. C. (2010), *No Safe Spaces: Re-Casting Race, Ethnicity, and Nationality in American Theater* (Ann Arbor, MI: University of Michigan Press).

Pawlyk, O. (2015), 'Seeking Ways to Bridge "Civilian-Military Gap"', *Military Times*, 21 March 2015, http://www.militarytimes.com/story/military/2015/03/21/veterans-natural-conversation-military-civilian-gap/25035857/, accessed 25 September 2016.

Pereira, M. (2002), '"When the Pear Blossoms/Cast Their Pale Faces on/the Darker Face of the Earth": Miscegenation, the Primal Scene, and the Incest Motif in Rita Dove's Work', *African American Review* 36/2: 195–211.

Perry, D. M. (2015), 'A New Right Grounded in the Long History of Marriage: Citing the Work of Historians that Demonstrates the Constant Evolution of the Institution, the U.S. Supreme Court Decides to Recognize a Constitutional Right to Same-sex Unions', *The Atlantic*, 26 June 2015, http://www.theatlantic.com/politics/archive/2015/06/history-marriage-supreme-court/396443/, accessed 11 October 2016.

Philipps, D. (2016), 'Wounded Warrior Project Spends Lavishly on Itself, Insiders Say', *The New York Times*, 27 January 2016, http://www.nytimes.com/2016/01/28/us/wounded-warrior-project-spends-lavishly-on-itself-ex-employees-say.html, accessed 13 July 2016.

Poole, W. (1990), 'Male Homosexuality in Euripides', in A. Powell, ed., *Euripides, Women and Sexuality* (New York: Routledge), 108–50.

Powers, M. (2009), 'Unveiling Euripides', *Journal of Dramatic Theory and Criticism* 23/2 (Spring): 5–20.

Powers, M. (2011), 'Syncretic Sites in Luis Alfaro's *Electricidad*', *Helios* 38/2 (Fall): 193–206.

Powers, M. (2014), *Athenian Tragedy in Performance: A Guide to Contemporary Studies and Historical Debates* (Iowa City, IA: University of Iowa Press).

Powers, M. (2015), 'Reclaiming Euripides in Harlem', in K. Bosher, F. Macintosh, J. McConnell, and P. Rankine, eds., *The Oxford Handbook of Greek Drama in the Americas* (Oxford: Oxford University Press), 595–610.

Preisser, A. (2017), Interview by Melinda Powers. Personal interview by email, 27 January 2017. New York.

Prentki, T. and Preston, S., eds. (2009), *The Applied Theatre Reader* (New York: Routledge).

Priest, D. and Hull, A. (2007), 'Soldiers Face Neglect, Frustration at Army's Top Medical Center', *The Washington Post*, 18 February 2007, http://www.washingtonpost.com/wp-dyn/content/article/2007/02/17/AR2007021701172.html, accessed 25 September 2016.

Prieto, A. (2000), 'Camp, *Carpa* and Cross-Dressing in the Theater of Tito Vasconcelos', in C. Fusco, ed., *Corpus Delecti: Performance Art of the Americas* (New York: Routledge), 83–96.

Propst, A. (2009), 'Classical Theatre of Harlem Founders Alfred Preisser, Christopher McElroen to Depart Company', *TheatreMania*, 2 November 2009, http://www.theatermania.com/new-york/news/11-2009/classical-theatre-of-harlem-founders-alfred-preiss_22528.html, accessed 11 December 2012.

Rabinowitz, N. S. (1995), 'How Is it Played: The Male Actor of Greek Tragedy: Evidence of Misogyny or Gender-Bending?', *Didaskalia Supplement*, 1 May 1995, http://www.didaskalia.net/issues/supplement1/rabinowitz.html#, accessed 15 February 2016.

Rabinowitz, N. S. (1998), 'Embodying Tragedy: The Sex of the Actor', *Intertexts* 2/1: 3.

Rabinowitz, N. S. (2015), 'Greek Tragedy, Enslaving or Liberating? The Example of Rita Dove's *The Darker Face of the Earth*', in K. Bosher, F. Macintosh, J. McConnell, and P. Rankine, eds., *The Oxford Handbook of Greek Drama in the Americas* (Oxford: Oxford University Press), 495–513.

Rabkin, G. (1984), 'Lee Breuer on *The Gospel at Colonus*', *Performing Arts Journal* 8/1: 48–51.

Rademaker, A. (2005), *Sophrosyne and the Rhetoric of Self Restraint: Polysemy and Persuasive Use of an Ancient Greek Value Term* (*Mnemosyne* Suppl. 259, Boston, MA, and Leiden: Brill).

Rankine, P. D. (2006), *Ulysses in Black: Ralph Ellison, Classicism, and African American Literature* (Madison, WI: University of Wisconsin Press).

Rankine, P. D. (2013), *Aristotle and Black Drama: A Theater of Civil Disobedience* (Waco, TX: Baylor University Press).

Rehm, D. (2014), 'A Conversation with the New Chairman of the National Endowment for the Humanities', https://dianerehm.org/shows/2014-11-20/a_conversation_with_the_new_chairman_of_the_national_endowment_for_the_humanities, accessed 1 March 2018.

Rehm, R. (1992), *Greek Tragic Theatre* (New York: Routledge).

Rehm, R. (2003), *Radical Theatre: Greek Tragedy and the Modern World* (London: Duckworth).

Revermann, M. (2006), *Comic Business: Theatricality, Dramatic Technique, and Performance Contexts of Aristophanic Comedy* (Oxford: Oxford University Press).

Revermann, M., ed. (2014), *The Cambridge Companion to Greek Comedy* (Cambridge: Cambridge University Press).

Riley, K. (2008), *The Reception and Performance of Euripides' Herakles: Reasoning Madness* (Oxford: Oxford University Press).

Roach, J. (1996), *Cities of the Dead: Circum-Atlantic Performance* (New York: Columbia University Press).

Roberts, S. and Baker, P. (2010), 'Asked to Declare His Race, Obama Checks "Black"', *The New York Times*, 2 April 2010, http://www.nytimes.com/2010/04/03/us/politics/03census.html, accessed 8 June 2014.

Rochel, A. (2007), Interview by Melinda Powers. Personal interview by telephone, 15 May 2007. New York.

Rochel, A. (2016), Interview by Melinda Powers. Personal interview by telephone, 18 May 2016. New York.

Rodríguez, J. M. (2003), *Queer Latinidad: Identity Practices, Discursive Spaces* (New York: New York University Press).

Román, D. (1995), 'Teatro Viva!: Latino Performance and the Politics of AIDS in Los Angeles', in E. L. Bergmann and P. J. Smith, eds., *¿Entiendes? Queer Readings, Hispanic Writings* (Durham, NC: Duke University Press), 346–69.

Román, D. (2005), *Performance in America: Contemporary U.S. Culture and the Performing Arts* (Durham, NC: Duke University Press).

Román, D. and Miller, T. (2002), 'Preaching to the Converted', in A. Solomon and F. Minwalla, eds., *The Queerest Art: Essays on Lesbian and Gay Theater* (New York: New York University Press), 203–26.

Romm, J. (2017), 'A Misguided Impulse to Update the Greek Classics', *The New Yorker*, 21 April 2017, http://www.newyorker.com/culture/cultural-comment/a-misguided-impulse-to-update-the-greek-classics, accessed 28 May 2017.

Rose, M. L. (2003), *The Staff of Oedipus: Transforming Disability in Ancient Greece* (Ann Arbor, MI: University of Michigan Press).

Rosello, M. (1997), *Declining the Stereotype: Ethnicity and Representation in French Cultures* (Hanover, NH: Dartmouth College Press).

Russo, V. (1981), *The Celluloid Closet: Homosexuality in the Movies* (New York: Harper & Row).

Rutherford, R. (2005), 'Preface to *Iphigenia at Aulis*', in J. Davie, ed. and trans., *Euripides: The Bacchae and Other Plays* (London: Penguin), 326–7.

Sager, R. (2017), 'Gentrification in L.A.'s Boyle Heights Leaves Some Latinos Threatened, Others Hopeful', *NBC News*, 14 November 2017, https://www.nbcnews.com/news/latino/gentrification-l-s-boyle-heights-leaves-some-latinos-threatened-others-n820381, accessed 29 June 2018.

Saltz, R. (2010), 'Medea Story Sways to a 19th-Century Island Rhythm', *The New York Times*, 25 March 2010, http://www.nytimes.com/2010/03/25/theater/reviews/25pecong.html, accessed 1 June 2014.

Sandahl, C. (2003), 'Queering the Crip or Cripping the Queer: Intersections of Queer and Crip Identities in Solo Autobiographical Performance', *GLQ: A Journal of Lesbian and Gay Studies* 9/1–2: 25–56.

Sandahl, C. and Auslander, P. (2005), *Bodies in Commotion: Disability and Performance* (Ann Arbor, MI: Michigan University Press).

Sanders, J. (2006), *Adaptation and Appropriation* (New York: Routledge).

Sanneh, K. (2016), 'What Do People Mean when They Say Donald Trump Is a Racist?', *The New Yorker*, 18 August 2016, http://www.newyorker.com/news/daily-comment/what-do-people-mean-when-they-say-donald-trump-is-racist, accessed 15 September 2016.

Sauter, W. (2000), *The Theatrical Event: Dynamics of Performance and Perception* (Iowa City, IA: University of Iowa Press).

Scarry, E. (1985), *The Body in Pain: The Making and Unmaking of the World* (Oxford: Oxford University Press).

Seaford, R., ed. and trans. (1997), Euripides: *Bacchae* (Warminster: Aris and Phillips).

Seidensticker, B. (1978), 'Comic Elements in Euripides' *Bacchae*', *American Journal of Philology* 99/3: 303–20.

Senelick, L. (2000), *The Changing Room: Sex, Drag and Theatre* (London: Routledge).

Setoodeh, R. (2009), 'Does Television's Gay Influx Promote Stereotypes?', *Newsweek*, http://www.newsweek.com/does-televisions-gay-influx-promote-stereotypes-76717, accessed 6 May 2016.

Sexton, D. (2008), 'Lifting the Veil: Revision and Double Consciousness in Rita Dove's "The Darker Face of the Earth"', *Callaloo* 31/3: 777–87.

Shakespeare, T. (2006), 'The Social Model of Disability', in L. J. Davis, ed., *The Disability Studies Reader*, 2nd edn (New York: Routledge), 197–204.

Shaw, L. and Dennison, S. (2005), *Pop Culture Latin America!: Media, Arts, and Style* (Santa Barbara, CA: ABC-CLIO, Inc.).

Shay, J. (1994), *Achilles in Vietnam: Combat Trauma and the Undoing of Character* (New York: Athenaeum).

Shay, J. (2002), *Odysseus in America: Combat Trauma and the Trials of Homecoming* (New York: Scribner).

Shay, J. (2014), 'Moral Injury', *Psychoanalytic Psychology* 31/2 (April): 182–91.

Sherman, N. (2015), *Afterwar: Healing the Moral Wounds of Our Soldiers* (Oxford: Oxford University Press).

Shuler, D. (2010), '*Pecong*: Revenge in Rhythm and Verse', *Examiner.com*, 10 March 2010, http://www.examiner.com/article/pecong-revenge-rhythm-and-verse, accessed 16 August 2014.

Sierra Leone Truth and Reconciliation Commission (2004), *Witness to Truth: Report of the Sierra Leone Truth and Reconciliation Commission*, vol. 3A (Accra: GPL Press), http://www.sierra-leone.org/Other-Conflict/TRCVolume3A.pdf, accessed 12 November 2012.

Simmons, P. (2008), 'Review of *Trojan Women*', *Curtain Up: The Internet Theatre Magazine of Reviews, Features, Annotated Listings*, 12 January 2008, http://www.curtainup.com/trojanwomencth08.html, accessed 11 December 2012.

Simons, M. (2013), 'EnGENDERED MEANINGS IN *OEDIPUS REX XX/XY*', Unpublished paper submitted to Melinda Powers for a course in the PhD Programme in Theatre at the CUNY Graduate Center.

Simons, M. (forthcoming 2018), 'EnGENDERED MEANINGS IN *OEDIPUS REX XX/XY*', *Didaskalia*.

Slater, N. W. (2013), *Euripides*: Alcestis. *Companions to Greek and Roman Tragedy* (London and New York: Bloomsbury Academic).

Slater, N. W. (2015), '"The Greatest Anti-War Poem Imaginable": Granville Barker's *Trojan Women in America*', *Illinois Classical Studies* 40/2 (Fall): 347–71.

Smith, G. (2013), *Working with Trauma: Systemic Approaches* (New York: Palgrave Macmillan).

Smith, M. (2010), 'Obama Census Choice African-American', *Huffington Post*, 2 April 2010, http://www.huffingtonpost.com/2010/04/02/obama-census-choice-afric_n_524012.html, accessed 8 June 2014.

Solomon, A. (1997), *Re-Dressing the Canon: Essays on Theater and Gender* (New York: Routledge).

Soloski, A. (2008), '*Trojan* Harlem: A Child Thirsts for Blood in an Uptown Euripides', *The Village Voice*, 22 January 2008, http://www.villagevoice.com/2008-01-22/theater/trojan-harlem, accessed 11 December 2012.

Sommerstein, A., ed. and trans. (1990), *Aristophanes* Lysistrata (Warminster: Aris and Phillips).

Sorkin, A. D. (2015), 'The Here and Now of Same-Sex Marriage', *The New Yorker*, 28 April 2015, http://www.newyorker.com/news/amy-davidson/obergefell-v-hodges-supreme-court-same-sex-marriage, accessed 9 October 2016.

Soyinka, W. (1976), *Myth, Literature and the African World*, 1st edn (Cambridge: Cambridge University Press).

Spindle, L. (2007), 'The Bacchae', *In Magazine* 9/25 (1 February 2007): http://www.inlamag.com/925/reviews/theatreR.html, accessed 4 November 2009.

Stanley, S. (2007), 'The Bacchae', *Stage Scene LA*, 2 February 2007: http://www.stagescenela.com/html/the_bacchae.html, accessed 4 November 2009.

Stedman, R. W. (1982), *Shadows of the Indian: Stereotypes in American Culture* (Norman, OK: University of Oklahoma Press).

Stephens, S. A. and Vasunia, P. (2010), *Classics and National Cultures* (Oxford: Oxford University Press).

Sterngold, J. (2000), 'February 6–12; L.A.P.D. Blues', *The New York Times*, 13 February 2000, http://www.nytimes.com/2000/02/13/weekinreview/february-6-12-lapd-blues.html, accessed 1 November 2009.

Stray, C. (1998), *Classics Transformed: Schools, Universities, and Society in England, 1830–1960* (Oxford: Oxford University Press).

Stuttard, D. (2014), 'Introduction', in D. Stuttard, ed., *Looking at* Medea: *Essays and a Translation of Euripides' Tragedy* (New York: Bloomsbury Academic), 1–10.

Sugrue, T. J. (2010), *Not Even Past: Barack Obama and the Burden of Race* (Princeton, NJ: Princeton University Press).

Svich, C. (2012), *Blasted Heavens: Five Contemporary Plays Inspired by the Greeks* (Roskilde: Eyecorner Press, University of Denmark).

Taaffe, L. K. (1993), *Aristophanes and Women* (New York: Routledge).

Taplin, O. (1986), 'Fifth-Century Tragedy and Comedy: A Synkrisis', *The Journal of Hellenic Studies* 106: 163–74.

Tomm, K. (2002), 'Enabling Forgiveness and Reconciliation in Family Therapy', *The International Journal of Narrative Therapy and Community Work* 1: 65–9.

Tompkins, J., ed. (2014), 'Theatre and Adaptation', special issue, *Theatre Journal* 66/4 (December).

Tulloch, J. (2005), *Shakespeare and Chekhov in Production and Reception: Theatrical Events and their Audiences* (Iowa City, IA: University of Iowa Press).

Turner, C. (2004), 'Fabulousness as Fetish: Queer Politics in *Sex and the City*', *The Scholar and Feminist On-Line*, Barnard Center for Research on Women 3/1 (Fall): http://sfonline.barnard.edu/hbo/turner_01.htm, accessed 3 April 2016.

Van Zyl Smit, B. (2014), 'Black Medeas', in D. Stuttard, ed., *Looking at Medea: Essays and a Translation of Euripides' Tragedy* (New York: Bloomsbury Academic), 157–66.

Vigil, J. D. (1988), *Barrio Gangs: Street Life and Identity in Southern California* (Austin, TX: University of Texas Press).

Weiss, H. (2013), 'Luis Alfaro Puts Chicago Spin on Classic Greek Tragedy', *Chicago Sun-Times*, 18 July 2013, http://www.pressreader.com/usa/chicago-sun-times/20130718/282037619769460, accessed 11 October 2016.

Wetmore, K. J., Jr. (2003), *Black Dionysus: Greek Tragedy and African American Theatre* (Jefferson, NC: McFarland).

Wetmore, K. J., Jr. (2013), *Black Medea: Adaptations for Modern Plays* (Amherst, NY: Cambria Press).

Wetmore, K. J., Jr. (2015), '"Aeschylus Got Flow!": Afrosporic Greek Tragedy and Will Power's *The Seven*', in K. Bosher, F. Macintosh, J. McConnell, and P. Rankine, eds., *The Oxford Handbook of Greek Drama in the Americas* (Oxford: Oxford University Press), 543–55.

Wiles, D. (2000), 'Burdens of Representation: The Method and the Audience', in D. Krasner, ed., *Method Acting Reconsidered: Theory, Practice, Future* (New York: St. Martin's Press).

Willis, A. T. (2005), 'Euripides' *Trojan Women*' (DPhil thesis, University of Oxford).

Wilmer, S. (2007), 'Women in Greek Tragedy Today: A Reappraisal', *Theatre Research International* 32/2 (July): 106–18.

Winkler, J. (1990), *The Constraints of Desire: The Anthropology of Sex and Gender in Ancient Greece* (New York: Routledge).

Wolfe, G. C. (1988), *The Colored Museum* (New York: Grove Press).

Wong, C. M. (2017), 'This Naked Calendar Celebrates Gay Men With "Ordinary" Bodies', *Huffington Post*, 'Queer Voices', 17 December 2017, https://www.huffingtonpost.com/entry/meatzine-naked-gay-men-calendar_us_5a303f0de4b01bdd765803f5, accessed 18 February 2018.

Woodruff, P., ed. and trans. (1998), *Euripides*: Bacchae (Indianapolis, IN: Hackett Publishing Company).

Woodruff, P. (2014), 'Introduction', in P. Meineck, trans., *Sophocles*: Philoctetes (Indianapolis, IN: Hackett Publishing Company), 20–62.

Worman, N. (2015), 'What Is "Greek Sex" for?', in R. Blondell and K. Ormand, eds., *Ancient Sex: New Essays* (Columbus, OH: Ohio State University Press), 208–302.

Worthen, W. B., ed. (2011), *The Wadsworth Anthology of Drama*, 6th edn (Berkeley, CA: Wadsworth Publishing).

Wrigley, A. (2011), *Performing Greek Drama in Oxford and on Tour with the Balliol Players* (Exeter: University of Exeter Press).

Young, H. (2009), 'Introduction', *Theatre Topics* 19/1 (December): xiii–xviii.

Young, H. (2010), *Embodying Black Experience: Stillness, Critical Memory, and the Black Body* (Ann Arbor, MI: University of Michigan Press).

Zaccaria, M. (2016), 'Philoctetes: A Soldier's Story', *Theatre Pizzazz*, 8 April 2016, http://www.theaterpizzazz.com/philoctetes-a-soldiers-story/, accessed 16 July 2016.

Zeitlin, F. (1980), 'The Closet of Masks: Role Playing and Mythmaking in the *Orestes* of Euripides', *Ramus* 9: 55–71.

Zeitlin, F. (1996), *Playing the Other: Gender and Society in Classical Greek Literature* (Chicago: University of Chicago Press).

Žižek, S. (1993), *Tarrying with the Negative: Kant, Hegel, and the Critique of Ideology* (Durham, NC: Duke University Press).

Index of Productions and Adaptations of Greek Dramas

This index references productions and adaptations mentioned in this book. The Archive of Performances of Greek and Roman Drama (www.apgrd.ox.ac.uk/) has more complete information on some of these productions. See also appendices A–G of Helene P. Foley's Reimagining Greek Tragedy on the American Stage *for further information on the reception of Greek tragedy on the US stage.*

Index